DATE DUE

E-Learning and Business Plans

National and International Case Studies

Edited by
Elaina M. Norlin and Tiffini A. Travis

THE SCARECROW PRESS, INC.
Lanham, Maryland • Toronto • Plymouth, UK
2008

SCARECROW PRESS, INC.

Published in the United States of America
by Scarecrow Press, Inc.
A wholly owned subsidiary of
The Rowman & Littlefield Publishing Group, Inc.
4501 Forbes Boulevard, Suite 200, Lanham, Maryland 20706
www.scarecrowpress.com

Estover Road
Plymouth PL6 7PY
United Kingdom

British Library Cataloguing in Publication Information Available

Library of Congress Cataloging-in-Publication Data

E-learning and business plans : national and international case studies / [edited
by] Elaina M. Norlin and Tiffini A. Travis.
    p. cm.
    Includes bibliographical references and index.
    ISBN-13: 978-0-8108-5195-5 (hardcover : alk. paper)
    ISBN-10: 0-8108-5195-4 (hardcover : alk. paper)
    eISBN-13: 978-0-8108-6229-6
    eISBN-10: 0-8108-6229-8
    1. Computer-assisted instruction—Case studies. 2. Employees—Training of—
Computer-assisted instruction—Case studies. 3. Internet in higher education—
Case studies. 4. Organizational learning—Data processing. I. Norlin, Elaina.
II. Travis, Tiffini A., 1971–.
    LB1044.87.E14 2008
    658.3'124—dc22   2008003163

♾ ™ The paper used in this publication meets the minimum requirements of
American National Standard for Information Sciences—Permanence of Paper
for Printed Library Materials, ANSI/NISO Z39.48-1992.
Manufactured in the United States of America.

Contents

Introduction

Elaina M. Norlin and Tiffini A. Travis

With the invention of desktop computers, electronic learning, or *e-learning*, has become a convenient learning tool of choice for individuals with busy schedules. For the past several years, there has been a continuous stream of much-needed innovation in the use of e-learning, which has now become second nature to both e-learning providers and users. A major growth area has been in distance learning, where prospective students have the choice of going back to school or taking continuing education classes from the comfort of home. Of course, distance education has been around for a long time, but with desktop computers and the Internet, students expect immediate access and gratification. But just as e-learning has enhanced and enriched our lives, challenges have increased as the creation of courses and e-learning material evolves. Technology, although it makes our lives easier, can come with a not-so-affordable price tag. After raising money to provide a costly e-learning initiative, how do creators of e-learning content know if their customers or target audience are really learning? Who is going to maintain the technology? Who will subsidize the upkeep costs? How do they know whether there is a better product on the horizon that can do it more cheaply and with a more advanced technology infrastructure?

This book was originally intended as a guide to conducting usability testing for e-learning products. We have written together before on the topic of usability testing and were approached to publish another book on the subject. We initially decided to approach the book by interviewing companies, libraries, and other groups who had large-scale e-learning products and writing a selection of case studies on successful projects. As we conducted our initial research, however, we found that many e-learning products were never completed because of a lack of funding, because the planning group lost interest, or because a bigger company announced they were going to make something bigger and better the next year. This was not big news, because experts commonly predict that 50 percent of all projects fail within the first five years. Yet we were disturbed by the number of projects that began and failed, usually costing hundreds of thousands of dollars. What was more disturbing was that many of the companies, libraries, or organizations could not tell you why the project failed. Therefore, we decided to restructure the book to talk more about the importance of planning, or in this case developing a business plan before launching into a large-scale and often expensive e-learning project.

The book is divided into two parts. The first part provides the background and context for the rest of the chapters. Chapters 1 through 4 set the foundation for the rest of the book. Chapter 1 examines e-learning users, while chapters 2 and 3 provide an overview of e-learning, some trends for the future, and the definition of e-learning for the purpose of this book. Chapter 4 provides an overview of a business plan modified for an existing company. This business-plan chapter also contains examples for people who need to see practical applications of the topics discussed. The second part of the book, chapters 5 through 10, contains national and international e-learning case studies.

Each case study is divided into potential components of a business plan. The areas covered in the case studies include vision and planning, management and personnel issues, usability and assessment, marketing, and financial feasibility.

The first case study, in chapter 5, focuses on the roles of planning and vision in the development of an e-learning project at Golden Gate University. Using the development of an online course, Competitive Core Research Skills, the author examines how effective planning in the beginning stages can affect the outcome and success of a project.

Chapter 6 features a case study that details a project at the University of Hertfordshire. The study emphasizes the importance of managing people in the development of a successful e-learning project.

In chapter 7, "Marketing Specialist Technology Information Services," Roddy MacLeod provides a case study of the marketing techniques used by the resource portal EEVL to promote both services and assessment of its success.

Chapter 8, "Structuring Interdepartmental Collaborations in E-Learning Design, Delivery, and Support," contains a key case study at the University of Glamorgan, which highlights the roles and management structure in an e-learning environment with special attention to design, usability, and long-term support of e-learning products and services.

In chapter 9, "A New Approach to E-Learning," the authors describe how the LCeL Project is developing pedagogically sound and strategically significant e-learning tools. Their strategy is to apply user-centered design approaches to best understand the learning needs, styles, and environment of learners, combined with the "balanced scorecard" approach to understanding the processes in which organizations identify their learning needs and expectations of e-learning tools.

The final chapter, "Maintaining Quality Education while Reducing Costs," introduces the process of redesigning stand-alone courses. The author shows the transition from traditional in-person courses to courses that use information technology. The main focus is on how the redesigns achieve cost savings as well as quality enhancements that contribute to improved student learning.

Each of the case studies focuses on a particular area of the study instead of providing an overview of the entire project. This approach will provide both some background about the authors' e-learning plans and specific information on how to market or develop a financial feasibility plan. This format also allows readers to contact specific authors for information on particular issues that might be stumbling blocks as they begin to write a business plan.

Overall, we hope that this book serves as food for thought as your business or organization begins to plan for an e-learning project. We have written it so more people can be successful in creating better and richer e-learning projects.

PART ONE

E-LEARNING IN THE 21ST CENTURY

1

Who Are E-Learners?

Rosemary McGill, California State University, Fullerton

Student population trends and learning motivations and styles are key factors to consider when planning e-learning programs. This chapter provides decision makers with an overview of some key demographics and learning information that will allow them to plan accordingly. E-learning offers flexibility in the time, place, and pace of instruction for students and faculty. Successful programs require that providers develop instructional environments adaptable to diverse student bodies. Understanding the motivation and competencies of e-learners is critical when deciding which courses to develop and how to design and implement programs.

A standard perception of online learners is of a female, older than "regular" students, employed, with some higher education and with family responsibilities. Increasingly, this profile is changing as are the demographics for all postsecondary education, which now has a majority of part-time, nontraditional learners who are working adults (Ausburn 2004). Reports show that as students encounter e-learning, they become more accepting of this method and more likely to take additional online courses. E-learners are pragmatic and use distance or online learning for its convenience of use. They take courses online because of a busy work/home schedule and because these courses fill a specific job-training requirement or educational need. Increasingly, this trend includes traditional students. Zemsky and Massy's 2004 Weatherstation Project reported that over 80% of the full-time students living on campus at three major research universities enrolled in e-learning courses that were specifically designed for part-time adult learners who were distant from campus (p. 51). Such students originally took a class because it fit their schedule, but they became more likely to take further classes.

Most market researchers expect considerable growth of online learning throughout the world. Eduventures, an education research firm, predicted that the online distance learning market, including corporate, government, and educational participants, would grow by more than 38% in 2004 (Botelho 2004). Increasingly, the corporate world and almost all for-profit education have readily adopted online learning, which has few geographic ties and therefore an expanding student pool. The challenge in the 21st century is not to decide why to have an online distance learning program, but how to design and implement successful, learner-centered education. Key demographics and learning styles will affect who your e-learners might be and how to design a successful course.

THE INTERNET

Use

Most e-learning uses the Internet. Internet World Stats data show that while continuing to have the smallest regional populations, North America (68%) and Australia (53%) lead all areas in the percentage of their population using the Internet. Asia, Europe, and North America have the greatest number of people online. The highest expected growth areas are the Middle East (392%), Latin America/Caribbean (304%), and Africa (430%), probably due to improved infrastructures, especially in telecommunications, and demand from citizens, businesses, and governments, as well as initiatives such as the ITU Connect the World program to end the digital divide.

Language

While English is usually considered the language of the Internet, 68% of Internet users are not native English speakers, although many are proficient (Internet World Stats). English dominance is likely to decrease as other-language resources are demanded for courses, and "popular" general information is added. Chinese, French, and Portuguese are listed by Internet World Stats as the fastest-growing languages on the Internet. Several studies have reported on the dramatic growth in China, Korea, and other Asian countries with financial, business, and management training e-learning (Payne 2002).

United States Internet Demographics

The Pew Internet and American Life Project presents a picture of the rapidly changing U.S. user, with the Internet used by 84% of those aged

18 to 29, 80% of those 30 to 49, and 67% of those 50 to 64. Approximately the same percentages of men and women use the Internet. The October 2005 Digital Divisions report shows growing participation in two groups: African-Americans and English-speaking Hispanics. Several studies have found that teenagers use the Internet more (for news, purchasing, banking, downloads, playing games, contacting friends, academics) than they watch television (Markoff 2004) and are increasingly identifying with the global marketplace, and less with the traditional family and school (Besley 2003).

Income and educational attainment continue to be the leading indicators of the digital divide—those with or without online technology access—among Americans under 65. In the more recent November Pew report (dated December 2005), only 29% of those without a high school diploma use the Internet, down from January. By contrast, 61% of high school graduates and 89% of those with some college education are Internet users. Providers need to consider whether their target population goes online. The new digital divide is connection: those with high-speed access are more likely to use the Internet than those with slower methods such as dial-up. Educators also need to determine whether they need to provide information and communication technology (ICT) skills training to enable their target audience to have a successful learning experience.

EDUCATION

Researchers have explored several trends in trying to determine the direction of higher education. Both nationally and internationally, enrollment in higher education is increasing. In many countries, much of the postsecondary, non-college education is vocational, technical, or certificated. In the United States, Howell et al. (2004) predicted a 16% increase in college and university enrollment and increased representation by gender (female), age (25+), and ethnicity in the next decade.

Gender and Ethnicity

Overall, world population statistics show equal or slightly higher numbers of females to males. A 2004 UNESCO report (p. 26) states that in most countries, gender parity in elementary education is at 44%, and only 13% of reporting countries have gender parity in the upper secondary level. This disparity can occur for both males and females, but is most commonly female.

In the United States, as postsecondary attendance has increased, so too have participation rates for several sectors. More women than men continue to enroll in college. In undergraduate education in the United States, 56% are female, and among students over age 29, 60% are female (National Center for Education Statistics 2005a). There has been a slow but continuing spread between male/female college participation rates (enrollment divided by total persons in group). In 1990 overall participation rates for the higher education population were almost the same, but by 2002 rates had spread to 42.8% for males and 47% for females (American Council on Education 2003–2004), and total minority enrollment numbers increased for minority females from 55% in 1980–1981 to 59% in 2002–2003.

Looking specifically at gender, there is a distinct difference, with a considerably larger proportion of all higher-education-enrolled minority groups, except Asian-Americans, being female. For example, proportionally, within the African-American population, more females are enrolled than are white females within the white population (Howell et al. 2003; Center for Labor Market Studies 2003; American Council on Education 2003 and 2004).

Enrollment for minority higher education has been increasing, 122% overall, with a 27% increase in college and university enrollment by 18- to 24-year-olds in the last 20 years (American Council on Education 2003, p. 5). However, differences occur in participation (enrollment divided by total persons in a group) by age and gender. With slight gains since the 1990s, white students (47%) still enroll in a greater percentage than Hispanics (32%) and African Americans (40%). One element common to all races is the higher female participation in this age group, with a male/female participation divide in whites (3%), African Americans (10%), and Hispanics (9%). The U.S. Hispanic population is expected to increase 63% by 2020, so even if the participation percentage does not grow, enrollment by this group will increase substantially.

Nontraditional Students

The National Center for Education Statistics (2005b) reports that nearly 75% of all undergraduates enrolled in institutions of higher education are "nontraditional." Nontraditional students are defined as having one or more of the following characteristics: don't enter postsecondary education in the same year they graduate from high school, attend school part-time, work full-time, are financially independent, have dependents, are single parents, and/or lack a high school diploma. Seventy-seven percent of 1999 graduates with a bachelor's degree attended two or more institutions, which could reflect several issues: cost, accessibility/schedule, first-in-the-family college student. E-learning enables colleges and universities to put their programs within reach of learners who need a high level of flexibility to complete a course.

Distance Education Participation

A 2005 NCES survey (2005b) reported that in 2002–2003, 36% of public school districts had students enrolled in distance education classes, 38% of public high school districts offered distance education courses, and about one-half of enrolled distance students took AP or college-level courses. Additionally, 46% of rural school districts had students in distance courses, compared to 28% of suburban and 23% of urban districts, with significantly higher enrollment in the southeast and central regions. An earlier NCES report (2004, p. 85) found that in 2000–2001, 56% of all higher education institutions offered distance courses, with an anticipated 12% adding courses within the next three years. Ninety percent of two-year and four-year public educational institutions offered online courses. Allen and Seaman (2004) reported that the number of private, for-profit schools offering courses increased dramatically, from 45% in 2002 to 89% in 2003. Associate's degree courses are the most popular, comprising about half of all online offerings from degree-granting institutions, and public postsecondary schools increasingly offer entire degree or certificate programs rather than sporadic classes.

Age

Older students or adult learners constitute approximately 42% of all students at both private and public higher education institutions and are the fastest-growing population in higher education (Aslanian 2001, p. 4). The number of 18- to 24-year-old students increased 41% between 1970 and 2000, while the number of adult students increased 170% (Aslanian 2001).

The age of online learners shows both the increasing acceptance by traditional students and the preference for online classes by older students. NCES reported that in 1999, 65% of those 18 or younger had enrolled in an online course, as had 57% of 19- to 23-year-olds, 56% of 24- to 29-year-olds, and 63% of those 30 and older (Palloff & Pratt 2003, p. 3).

E-LEARNERS

Economic necessity and the rapidly changing job market make continuing education of increasing importance. E-learners want "options, choices and personalization of learning opportunities" (Ausburn 2004, p. 14), and they share adult learner characteristics of "need-to-know, immediacy of application, sharing of life experiences as a source of knowledge, independence and self-direction, and ownership of one's own learning" (p. 2).

Business/Industry

Mungania's 2003 international study of barriers to e-learning focused on the business world and identified self-efficacy, computer competence, and training as statistically significant predictors of e-learning success. Common demographics such as age, gender, ethnicity, and marital status were not considered significant, although there are several important correlates such as ethnicity and level of education, and gender and computer skills and/or training.

Gallaher and Wentling (2004) determined that of various general demographic variables (gender, age, employment, etc.) influencing the rate of adoption of e-learning, only two, education level and Internet use, were significant. Recent research by Zhang further supports this (2005). What had greater impact was the culture of a professional group. For example, marketing and finance professionals had been early adopters of e-learning and late adopters of human resources (p. 82). Providers (industry management) rank the quality or reputation of the online teaching as the highest priority (Martin & Jennings 2002, p. 31), while users are most concerned with communication, technical ability, and relevance.

Learning Styles: Male and Female

As colleges and universities develop courses for e-learning, one must consider the potential impact of gender on adult learning styles. In the 2002 study conducted by Lynna Ausburn, both genders placed high value on effective communication with online instructors and classmates. Additionally, both desire customization of learning opportunities. However, there were some noticeable differences. When asked to rank the importance of various course goals, responses were weighted toward technology for males (desire to expand technology skills and for fast and effective assistance) and belonging and involvement for females (p. 12).

Preliminary research of Blocher et al. (2002, p. 7) on online M.Ed. students, using the Motivated Strategies Learning Questionnaire (MSLQ), showed a high intrinsic goal orientation of 6.57, and lower extrinsic goal orientation of 4.14.

Patrick Sullivan conducted a study of e-learning experiences among students at the Manchester Community College in Manchester, Connecticut. He found that both male and female students considered the lack of in-person interaction a downside to the online environment; they missed the face-to-face class interaction and exchange of ideas. He found that the women students mentioned family or children five times more frequently than did men as a factor for regarding the flexibility of online courses positively, a natural extension of the reality that female distance students tend to have family responsibilities while traditional students and male students in general have fewer family responsibilities.

Males are often viewed as having more positive attitudes to computers than do females, but this could be based on familiarity. Females use computers less, and when they do, it is more for educational purposes, while males tend to use the computer for information and games (Javid 2001, p. 194). This has direct impact on e-learning self-efficacy (Mungania 2003).

The 2004 study of business and accounting students by Holcomb et al. reported "no statistically significant gender difference for technology self-efficacy, distance education self-efficacy, or self-regulation skills" (p. 9). This population of younger students, used to computers, spreadsheets, and databases, might be reflective of the coming more computer literate population. Ong & Lai's (2004) study of Taiwanese workers in international companies found that men rated computer self-efficacy higher than did women and that they were looking for pragmatic "perceived usefulness" (e.g., increased performance) reasons to use online systems (p. 12). Correspondingly, the lower self-efficacy found in women more strongly influenced their perceived usefulness and perceived ease-of-use ratings (p. 4). But POEBI had a higher scoring by men (p. 9).

Carlson and Firpo's (2001) report on computer use in schools in Africa, Latin America, and the Middle East tends to support the idea that the difficulty of acquisition of computer skills and related use in learning is overrated, and that for participants the greatest perceived impact was the ability to get better jobs, followed by improved communication and reasoning skills (p. 92). They also reported that although the majority of teachers felt no gender differences, of those who did, the impact was usually greater on the girls in the areas of communication skills and attitudes to school.

The 2001 Moskal and Dziuban study of courses at a large Florida university showed some distinct differences between online and traditional-class demographics. Web-based classes were 73% female, compared to 57% female in face-to-face courses, which was almost identical to overall enrollment for females. They found that the Web-based students were older (mean = 30) than the face-to-face students (mean = 24). They also found that 51% of the female students were employed full-time, compared to 42% of the males (p. 166).

Halsne and Gatta (2003) found that online students had a more visual learning style than traditional students, who had high auditory and kinesthetic learning styles. Web-site design, and presumably other online programs, also has a gender component. A recent University of Glamorgan study (Key 2005) found that women generally prefer color and informal presentations; men, darker colors, horizontal lines, formal type, and expert language. They found that each gender preferred pages designed by their own gender. They also found that 94% of university websites have a masculine bent, while only 2% reflect female preferences. Given the importance of hybridized courses, which use a variety of technologies for successful online learning, designers and teachers should look carefully at creating effective interfaces.

Digital Natives and Digital Immigrants

> Today's average college grads have spent less than 5,000 hours of their lives reading, but over 10,000 hours playing video games (not to mention 20,000 hours watching TV). Computer games, email, the Internet, cell phones and instant messaging are integral parts of their lives.—Marc Prensky

Marc Prensky coined the terms "digital natives" and "digital immigrants." Students categorized as digital natives "are all 'native speakers' of the digital language of computers, video games and the Internet." These students are typically under the age of 30 and are known for their skills at multitasking and parallel-processing. They usually prefer seeing graphics before text, are used to receiving information instantaneously, and are very comfortable working in hyperlinked environments. If completing course-related work online, they might expect to receive frequent rewards or feedback.

Students older than 30 who were not born into the digital world but have adapted to it later in life are referred to as digital immigrants. They use technology but retain, to some degree, habits associated with their predigital past. For example, the immigrant may prefer to print out a document written with computer word-processing software to edit it, rather than just editing it onscreen.

When designing e-learning courses for digital natives, it is important to determine what students expect from e-learning and how they currently enjoy using technology. "They want to be connected, principally to one another. They want to be entertained by games, music, and movies. And they want to present themselves and their work."

CULTURES AND ASSOCIATED LEARNING STYLES

The need for e-learning is a global concern, closely related to changing technology, computer skills (or lack of needed skills), competition, demographics, and topics and changes in the workplace. Although there are many international programs, businesses and business higher education remain the leading users of e-learning and e-learning products. Business courses have found students around the world, but local market demands, such as foreign-language courses, which are common in Japan, may be unique to a culture or country (Zemsky & Massy 2004, p. 54).

Differences occur within groups such as the European Union, where France and Germany are far less accepting of distance education than the United Kingdom and the Scandinavian countries, where distance programs are well integrated within learning as a whole (Martin & Jennings 2002, p. 43). Several studies have explored how cultural factors can impact one's ability to gain knowledge in an e-learning environment. Wilson (2001) described this as "cultural distance" based on organizational, linguistic, cognitive, and motivational forces.

Wong & Trinidad (2004) contend that cultural differences can explain the wide gap that exists between the learning styles of students from Western countries and those from China and Hong Kong. Student/instructor roles are influenced by Chinese Confucian-heritage culture, in which students are taught to exhibit learning behavior that is considered passive, reactive, uncritical, and noncollaborative by Western standards. They conclude by recommending that e-learning courses be designed to exploit synchronous rather than asynchronous technologies that will enhance communication and interaction, and ultimately reduce the cultural gap between Western learners and those from China and Hong Kong (p. 11).

Separate from the broad and comprehensive country-specific "business system" approach discussed in the Martin & Jennings report are more concentrated foci such as the EMILE Project, Comparative Report (2002). This named four distinct educational "cultural groups" found in 23 European Union countries and stated that "schooling of the Germanic, Scandinavian, Anglo-Saxon or Latin type is regularly adapted to a nationally-oriented environment and cultural tradition. This is why formulas that are successfully applied by one are not necessarily applicable to another" (p. 37). Barron's 2003 report showed several geographic or cultural differences. U.S. and Canadian users rated their e-learning experiences highest, while Asia/Pacific respondents were least favorable. Again, Asians reported a greater need for personalization and synchronous tools than did North American or European users (p. 4).

In the seminal works by Geert Hofstede (2001) on cultural differences in thinking and work-related preferences, he categorizes those differences along five dimensions: power distance index (PDI), uncertainty avoidance index (UAI), individualism (IDV), masculinity (MAS) and long-term/short-term orientation (LTO). Hofstede's research reinforces the implications these cultural dimensions have on teaching and learning.

Countries with high PDI scores typically prefer an emphasis on student conformity, while those with low PDI scores may stress student-centered learning. Students from high UAI countries may have a greater fear of failure and a preference for clear instructions. High IDV scores might reflect a student's propensity for individual initiative and participation, where low-IDV countries may prefer an emphasis on maintaining class harmony in the e-learning environment. Students from those countries with high, "competitor" MAS scores may aspire for recognition that would be less desirable among students from countries with low, "nurturing" MAS scores. High LTO scores might reflect values of cooperation, respect for authority figures, and perseverance, as opposed to low scorers' greater uncertainty and need for "flexible" teaching and answers.

Each dimension is discussed below and includes a partial listing of countries at the highest and lowest rankings. Although culture does not explain all differences in individual learning styles, it should be taken into consideration when designing an e-learning class environment.

SELF-EFFICACY AND MOTIVATION

Bandura defined self-efficacy as "a person's judgment of their ability to organize and execute courses of action required to attain specific types of performances" (1986). Willingness to try and likelihood of success have direct co-relates to self-efficacy and intrinsic and extrinsic motivations. Demographically, age, gender, economic and educational levels all have impact on self-efficacy.

E-learners have a common interest in communication and having interesting classes. They differ by gender and self-efficacy, but tend to have similar reasons for taking classes—convenience of time, place, and flexibility. Blocher's reported high Intrinsic Goal Orientation of 6.57 to the lower ego 4.14 is ideal for distance education. Not unexpectedly, course relevancy is usually cited as the primary motive for online learning, followed by self-competence, reinforcement, and course interest (Laszlo and Kupritz 2003, p. 69). The most important characteristics for successful learning were receiving frequent instructor feedback and interesting (stimulating or arousing curiosity) course materials. Stafford (2005) reports that a combination of student ability (technology savvy) and social factors (interaction, feedback, etc.) demands a relevant, content-driven site "highly relevant, easy to use, and effective to search" to support motivation.

The digital divide is narrowing in most developed countries, and since computer access, a fast Internet connection, and good computer skills increasingly are the prerequisites for e-learning, this expands the e-learning world. Although there are age and gender differences between campus and distance students (Richardson et al. 1999; Richardson 2005), reports indicate that this has little influence on success, and more on the way students study—or to say this in another way, people adapt. Despite some common negative perceptions of women and technology, Christensen et al. (2001) reported that demographic differences such as gender and age are not strongly related to positive technical attitudes and receptivity to distance learning. They found that it is the perceived usefulness of the technology that determines attitudes, and that it can be influenced by experience and personal knowledge. Moreover, as technology increasingly allows distance classes to have many of the same learning-style flexibilities as traditional classes, there is increased satisfaction with the courses. Several studies support the positive-to-neutral effect of technology on learning (Pulichino 2005; Ali & Elfessi 2004; Gustafson 2003–2004).

Despite some ongoing hesitation about their computer competencies, users readily learn and adapt to new programs and systems (Mao & Brown 2005), and most skills are self- or peer-taught. Since there is a greater likelihood of a student taking repeated online classes, the need to learn the software diminishes, and self-efficacy increases (Carlson & Firpo 2001). As the Internet grows, as the user population increases, as the "millennials" age, technology self-efficacy is less likely to be a problem in the industrialized world, although in developing countries it will continue to be an issue. Ability to write is probably more important, since so much online is dependent on this form of communication.

While differences in learning motivation and styles are often based on age and life experiences, similarities occur in all demographic groups. Older students tend to be more self-directed, problem-centered, and looking for relevance or practical applications for their learning (Crawford 2004), but Frank et al. (2003) reported that the e-learning achievement of 11- to 12-year-olds is strongly influenced by self-direction and strong individual responsibility. He also reported another commonality with adult learners—social communication concerns. Interaction between student and teacher, and student to student, is a priority across all demographics (Ausburn 2004; Wong & Trinidad 2004; Frank et al. 2003).

There is some evidence that while age, GPA, and gender have little impact on perceived learning, and therefore performance, active instructor interaction is extremely important (Marks et al. 2005). The greater the internal locus of control, a learned trait, the more engaged and self-directed and successful a student will be. Consistent reinforcement for accomplishments is more likely to produce this than sporadic reinforcement. Students are thus more likely to remain in a class and continue using online courses (Parker 2003).

There is also a strong association between perceptions of the academic quality of courses in distance education and the study styles learners adopt (Richardson 2005). Successful online students seem to be more intrinsically motivated (Zhang 2005), which may explain their willingness to adapt. But even so, designers and teachers need to keep student competencies and objectives, learning strategies, and cultures in mind as they develop, refine, and market programs. Retaining students is primarily accomplished through satisfaction with the class, which is achieved by having a successful and interesting experience and by the quality of the education received (Zhang 2005; Parker 2003). The former can be accomplished by working to assure a student's "comfort" or trust level, primarily with the technologies employed and their online community (O'Brien & Renner 2002).

CONCLUSION

Today, social, technological, and economic drivers are transforming education systems around the world. . . . As local economies turn global, the development of a technologically skilled workforce becomes a worldwide concern; and as human capital becomes the chief source of economic value, education and training become lifelong endeavors for the majority of workers.—Peter J. Stokes, Eduventures.com, June 2000

There are some differences between online and traditional students: gender, age, income, marital status, some college classes, learning styles. Evans and Haase (2001) reported that business and management students were interested in online education more than in any other discipline. They also found that this was an older age group, employed, with relatively high incomes. The traditional North American college-age students were, at least initially, less interested, due to a perceived lack of personal contact with faculty and students, loss of campus experiences, and concerns about the quality of online education and their own ability to self-regulate for a successful learning experience.

These differences can often explain the online choice: age means more life experiences and responsibilities (time); motivation often comes from a practical desire to improve existing work positions and to get ahead; often for credit but not degree programs (focused, work-related); different study styles based on previous experiences. Both in-person and distance students are looking for the conveniences of a workable schedule and credit classes, and increasingly the former views online classes as "just another format," but one that can work with their life and lifestyle. The instructor must always bear in mind Ryan's (2001, p. 54) three factors for a potential student to consider—motivation, time, online comfort level.

Discovering who the e-learners are helps shape content development and information architecture, and it is an integral part of the business planning process.

REFERENCES

Ali, A., & Elfessi, A. (2004). Examining students performance and attitudes towards the use of information technology in a virtual and conventional setting. *Journal of Interactive Online Learning, 2*(3). Retrieved July 5, 2005 from http://www.ncolr .org/jiol/issues/PDF/2.3.5.pdf.

Allen, E. I., & Seaman, J. (2004). "Entering the mainstream: The quality and extent of online education in the United States, 2003 and 2004." Retrieved July 1, 2005 from http://www.sloan-c.org/resources/entering_mainstream.pdf.

American Council on Education. (2003). *Minorities in higher education: Annual status report 2002–2003* (20th ed.). Washington, D.C.: American Council on Education, Office of Minority Concerns.

———. (2004). *Minorities in higher education: Annual status report 2003–2004* (21st ed.). Washington, D.C.: American Council on Education, Office of Minority Concerns. Retrieved July 3, 2005 from http://www.ge.com/foundation/ minorities.pdf.

Aslanian, C. (2001). *Adult students today.* New York: The College Board, 2001.

Ausburn, L. (2004). Gender and learning strategy differences in nontraditional adult students' design preferences in hybrid distance courses. *Journal of Interactive Online Learning, 3*(2). Retrieved July 5, 2005 from http://www.ncolr.org/jiol/issues/ 2004/fall/06/index.pdf.

Barron, T. (2003). LoD survey: Quality and effectiveness of e-learning. *Learning Circuits* (May 16, 2003). Retrieved July 12, 2005 from http://www.learningcircuits .org/2003/may2003/qualitysurvey.htm.

Besley, A. C. (2003). Hybridized and globalized: Youth cultures in the postmodern era. *Review of Education, Pedagogy, and Cultural Studies, 25*(2), 153–177.

Blocher, J. M., Sujo de Montes, L., Willis, E. M., & Tucker, G. (2002). Online learning: Examining the successful student profile. *Journal of Interactive Online Learning, 1*(2). Retrieved July 12, 2005 from http://www.ncolr.org/jiol/issues/2002/fall/02/ index.pdf.

Botelho, G. (2004). Online schools clicking with students. CNN.com. Retrieved May 14, 2005 from http://www.cnn.com/2004/EDUCATION/08/13/b2s.e-learning/.

Carlson, S., & Firpo, J. (2001). Integrating computers into teaching: Findings from a 3-year program in 20 developing countries. In L. R. Vandervert, L. V. Shavinina, & R. A. Cornell (eds.), *Cybereducation: The future of long-distance learning* (pp. 85–114). Larchmont, N.Y.: Mary Ann Liebert, Inc.

Center for Labor Market Studies. (2003). *The growing gender gaps in college enrollment and degree attainment in the United States and their potential economic and social consequences.* Retrieved April 6, 2005 from http://www.brtable.org/pdf/943.pdf.

Christensen, E. W., Anakwe, U. P., & Kessler, E. H. (2001). Receptivity to distance learning: The effect of technology, constraints, and learning preferences. *Journal of Research on Computing in Education, 33*(3), 263–279.

Crawford, D. L. (2004). *The role of aging in adult learning: Implications for instructors in higher education.* Retrieved May 28, 2005 from http://www.newhorizons.org/ lifelong/higher_ed/crawford.htm.

EMILE Project. (2002). *The introduction of ICT into primary and secondary schools: A comparative report from six European countries.* Retrieved July 30, 2005 from http:// www.scotland.gov.uk/Resource/Doc/933/0007617.doc.

Evans, J. R., & Haase, I. M. (2001). Online business education in the twenty-first century: An analysis of potential target markets. *Internet Research: Electronic Networking Applications and Policy, 11*(3), 246–260.

Frank, M., Reich, N., & Humphreys, K. (2003). Respecting the human needs of students in the development of e-learning. *Computers & Education, 40*(1), 57–70.

Gallaher, J., & Wentling, T. L. (2004). The adoption of e-learning across professional groups. *Performance Improvement Quarterly, 17*(3), 66–85.

Gustafson, K. (2003–2004). The impact of technologies on learning. *Planning for Higher Education, 32*(2), 37–43. Available online from the Wilson Education Web database.

Halsne, A. M., & Gatta, L. A. (2003). *Online versus traditionally-delivered instruction: A descriptive study of learner characteristics in a community college setting.* Retrieved August 7, 2005 from http://www.westga.edu/%7Edistance/ojdla/spring51/halsne51.html.

Hofstede, G. H. (2001). *Culture's consequences: Comparing values, behaviors, institutions, and organizations across nations* (2nd ed.). Thousand Oaks, Calif.: Sage.

Holcomb, L. B., King, F. B., & Brown, S. W. (2004). Student traits and attributes contributing to success in online courses: Evaluation of university online courses. *Journal of Interactive Online Learning, 2*(3). Retrieved May 19, 2005 from http://www.ncolr.org/jiol/issues/2004/winter/04/index.pdf.

Howell, S. L., Williams, P. B., & Lindsay, N. K. (2003). Thirty-two trends affecting distance education: An informed foundation for strategic planning. *Online Journal of Distance Learning Administration, 6*(3). Retrieved October 29, 2005 from http://www.westga.edu/~distance/ojdla/fall63/howell63.html.

ITU, International Telecommunication Union. *Connect the World Initiative.* http://www.itu.int/home/index.html.

Internet World Stats. http://www.Internetworldstats.com/stats.htm.

"Japan E-Learning 2005–2009 Forecast." Retrieved June 19, 2005 from http://www.marketresearch.com/map/prod/1102414.html.

Javid, M. A. (2001). Edmonds and Kamiak cyberschools: Two innovative emerging models for cybereducation. In L. R. Vandervert, L. V. Shavinina, & R. A. Cornell (eds.), *Cybereducation: The future of long-distance learning* (pp. 185–217). Larchmont, N.Y.: Mary Ann Liebert, Inc.

"Key Website Research Highlights Gender Bias. (August 17, 2005). University of Glamorgan. Retrieved August 18, 2005 from http://www.glam.ac.uk/news/releases/003056.php.

Laszlo, F., Jr, & Kupritz, V. W. (2003). The identification of online learning motives in use by undergraduate students. *Delta Pi Epsilon Journal, 45*(1), 63–72.

Mai, J.-Y., & Brown, B. R. (2005). The effectiveness of online task support vs. instructor-led training. *Journal of Organizational and End User Computing, 17*(3). Available online from the ABI/INFORM Global database.

Markoff, J. (2004). Internet use said to cut into TV viewing and socializing. *New York Times*, December 30.

Marks, R. B., Sibley, S. D., & Arbaugh, J. B. (2005). A structural equation model of predictors for effective online learning. *Journal of Management Education, 29*(4), 531–563.

Martin, G., & Jennings, A. (2002). *The adoption, diffusion and exploitation of e-learning in Europe.* Scottish Enterprise. May 16, 2005. Retrieved May 30, 2005 from http://www.scottish-enterprise.com/publications/the_adoption,_diffusion_and_exploitation_of_e-learning_in_europe.pdf.

Moskal, P. D., & Dziuban, C. D. (2001). In Vandervert L. R., Shavinina, L. V., and Cornell, R. A. (eds.), *Present and future directions of assessing cybereducation: The changing research paradigm* in *cybereducation: The future of long-distance learning.* Larchmont, N.Y.: Mary Ann Liebert, Inc.

Mungania, P. (2003). *The seven e-learning barriers facing employees.* Retrieved June 23, 2005 from http://www.aerckenya.org/docs/E-learningReport.pdf.

National Center for Education Statistics. (2004). *The condition of education 2004.* Washington, D.C.: U.S. Dept. of Education, Office of Educational Research and Improvement, National Center for Education Statistics. Retrieved June 21, 2005 from http://nces.ed.gov/pubs2004/2004077.pdf.

———. (2005a). *The condition of education 2005.* Washington, D.C.: U.S. Dept. of Education, Office of Educational Research and Improvement, National Center for Education Statistics.

———. (2005b). *Distance Education Courses for Public Elementary and Secondary School Students: 2002–03.* Retrieved June 21, 2005 from http://nces.ed.gov/pubs2005/2005010.pdf.

O'Brien, B. S., & Renner, A. L. (2002). *Online student retention: Can it be done?* Retrieved from http://www.aace.org/DL.

Ong, C.-S., & Lai, J.-Y. (2004). Gender differences in perceptions and relationships among dominants of e-learning acceptance. *Computers in Human Behavior, 22*(5), 816–829.

Palloff, R. M., & Pratt, K. (2003). *The virtual student: A profile and guide to working with online learners* (1st ed.). San Francisco: Jossey-Bass.

Parker, A. (2003). Identifying predictors of academic persistence in distance education. *USDLA Journal, 17*(1). Retrieved August 7, 2005 from http://www.usdla.org/html/journal/JAN03_Issue/article06.html.

Payne, C. (2002). The e-learning market in Asia-Pacific. *Asia-Pacific Insights.* Retrieved August 13, 2005 from http://www.apconnections.com/perspective/02-March.html.

PEW Internet & American Life Project: Demographics of Internet users. Retrieved June 13, 2005 from http://www.pewinternet.org/trends/User_Demo_05.18.05.htm.

PEW Internet & American Life Project: Digital Divisions. Retrieved December 2, 2005 from http://www.pewinternet.org/pdfs/PIP_Digital_Divisions_Oct_5_2005.pdf.

Prensky, Mark. (2001). Digital natives, digital immigrants. *On the Horizon 9*(5). Retrieved June 3, 2005 from http://www.twitchspeed.com/site/Prensky-Digital Natives,Digital Immigrants-Part1.htm.

Pulichino, J. (2005). *Current trends in e-learning research report.* The E-learning Guild. Retrieved May 29, 2005 from http://www.e-learningguild.com/pdf/1/mar05-trends.pdf.

Richardson, J. T. E. (2005). Students' perceptions of academic quality and approaches to studying in distance education. *British Educational Research Journal, 31*(1), 7–27.

Richardson, J. T. E., Morgan, A., & Woodley, A. (1999). Approaches to studying in distance education. *Higher Education, 37*(1), 23–35.

Ryan, S. (2001). Is online learning right for you? *American Agent & Broker, 73*(6). Available online, from ABI/Inform Global database.

Stafford, T. F. (2005). Understanding motivations for Internet use in distance education. *IEEE Transactions on Education, 48*(2), 301–306.

Stokes, P. (2000). *E-learning: Education businesses transform schooling.* Eduventures.com.
Retrieved May 2005 from http://www.eduventures.com/pdf/doe_e-learning.pdf.

UNESCO. (2004). *Global monitoring report: Education for all.* Paris: UNESCO from
http://portal.unesco.org/education/en/ev.php-URL_ID=35874&URL_DO=DO_
TOPIC&URL_SECTION=201.html.

Wilson, M. S. (2001). Cultural considerations in online instruction and learning.
Distance Education, 22(1), 52–64.

Wong, L. F., & Trinidad, S. G. (2004). Using Web-based distance learning to reduce
cultural distance. *Journal of Interactive Online Learning, 3*(1). Retrieved June 20,
2005 from http://www.ncolr.org/jiol/issues/2004/summer/02/index.pdf.

Zemsky, R., & Massy, W. F. (2004). *Thwarted innovation: What happened to e-learning
and why.* The Learning Alliance. Retrieved June 11, 2005 from http://www.irhe
.upenn.edu/WeatherStation.html.

Zhang, Y. (2005). Distance learning receptivity. *Quarterly Review of Distance Education, 6*(1), 45–53.

2

What Is E-Learning?

Tiffini Travis, California State University, Long Beach

Ask 10 different people to define e-learning and you will get 10 different answers. The most common definition is using technology to enhance learning. However, technology and learning take many forms, are used on many scales, and can be delivered for entirely different outcomes. Before we can accurately define e-learning, it's important to discuss the state of the industry, who is using e-learning, and elements of e-learning that distinguish good products from products that don't work. This chapter seeks to give a general overview of e-learning to provide context for the case studies presented in this book. By examining the state of the e-learning industry and elements of best practice, we set the stage for exploring the benefits of developing business plans in the context of e-learning.

E-LEARNING, THE INDUSTRY

Categories of service in the e-learning space include "portals, content providers, learning customization service providers, learning management software providers and specialist technology companies" (Morgan 2001). The e-learning industry can be divided into two categories—educational services and applications software. Educational services can be defined as companies that provide both platform and content, while applications software providers supply the platform, but not content. According to Datamonitor market analysis, the global education services sector consists of private universities, providers of educational seminars and correspondence teaching, educational materials, technical education, driving schools, language schools, and schools for recreational activities (Datamonitor 2005).

Table 2.1.   Global Education Services Sector, 2004

Category	% Market Share
Technical and trade schools	24.5
Business schools and computer and management training	23.9
Educational support services	19.6
Other	32.0
Total	100.0

Source: Datamonitor

Both educational services and software applications industries have seen steady growth over the last five years. The traditional education field is still one of the largest consumers and producers of e-learning. In 2004, the sector's value globally increased by 8.4% to $110.6 billion. Technical and trade schools account for the largest share of the sector, generating total revenue of $27.2 billion in 2004, equivalent to 24.5% of the sector's total value. (See table 2.1.) The United States remains the largest market for educational services; however, the market in Asia has increased significantly, with a 33% market share in 2004. (See table 2.2.) This is due to a higher demand for skilled employees, the increased use of online distance-education courses, and a greater need for English-language training.

Based upon sales, the largest U.S. company in this industry is the Apollo Group, creators of popular online-only schools, including the University of Phoenix, the Institute of Professional Development, and Western International University. Their revenue was as much as $1.8 billion, an increase of 34.3% from the previous year (Datamonitor 2005).

The majority of e-learning in the private sector uses various software applications. Primary products include learning management systems (LMS), intranets, conference systems, and other courseware systems. The market size for LMS producers in the United States was over $350 million in 2003 (Spangler 2004).

Table 2.2.   Global Education Services Sector Segmentation, 2004

Geography	% Market Share
United States	34.3
Asia-Pacific	33.0
Europe	25.2
Rest of the world	7.5
Total	100.0

Source: Datamonitor

Typical of most technology-driven industries, e-learning has shown a tendency toward market consolidation. Global information technology research firm Gartner has predicted that 25% of vendors in the market may be acquired by others by 2006. Already this is evident in the acquisition of smaller LMS providers by larger companies. Within the last two years notable companies have been bought out by others; SumTotal purchased Pathlore, Blackboard purchased WebCT, Saba purchased Sentra, and Huveaux purchased Epic.

By 2008 the total e-learning market should more than double in value, rising to $13.5 billion in the U.S. and $21 billion globally (Tucker 2005). The obvious advantage of using an online platform to reach large numbers of students or employees who may or may not be in one centralized location is the lower cost and flexibility. This has led to an increased use by schools and corporations providing more educational content via the Internet. For educators e-learning on the Internet offers the advantage of reaching students outside of the classroom and getting people to enroll regardless of physical location and work/home schedules. For corporations, e-learning offers the opportunity to reduce travel expenses and salaries for in-person instructors, and leads to increased productivity. What has been emerging in recent years is an expansion of e-learning not only to enhance the learning process but to satisfy needs not being met due to a lack of skills or funding within an organization. Both advantages translate to increasing profits and efficiency. The rush to develop e-learning has led to the creation of innovative products and not-so-innovative products. With more choices, as well as a growing body of research regarding the most effective way to provide learning online, it has become increasingly difficult to select the best e-learning products for users.

THE LANDSCAPE OF E-LEARNING

Higher Education

The primary users of e-learning are as varied as the products they are buying. Internationally, almost all countries are involved in some sort of e-learning effort, whether it is at the level of the company, government, or higher education.

Universities and colleges have always been at the forefront of using e-learning. The latest distance-learning statistics for the United States indicate that in 2001, 90% of public two-year and 89% of public four-year institutions already offer distance-education courses (Waits and Lewis 2003). Online learning accounted for 90% of distance learning at these same institutions. Concurrently, 57% of Canadian universities offered online courses, and 34% of Japanese universities used the Internet for learning. Exporting e-learning has become very profitable for many Western countries. The U.S., Australia, the UK, Germany, and the Netherlands are countries profiting from the export of higher-education e-learning projects. In 2002, the U.S. was the largest provider of distance learning, with the UK, Canada, Germany, and France following closely behind (van der Wende 2002).

Government

Public sector e-learning is a growing area of the market mainly due to its cost-cutting benefits and capacity to reach large numbers of tax-paying citizens. Governments are providing on-the-job training for their employees as well. Developing countries rely on e-learning and funding by outside agencies to increase access to education as well as training for government staff. E-learning has afforded countries the means to train staff without the expense of travel or importing experts to provide in-house training. Efforts undertaken by the World Bank illustrate this form of third-party service. It recently launched a global learning management system to educate service workers and the public on a variety of topics, including HIV prevention and city development.

African countries are primary examples of using e-learning to reach rural or economically disadvantaged peoples. They have been developing e-learning endeavors to meet the overwhelming need to raise the educational attainment of citizens. While distance education has been around for more than 65 years in some areas, the transition to online learning has expanded the possibility of meeting the educational goals of the countries. Currently, African governments can spend as much as 25% of their budgets on education, so the move to e-learning is appealing.

Another region using e-learning to further government objectives is the United Arab Emirates. The city of Dubai has taken a lead in the region by deploying eGovernment applications and is among the first few governments in the world to provide such integrated services to its citizens. The government portal is "a single contact point masking the complexity of the bureaucratic procedures, and guiding access to all services in the easiest possible way" (Al-Bawaba 2006).

Partnerships

The use of e-learning in governments and academic institutions is not mutually exclusive. Both sectors are seeing the advantages of developing partnerships to facilitate e-learning on a broader scale. Consortia have become an essential element of successful e-learning. For some governments it is a way to shift from a labor force to a knowledge-based workforce without losing educated populations to Western countries. Developing countries in particular are using partnerships to increase the reach of their e-learning efforts. Africa and China have been collaborating with higher-education institutions in the U.S., Australia, and the UK. In China, CERNET was developed to facilitate distance learning, and as of 2002 had 932 colleges connected to their network, with over 80,000 users connected countrywide (Kang 2005). Today, China has 15 million students enrolled in postsecondary education. To meet growing demand, CERNET recently joined forces with e-learning software provider Blackboard to develop online courses to increase the reach of China's e-learning efforts (Blackboard 2006). Additionally, the European Union (EU) and China have been working on joint efforts to "pave the way to the development of new education and training programs applicable to the EU and Chinese environments, bridging the current gap between EU and Chinese open and distance education models and strategies" (International Council for Open and Distance Education n.d.). Global Universitas 21, founded in 2001, is the online version of the widely successful international consortium Universitas 21, created by the University of Melbourne. Likewise, projects like the African Virtual University, with 53 participating institutions in 27 countries, are continuing to showcase e-learning success (African Virtual University 2005).

Corporate

While the major users of e-learning traditionally have been universities and distance-learning programs, the private sector has recognized the value of e-learning to meet required compliance training and professional development. Compliance training includes discrimination and sexual harassment training modules, certificated tasks, and IT training. E-learning as a professional development tool has been used by organizations to allow members to update skills or to fulfill credit. In the United States, the American Library Association has offered webcasts of presentations that allow for interactive discussions via email and online surveys. The Dental Channel in the UK has used e-learning to train dentists in endodontics. The success of their endeavor can be seen in the use of their training modules by 25% of dentists in England and Wales (E-learning Age 2005). Likewise, Doctors .net.uk developed an e-learning program called *Incident Management*, to train doctors to respond to disasters. They were able to achieve resounding effects. In one year, over 4,452 general practitioners completed the training, and "97.3% of participants reported that the training increased their knowledge of the steps to take to prepare their practice and staff for a chemical or infectious disease incident" (Doctors.net.uk 2006).

The growing importance of corporate e-learning is also evident. According to the International Data Group (IDC), nearly 80% of all companies and 90% of organizations with 10,000 or more employees are either currently creating e-learning objects internally or are planning to do so in the future (Britt 2004). In a study of Fortune 500 companies conducted by Larstan Business Reports, 85% said they planned to expand the role of e-learning (Archibald 2005). Many of these companies believe that eventually, half of their training budgets will be devoted to e-learning. Notable industry leader 3COM has dedicated 75% of its training budget specifically to computer-based learning (Allen 2003). In the UK, training has become a primary area of focus for businesses. The 2004 National Employers Skills Survey showed that 64% of respondents offered some type of training to remedy skill deficiencies in their organizations. Forty-eight percent of respondents had a formal training plan in place, while 59% identified training with new technology as one of the areas being taught. The calculated cost of training was roughly 205 GPB ($362 USD) per worker (Learning and Skills Council 2005).

Course Management Systems (CMS) and
Learning Management Systems (LMS)

The diverse field of users of e-learning has resulted in growth in the number of e-learning products available for purchase. The primary tools used to facilitate e-learning are course management systems (CMS) and learning management systems (LMS). Commonly used related terms include learning content management system (LCMS), managed learning environment (MLE), and virtual learning environment (VLE). *LMS* and *enterprise course management systems* are often interchangeable (Long 2001). The EDUCAUSE Evolving Technologies Committee offers a reliable definition of a CMS: "it provides an instructor with a set of tools and a framework that allows the relatively easy creation of online course content and the subsequent teaching and management of that course, including various interactions with students taking the course" (Meerts 2003). Blackboard, WebCt, and Desire2Learn are examples of commercially available course management systems. Moodle, Sakai, Angel, and Bodington are examples of open source management systems. Examinations of the definitions proffered above exemplify/reflect the following similarities: these systems are tools-based software, providing instructors and trainers with a straightforward approach for developing teaching material and offering a multifaceted, interactive learning environment for students. Typical components of C/LMS include uploading of course materials—syllabi, assignments, etc.—in a variety of formats (MS Word, PowerPoint, Excel), asynchronous communication tools such as bulletin boards and email, assessment tools (online quizzes and tests), and administration tools enabling instructors to record grades and track each student's progress throughout the course.

Much of the literature focuses on distinguishing between these two types of systems, so it is practical to review the major arguments. Saul Carliner, educational technology professor, posits that LMS and CMS have many similar components on the surface but that in order to select the most appropriate system for an institution or an organization's needs, it is useful to know the differences. One distinction that he points out is that CMS were designed to support teaching and learning for classrooms in academic environments, and LMS for corporate training (Carliner 2005). Carliner expounds on features and challenges to users for each of these types of systems. CMS provide a fluid mechanism for faculty to input and manage course materials through the use of templates, thus making CMS a popular choice for instructors. This same ease in functionality can pose challenges, such as diminished flexibility in revising course design features and labels, and restrictions on interactivity; instructors are unable to create instructional activities using external tools like Flash or Dreamweaver within the system; rather, they must develop and house them in other virtual locations (Carliner 2005). LMS distinguish themselves from CMS by providing software for registering students, tracking participation, "skills management," and "process charges for courses" (Carliner 2005).

There are key areas that should be considered when evaluating off-the-shelf products or open source systems. In a 2006 study of L/CMS, administrators, faculty, and students identified strengths and weaknesses of current systems. Three issues emerged from these stakeholders' feedback: compatibility and interoperability, usability, and smartness/dumbness. In terms of compatibility, a number of administrators felt it important to examine open source options to tackle this challenge, while others were skeptical about reliability. Integration with other systems was a factor, and "browser incompatibility" problems surfaced during discussions with administrators (Jafari, McGee, and Carmean 2006, 52–54). These same stakeholders expressed their aspirations for the next-generation e-learning environment, covering five areas. Smart systems—Faculty and students would like more intuitive systems that pick up on the habits of users, remember them, and make adjustments to cut down on repetitive tasks. In general, they wanted "more control"—they need enhanced capabilities to "track and analyze students' work across system functions" (Jafari, McGee, and Carmean 2006, 56). Environment—Administrators want an "immersive" environment that could "support games, worlds . . . and Faculty are requesting access to more entities on campus and tools-integration" (Jafari, McGee, and Carmean 2006, 52–54). Archives and storage—Administrators desire "new and improved ways to migrate, transport, extract compact and back up course content. . . . Students want to "access and store content over the duration of their degree work . . . and to be able to return to a former course and

locate materials" (Jafari, McGee, and Carmean 2006, 52–54). Multi-Modal/
Multimedia—This involves both communication channels and collaborative tools. Students would like to be able to utilize the software that is au
courant to them: chat, IM, podcasts, Skype. Faculty also want these types of
tools integrated into the management system, along with more collaborative tools such as Flickr, wikis, dellicio.us, and the like (Jafari, McGee, and
Carmean 2006, 52–54). Mobile computing—Both faculty and students
desire to be freed of spatial boundaries. They want to be able to use PDAs
and smart phones to access relevant course materials and to receive email
(Jafari, McGee, and Carmean 2006, 52–54).

In addition to these identified traits, e-learning producers should carefully evaluate content, design, and the future applications available in this
rapidly changing environment.

Best Practices for E-Learning Content

It is important that e-learning developers consider their content. In the
initial phases of Web-based e-learning, instructors merely included things
they formerly used in other formats. Not only did they fail to utilize the
tools available in an online environment, but also they neglected to modify
their content to fit the new needs of their target audience. Likewise, the
ability to modify design of content was lacking in many first-generation
products. Instructional design should take basic principles such as layout
and the density of text into consideration. An exemplary e-learning tool
will allow the tailoring of content. A good system will facilitate learning by
accounting for multiliteracies and different learning styles of an audience.
Collaborative learning via discussion groups, IM, blogs, facilitators, etc., is a
key support for learning outside of the text and graphics delivered through
a learning system.

Whether purchasing or developing original content, one must determine
the potential cost of modifying the system in the future. For example, the
company Rent-A-Center contracted with an e-learning services provider to
convert its existing training materials into 12 hours of content. According
to the company, this conversion cost 50% more than what it spent on the
learning management system itself (Spangler 2004).

Content design should match the type of e-learning being provided. If
there are large blocks of information, then a formal course is the preferred
option. Segments of information used for quick training can be formatted
in a smaller "rapid e-learn" design. Rapid e-learning is point-of-need for
particular tasks rather than entire courses on a particular topic (Archibald
2005). Minitutorials on topics such as how to sell items on eBay or use a
research database are simpler, less costly versions of e-learning designed to
meet task-oriented needs rather than to expand knowledge. This point-of-

need trend can be seen with the development of Giunti Labs' creation of the eXact iTutor, which is a wearable learning platform allowing for hands-free learning on a factory floor. This innovation can be used for all types of training where performance of the task is integrated into the learning process. Giunti is on the frontlines of integrating gaming technology into e-learning (E-Learning Age 2005).

Effective e-learning should allow for content to adapt with evolving technologies. Podcasting and gaming technologies have been integrated into current learning systems and diversify the delivery of content. Organizations are now experimenting with PDAs and other handheld tools for facilitating the online learning experience. New technologies can take e-learning off the desktop and allow for lifelong learning in a car, on a plane, or on a remote island.

The use of learning objects in designing content allows for the packaging and repackaging of information independent of the form new technologies may take. Regardless of format, e-learning should account for individual learning goals and allow students the means to demonstrate their understanding of the content presented. A sound pedagogy will result in a meaningful experience for both providers and learners. Content for an e-learning site should contextually resonate with the user. According to the EPIC survey on the future of e-learning, respondents believed the most likely reason e-learning was successful in their organization was content—above effective management, buy-in, and good learner support (Clark and Hooley 2003).

Developing a social learning experience for users is one difficult aspect of e-learning. Often, users will be isolated from virtual classmates and never meet the instructor in person. There are two basic types of learning online—asynchronous and synchronous. Interactive learning can be achieved by providing a blended learning experience or utilizing online social networking tools. The Open University of the UK uses blended learning for half of its 375 courses (NIACE 2005). Blended, hybrid, blended e-learning, mixed-mode: all are terms connoting the concept of combining multiple methods of instruction delivery. A closer examination of variances in meaning of this concept will elucidate the value of this alternative online learning strategy.

In addition, the generic definition of blended learning, which is melding face-to-face instruction with online delivery modes, addresses other important factors that need to be taken into account. This definition, derived from the business arena, refocuses the emphasis on business learning objectives and outcomes rather than on the technology-based delivery mode: "Blended learning focuses on optimizing achievement of learning objectives by applying the 'right' learning technologies to match the 'right' personal learning style to transfer the 'right' skills to the 'right' person at the 'right time'" (Singh and Reed 2001, 1). The essential elements of this definition are grounded in the idea that learning objectives and delivery modes should be in balance; individuals' learning styles must be acknowledged and considered in the design process; constructivist theories such as taking into account prior knowledge of the learner must be integrated into the learning experience; and just-in-time and "just-what-I-need" strategies should be factored into curriculum and delivery planning (Singh and Reed 2001, 2). Hybrid learning aims to combine the best of both traditional and online learning activities.

Models

Enterprises and academia are investigating the efficacy of utilizing blended learning strategies. Models of blended e-learning abound. Dimensions of blending applied to a business context include melding offline and online learning, combining traditional classroom methods with virtual approaches; self-paced and live, mixing "solitary, on-demand" learning with collaborative learning; and structured and unstructured learning, which incorporates both formal (e.g., classes, tutorials) and informal learning activities, such as creating "knowledge repositories for capturing conversations and casual meeting that result in some training" (Singh and Reed 2001, 2). The most prevalent uses of blended training by corporations are "sales force training, new product rollout, skill/software updates, new employee orientation & human resources and personal & professional development" (New Jersey Institute of Technology n.d.) Companies using blended learning currently include Roche, Kinko's, Cisco, Siemens, Verizon, NCR, and Novell. Hybrid learning has proven to be beneficial because it improves learning effectiveness by offering multiple learning strategies; extends the reach because students have more options for learning situations; and optimizes development and deployment cost and time.

On the academic front, as part of a Pew Grant Program on Course Redesign, 30 institutions participated in a hybrid instruction project (Pew Grant Program on Course Redesign 2001–2002). Five models were utilized in that project. Six schools implemented the supplemental approach, whereby the traditional classroom structure is maintained, supplemented by "web-based, out-of-class activities." The University of New Mexico (UNM) and Carnegie Mellon University were among those who participated in this model. At UNM, students in a general psychology class attended lectures once a week, participated in undergraduate teaching-assistant-led labs, and completed Internet/CD-ROM quizzes and self-paced activities.

The replacement model, which reduces class meetings and replaces them with either online, interactive activities or a significant revision of in-class activities, was the preferred method for 15 of the participating institutions. Brigham Young, the University of Wisconsin-Madison, Portland State University, and Penn State University were among the schools piloting this type of hybrid.

As an alternative to e-learning models, blended learning models offer additional choices for trainers and instructors to be responsive to trainees'/students' learning styles and to improve learning outcomes.

A community of practice can allow for interaction between instructors and other learners in an online-only situation. To facilitate learning, a community of practice should be an objective for anyone designing an e-learning environment. To incorporate a community of practice, instructional design "should foster a sense of *belonging* so that newcomers and less experienced members can feel comfortable asking for help and learning alongside more experienced members" (Farmer 2005, 85). The EPIC survey identified e-tutors, threaded discussion groups, virtual classrooms, email, and chat to be most effective in facilitating a collaborative learning environment (Clark and Hooley 2003).

Design

E-learning is available in a variety of formats, from off-the-shelf learning management systems to simple intranet and CD-ROM products (Clark and Hooley 2003). They can be bought commercially or developed in-house. Apart from the option in which you select to invest, the design should reflect the needs of your users. In this age of global e-learning, culture and learning styles are increasingly important. Research has found that Java and HTML features such as pop-ups can "confuse the non-western reader" (Friesner and Hart 2004, 84). The same researchers note that there is evidence of cross-cultural differences in website designs for Western and Chinese sites.

In the Australian Flexible Learning Framework Toolbox series, content and design were specifically developed to address the observed learning differences evident in the aboriginal population. According to a commissioned report evaluating the courses, indigenous learning styles should be accommodated in the way we build e-learning content, including how we use text on screens, the type and amount of multimedia interactivity and the approach to learning and its scaffolding" (Bamblett 2005, 3).

It is useless to build a product that your target market cannot use. A pretty website does not automatically mean your learners will understand how it works. A good product should be graphically pleasing, interactive, and platform-independent, and should provide an optimal learning environment. User interface design can help you reach your learning outcomes.

One benefit of e-learning is the ability to "take advantage of the interactive, learner-driven opportunities created by Internet- and Web-based technology" (Morgan 2001). An easy way to ensure a product is meeting learning outcomes is to continually test the product with user feedback. Usability testing can be a low-cost resource for evaluating any e-learning tool. Journalist Todd Spangler recounts the story of a major company that designed an e-learning system to train as many as 20,000 employees. After implementing the program, the company discovered that its users were confused by the design of the system, which didn't identify which of the 2,700 courses the employees were to take (Spangler 2004). Usability testing would have identified this flaw and saved this company money and time in the development of its e-learning system.

Products should also be customizable, with the flexibility to meet the needs of the chosen audience. Information architecture is an important component of e-learning, because it will determine the navigation and organization of a product. Scalability is an important aspect of information architecture. A product should be able to evolve from the second to the fifth generation of e-learning. By ensuring an e-learning program can adapt to new technologies, the learning process can easily be altered as the virtual learning environment changes. An applications software company should be able to provide its plan for the next five years. Off-the-shelf LMS systems should allow the ability to invest more in content and marketing, allowing more flexibility in the long run. Relying solely on the functionality of the current system may result in purchase of a product that is too costly to upgrade and too labor-intensive to convert in the future. Be wary of the term *beta* before the name of a product; many organizations have belatedly found that reinventing the wheel can be costly. Determining how often a system will need to be upgraded or significantly changed will help guide the product selection process.

Lessons Learned: UK E-University

The most glaring example of the pitfalls in e-learning development rests at the door of the UKeU, a government funded e-learning endeavor. The UKeU project was done to further e-learning opportunities in the United Kingdom. However, it was developed without input from its primary users—students and university administrators. It was created using a custom system that ended up costing 50 million GPB. This cost overrun was primarily based in the formation of infrastructure and course development. In the end, only 16 courses (the administrators had projected 40) went online and only 900 students were ever enrolled. Critics blamed poor business planning. The committee gathered to investigate the poor results of the project identified these reasons for its failure: it took a supply-driven rather than a demand-led approach; UKeU pursued a narrow concept of e-learning; lacked marketing and market research; and placed too much emphasis on the development of the technology platform. The lessons learned from the UKeU debacle are being used by the government to prevent future problems in e-learning development (House of Commons 2005).

Interoperability and Standards

Interoperability has become a growing concern in the e-learning industry. It is "a key to the successful implementation of an e-learning environment" (Collier 2002). More and more companies are seeing the value of integrating their e-learning into preexisting company infrastructure such as intranets or other knowledge management systems. Whether or not other systems work with e-learning software needs to be considered when buying or developing an e-learning product. One reality that is driving the push for interoperability is the lack of standards in the e-learning field. "E-learning is in the transition from the lawless 'before standards' state to a more stable 'with standards' state" (Collier 2002). In a white paper, Sun Microsystems noted that the benefits of standards affect both the end-user and the vendors. From a consumer perspective, it discourages proprietary development of e-learning products and lowers cost. From the producer's perspective, it creates a standardized method of interoperability, eliminating the need to develop proprietary interfaces and products. Likewise, Josh Bersin, a leading expert on the e-learning industry, thinks one of two things will have to happen before standards can drive interoperability: either one vendor will have to dominate the market, or another organization, like IEEE, will have to get involved and mandate the precise way standards are implemented (Boehle 2005).

According to a Sun Microsystems analysis, industry standards will also allow for standardized learning object metadata, content packaging, learner profiles, and technical architecture (Collier 2002). IEEE and ISO are the current leaders in the development of international accredited standards; however, other notable groups working on standards include IMS Global Learning Consortium, the Advanced Distributed Learning (ADL) Initiative, Education Network Australia, and the European Commission Prometheus project.

Perhaps the most prominent set of standards has been the Sharable Content Object Reference Model (SCORM) standards developed by the ADL Initiative. They define SCORM as "a collection of standards and specifications adapted from multiple sources to provide a comprehensive suite of e-learning capabilities that enable interoperability, accessibility and reusability of Web-based learning content" (Advanced Distributed Learning 2005). It allows multiple learning objects to be reused regardless of the LMS system and regardless of the original source of content. Unfortunately, there is currently no way to verify compliance of these standards for a product, and SCORM has not been adopted universally.

The latest generation of e-learning platforms has focused more on integration and interoperability. Open architecture and standards are integral to ensuring the ability of e-learning products to work seamlessly regardless of their size, scope, or brand. Open architecture will allow systems to be integrated with or added onto products developed by multiple vendors. Like other open source technologies, open architecture and standards can take e-learning in an entirely new direction and further enhance its cost efficiency.

Internationally, 23 different bodies are identified as developing e-learning standards at either the local or the international level. This may point to problems of adopting standards in the future, when so many standards will be competing with one another for industry dominance. This will lead to difficulties in creating culturally neutral standards, which may also affect the local and international adoption of standards by smaller software companies (Collier 2002).

Cost

Developing the infrastructure, programming, or purchasing the software and hardware to use for e-learning is only the first step in the cost process. There is additional cost with the conversion of content and in maintenance. When purchasing or developing a product it is important to examine what is needed once the product is up and running. Staffing is a hidden cost in e-learning that people often fail to account for. Staff needs to be available for maintaining the technological aspects of e-learning, from keeping servers running to handling upgrades to software or software conversion. Future replacement of hardware or upgrading software is not always accounted for in the initial stages of development. Analysts estimate that the cost for online courses can range between $10,000 and $50,000 USD per hour of e-learning. This becomes problematic when technical problems occur unexpectedly. Properly forecasting a budget for e-learning past the start-up costs will ensure there are funds for these hidden or unforeseen costs.

While the efficiency of using e-learning pays for the cost of some systems, there are other innovative ways to recoup initial outlay of funds. In the publicly funded world of e-learning, more organizations are moving toward public/private partnerships to allay the costs of developing large-scale e-learning initiatives. For example, the African Virtual University is partnered with companies like Microsoft and other universities worldwide (African Virtual University 2005). In the report on the UKeU project, the lack of private funding was cited as a primary reason for its failure (House of Commons 2005).

In addition to partnerships, cost recovery methods include marketing custom products to other industry companies. Such is the case with Turner

Construction. They developed a series of e-learning modules to train workers and then sold the intellectual content to other construction companies. As a result, the company has recouped the funds used to create their e-learning tools (Boehle 2005). Marketing content to other organizations may be a viable option for increasing return on investment.

Assessment

The last factor in selecting a good e-learning product is the ability to assess its usefulness for an organization. Assessment is an ongoing process. As technologies evolve there is a need for reevaluating products and learning outcomes of your target audience. Do they really learn? Do they even finish taking the course? Can they demonstrate their learning? Does it meet your goals and objectives? Find or develop a product that allows for tracking of users, compiling of data, and generation of reports at the individual and institutional levels. This will aid in evaluating the effectiveness of an e-learning product. So what is the definition of e-learning anyway? Here are some choices:

> E-learning is a learning system that uses electronic mediums (e.g., cable TV, the Internet, or palm-held computers) for human learning.—*The Greenwood Dictionary of Education*

> E-learning is learning facilitated and supported through the use of information and communications technology; e-learning can cover a spectrum of activities from supported learning, to blended learning (the combination of traditional and e-learning practices), to learning that is entirely online.—University of Bath CMS glossary

Regardless of the definition used to describe e-learning, it should "have a constructivist approach, evoke intrinsic motivation, make learning a social and private activity, allow for experiential learning, take a reflective approach, and most importantly not be linear" (Hamid 2001, 315). E-learning should incorporate a meaningful learning experience and ensure quality content and flexibility for the learner. It should take into account the readiness, needs, and support of the learner. Technology should be seamless and not the focus of e-learning, but a tool to enhance the learning of the student, whether the student is in an academic, vocational, or lifelong learning environment. The current state of the e-learning field is ripe for meeting all of these criteria and should continue to do so as it matures and as companies employ more standards and open architecture designs.

When preparing for e-learning projects, it is important to account for specific elements unique to technology planning. Components that are unique to business plans for e-learning include: content, evolving technologies, costs, user interface design, information architecture, and teaching effectiveness. Always keep in mind that the overall purpose of creation and planning for e-learning is to help people learn online *better*. The case studies presented in this book will illustrate the best practices for e-learning and, more importantly, the steps for creating success using business planning principles.

REFERENCES

Advanced Distributed Learning. "Advanced Distributed Learning." http://www.adlnet.org/ (November 18, 2005).

African Virtual University. "African Virtual University." (December 4, 2005).

Al-Bawaba. "Dubai eGovernment Announces Major e-Learning Initiative in Celebration of DSF 2006." (Jan. 2, 2006): 1, http://proquest.umi.com.

Allen, Michael. "The Lessons of E-Learning." *Optimize* (Dec. 2003): 51, http://proquest.umi.com/.

Archibald, Diane. "Rapid E-Learning: A Growing Trend." http://www.learningcircuits.org/jan2005/archibald.htm (November 28, 2005).

Bamblett, Esme. "Indigenous Australian Delivery Trials of Flexible Learning Toolboxes." Australian Flexible Learning Framework. http://www.flexible-learning.net.au/toolbox/documents/pdfs/indigenous_deliverytrials.pdf (January 28, 2006).

Blackboard. "Blackboard Accelerates e-Learning in China." Blackboard press archive. www.blackboard.com/company/press (January 12, 2005).

Boehle, Sarah. "The State of the E-Learning Market." *Training* 42, no. 9 (Sept. 2005): 12, http://proquest.umi.com.

Britt, Phil. "E-learning on the Rise: Companies Move Classroom Content Online." *EContent* 27, no. 11 (Nov. 2004): 36, http://proquest.umi.com/.

Carliner, Saul. "Course Management Systems versus Learning Management Systems." *Learning Circuits*, November 2005. http://www.learningcircuits.org/2005/nov2005/carliner.htm (August 8, 2006).

Clark, Donald, and Andrew Hooley. *EPIC Survey 2003: The Future of E-Learning*. Epic Group Plc, 2003 (December 10, 2005).

Collier, Geoff. "E-learning Interoperability Standards. in Sun Microsystems, Inc. 2002" (cited November 1, 2005). Available from http://www.sun.com/products-n-solutions/edu/whitepapers/pdf/e-learning_Interoperability_Standards_wp.pdf.

Collins, John, and Nancy Patricia O'Brien, eds. *Greenwood Dictionary of Education*. Westport, Conn.: Greenwood Press, 2003.

Datamonitor. "Global Education Services: An Industry Profile." www.datamonitor.com (November 10, 2005).

"Doctors.Net.UK." http://www.doctors.net.uk/ (January 20, 2006).

EduTech Wiki. "Learning Management System." http://edutechwiki.unige.ch/en/LMS#List_of_Free_.2F_Open_Source_Softwares (August 6, 2006).

ELearning Age. "2005 E-Learning Awards." *ELearning Age* (Oct. 2005): 19, http://proquest.umi.com/.

Farmer, Lesley J. "Community of Practice." In *Technology-Infused Instruction for the Educational Community: A Guide for School Library Specialists*. Lanham, Md.: Scarecrow Press, 2005.

Friesner, Tim, and Mike Hart. "A Cultural Analysis of E-Learning for China." *Electronic Journal on E-Learning* 2, no. 1 (2004): 81–88 (November 19, 2005).

Hamid, Azma Abdul. "E-Learning: Is It the 'E' or the Learning That Matters?" *Internet and Higher Education* 4, no. 3–4 (2001): 311–316.

House of Commons. "UK e-University: Government's Response to the Committee's Third Report of Session 2004–05." http://www.publications.parliament.uk/pa/cm200506/cmselect/cmeduski/489/489.pdf (December 10, 2005).

International Council for Open and Distance Education. "The DEC eLearn Project." http://www.icde.org/oslo/icde.nsf/ (November 18, 2005).

Jafari, Ali, Patricia McGee, and Colleen Carmean. "Managing Courses, Defining Learning: What Faculty, Students, and Administrators Want." *EDUCAUSE Review* (July/August 2006): 52–54. http://www.educause.edu/ir/library/pdf/ERM0643.pdf (August 8, 2006).

Kang, Feiyu. "E-Learning in China: Recent History and Current Situation." eChina–UK eLearning Programme. http://www.echinaprogram.org/downloads/feiyuKANG.ppt (December 15, 2005).

Learning and Skills Council. "National Employers Skills Survey 2004." http://readingroom.lsc.gov.uk/lsc/2005/research/commissioned/national-employers-skills-survey-main-report-2004.pdf (December 19, 2005).

Long, Phillip D. "Learning Management Systems (LMS)." In *Encyclopedia of Distributed Learning*. Thousand Oaks, Calif.: Sage, 2004.

Meerts, John. "Course Management Systems." EDUCAUSE Evolving Technologies Committee, October 20, 2003. http://www.educause.edu/ir/library/pdf/DEC0302.pdf#search='meerts%20evolving%20course%20management%20systems' (August 8, 2006).

Morgan, Gareth. "Thirteen 'Must Ask' Questions about E-Learning Products and Services." *Learning Organization* 8, no. 5 (2001): 203. http://proquest.umi.com/.

New Jersey Institute of Technology. "Hybrid Learning." http://media.njit.edu/hybrid/defined.php (April 2, 2008).

NIACE. "What Is Online Learning?" NIACE Briefing Sheet 56. http://www.niace.org.uk/information/Briefing_sheets/56-What-is-online-learning.pdf (January 28, 2006).

Pew Grant Program on Course Redesign. "Project Descriptions." (2001–2002). National Center for Academic Transformation. http://www.center.rpi.edu/PCR/Proj_Desc.htm (August 20, 2006).

Singh, Harvi, and Chris Reed. "A White Paper: Achieving Success with Blended Learning." http://www.e-learningsite.com/download/white/blend-ce.pdf#search=%22singh%20reed%20%22blended%20learning%22%22 (August 14, 2006).

Spangler, Todd. "Lessons from the Virtual Classroom; E-Learning Software Can Let Organizations More Efficiently Manage Their Training and Enable Them to Offer Tutorials over the Web." *Baseline* 1, no. 31 (June 1, 2004): 72. http://proquest.umi.com.

Tucker, Michael A. "E-Learning Evolves." *HRMagazine: On Human Resource Management* 50, no. 10 (Oct. 2005): 74. http://proquest.umi.com.

van der Wende, Marijk. "The Role of US Higher Education in the Global E-Learning Market." Center for Studies in Higher Education. repositories.cdlib .org/cshe/CSHE1-02 (November 20, 2005).

Waits, Tiffany, and Laurie Lewis. *Distance Education at Degree Granting Post-Secondary Institutions 2000–2001*. Washington, D.C.: U.S. Department of Education, National Center for Education Statistics, 2003.

University of Bath Computing Services. "CMS Glossary." http://internal.bath.ac.uk/ web/cms-wp/glossary.html (December 20, 2005).

3

E-Learning Tools

Current and Emerging Technologies

Stephanie Sterling Brasley,
University of California, Los Angeles

When designing for e-learning environments, it is important to identify and select appropriate e-learning tools to fulfill learning objectives. This chapter will provide a brief overview of e-tools that are in current use as well as those that show promise for providing a rich and rewarding e-learning experience. This review is not intended to be comprehensive in scope, but rather seeks to provide a point of entry to educators and non-profit organizations planning e-learning ventures. Before delving into the tools, it is useful to note that as these software and Web-based technologies are discussed, it is important to keep in mind that e-learning experts aren't in agreement about what these tools are called or their value for the e-learning environment.

CURRENT E-LEARNING TOOLS

Learning Objects (LOs) and Low Threshold Applications (LTAs)

As with other e-learning tools, there has been a proliferation of definitions for learning objects. Dr. David A. Wiley, who has written extensively on this topic, uses this definition: "Learning Objects are defined here as any entity, digital or non-digital, which can be used, re-used or referenced during technology supported learning" (Wiley 2000, 4). Rory McGreal examined the varying definitions; "asset, content object, information object, knowledge object, learning resource, reusable learning object, unit of learning" are but a few of the terms used to describe a learning object. Despite the differences of opinion by key e-learning specialists, he identifies "four different types of meaning . . . that range from general to the particular. There are 1) objects that could be anything; 2) objects that could be anything digital; and 3) digital objects that have been designed with an ostensible learning purpose or outcome; 4) other objects that are specific to a single approach or proprietary standard" (McGreal 2002).

When considering whether to create learning objects for e-learning, recognize that they should be granular, small, and reusable in different learning situations, and deliverable over the Web, enabling many people to access them simultaneously (Wiley 2004, 7). Because learning objects are designed to be reused and applied to multiple learning contexts, they offer a number of advantages to those who wish to engage in designing them. Advantages include flexibility, ease in updating, searching, and content management, customization, interoperability, facilitation of competency-based learning, and increased value of content (due to reusability) (Longmire 2000). When authoring learning objects for e-learning, one must consider both the content and the metadata tags used to describe the LO.

Low Threshold Applications

"A Low-Threshold Application (LTA) is a teaching/learning application of information technology that is reliable, accessible, easy to learn, non-intimidating and (incrementally) inexpensive. Each LTA has observable positive consequences, and contributes to important long term changes in teaching and/or learning. . . . the potential user (teacher or learner) perceives an LTA as NOT challenging, not intimidating, not requiring a lot of additional work or new thinking. LTAs . . . are also 'low-threshold' in the sense of having low INCREMENTAL costs for purchase, training, support, and maintenance" (Gilbert 2002). LTAs are a reasonable alternative to some of the e-learning tools discussed that require many more resources. LTAs "have a low entry cost, are easy to learn, are not intimidating, reliable and have observable, positive consequences" (Gilbert 2002).

EMERGING TECHNOLOGIES

Web 2.0

When Tim Berners-Lee invented the World Wide Web in 1989, he had a vision for an interactive web. As the Web has developed, it has been, in large part, read-only. One barrier to realizing this "collaborative medium . . . where we can all meet and read and write" (Carvin 2005) according to Berners-Lee's vision is that writing to the Web required knowledge of HTML. Fast-forward the last 10 years to the emergence of tools that transform the way in which information is created, distributed, and shared. This is the Read-Write Web, or Web 2.0 (Richardson 2006, 1–2).

Similar to the myriad discussions about the meaning of e-learning and the current technologies reviewed above are conversations about Web 2.0, social software, and the like. Stephen Downes, researcher at the National Research Council of Canada, posits that with revolutionary changes made to the World Wide Web, mainly in the form of Web 2.0 tools, e-learning can now be called "E-Learning 2.0" (Downes 2005). A fundamental distinction between the Web 1.0 and the Web 2.0 (a term coined by Tim O'Reilly Media) is that the latter can be viewed as a "social revolution" (Downes 2005). This revolution has many supporters; few agree, however, on what it is. Web 2.0 has been described in the literature as "a set of principles and practices," an attitude, a philosophy, and a phenomenon, to name a few. While definitions abound, it is useful to examine some of them to provide a context for the tools and concepts to be explored later in this chapter. According to Wikipedia, Web 2.0 is "a supposed second-generation of Internet-based services that let people collaborate and share information online in new ways—such as social networking sites, wikis, communication tools, and folksonomies" (Wikipedia). (Note: Due to the practice of editing of the Wikipedia, other definitions may be noted in the literature.) According to O'Reilly, "you can visualize Web 2.0 as a set of principles and practices that tie together a veritable solar system of sites that demonstrate some or all of those principles at a varying distance from the core" (O'Reilly 2005). According to O'Reilly, Web 2.0 was conceived through a brainstorming session. Participants attempted to provide meaning to this term by listing characteristics of Web 1.0 and Web 2.0. The former is exemplified by these products and tools: Double Click, Ofoto, Britannica Online, content management systems, directories, and personal websites. Conversely, Web 2.0 is exemplified by Google AdSense, Flickr, Wikipedia, wikis, tagging (folksonomies), and blogging.

Stephen Abram, VP at Sirsi, characterizes the Web in terms of temperature: it is either hot or cold. Interactivity is what creates a "hot web" and Web 2.0. "It's about conversations, interpersonal networking, personalization, and individualism" (Abram 2005). Social software, a major component of Web 2.0, epitomizes the characteristics Abram describes.

Social publishing tools (e.g., RSS, blogs, wikis), classification systems (e.g., bookmarking tools, folksonomies), mobile learning devices (e.g., PDAs, podcasts) have been embraced heartily by many K–16 educators. Bernie Dodge, known widely for creating the concept of webquests, cautions educators about accepting new technologies prematurely, "forcing these tools into being curricularly useful. . . . Early adopters rush to embrace them without thinking through their pedagogical purpose" (Kasman Valenza 2006, 6). Lisa Neal, editor-in-chief of *eLearn Magazine*, echoes his sentiments in her piece on e-learning predictions for 2006. She explains: "Technology, no matter how innovative, is just an enabler. New technologies only succeed if they help people learn" (Neal 2005). When selecting e-learning tools, the needs of the learner should take the highest priority. The remaining chapter content is devoted to a brief review of emerging technological tools that can be used to create learner-centered instruction activities.

Weblogs, or Blogs

Weblogs (blogs), like wikis, are social publishing tools. While wikis are written collaboratively (they can be edited by multiple users), blogs are personal websites written by anyone interested in publishing journal-like entries on the Web. The content is organized in reverse chronological order. Some are personal commentaries; others resemble newsletters or columns. Most include links to other relevant information. People who create blogs are referred to as "bloggers." The Pew Internet and American Life Project issued a data memo on the "State of Blogging" in January 2005. Two surveys revealed that 8 million Americans have created blogs, up from 3 million in February 2004 (Pew Internet and American Life Project 2005, 2004).

Rebecca Blood provides an interesting history of weblogs and their purpose. She comments: "The original weblogs were link-driven sites. Each was a mixture in unique proportions of links, commentary, and personal thoughts and essays" (Blood 2000). Currently, social bookmarking tools, such as del.icio.us, have taken over this function, and blogs have moved to news or social commentary. This transition began after the 9/11 tragedy, in which much of what was occurring was reported in the blogosphere before it was reported in traditional news sources, along with personal observations. It allowed people immediate access to the events unfolding in the days following. Essentially, blogging is "personal publishing" (Downes 2004).

Similar to wikis, blogs owe their popularity to their ease of use. Blogs can be created either by utilizing hosting services or via software installed on a computer. Hosting services, which provide access to all components needed for creating a blog, offer potential bloggers a straightforward experience. Blogger, LiveJournal, and TypePad are examples of major blog-creation sites. Movable Type, WordPress, and Radio Userland are examples of desktop software. Some of the more popular weblog search sites include Blogger.com's search, Technorati, Feedster, Google Blog Search, Daypop, and Yahoo! News and Blog Search.

Blogs in Education

Google and Yahoo searches of the phrases "education weblogs" and "education blogs" reveal hundreds of thousands of blogs devoted to educational pursuits, at all levels, worldwide. The ease of use of weblogs has prompted many instructional experiments that are well-documented in the literature. For example, Henry Farrell, political scientist and Crooked Timber blog member, describes five uses of weblogs in the classroom (Farrell 2003). This author would argue that these ideas can be incorporated, with slight revision, into e-learning situations. At the most basic level, blogs can replace static webpages easily, without authors needing competency with web-authoring software. The comments section can be used by an instructor to collocate answers to questions in one location instead of responding to individual student queries by email. Next, instructors can use blogs to compile topically based links that complement information presented in a formal lecture. Blogs can be used to organize class discussions by having students post comments to an instructor-posed question. Other educators, like Mireille Guay, point to the increased participation of and interaction among students as a prime advantage of this technological medium. As with the Internet when it was born, blogs as collaborative publishing tools enable verbose and shy students equal opportunities to voice their opinions (Downes 2004, 18). Finally, Farrell lists student-created weblogs as the most challenging and creative use of this social software. Writing assignments lend themselves well to working within a weblog environment. Learners can write within the blogs, engage in peer-editing activities, and post and store their final products online. Richardson presents additional creative uses for weblogs: "class portal," "online filing cabinet," "blog portfolio," and "collaborative space" (Richardson 2006, 21–24).

Wikis

Leuf and Cunningham, creators of the wiki concept, define a wiki as "a freely expandable collection of interlinked webpages, a hypertext system for storing and modifying information—a database, where each page is easily edited by any user with a forms-capable Web browser client" (Leuf and Cunningham 2001, 14). Sloan offers a slightly different definition: "A wiki (sometimes spelled 'Wiki') is a server program that allows users to collaborate in forming the content of a Web site. With a wiki, any user can edit the site content, including other users' contributions, using a regular browser. Basically, a wiki Web site operates on a principle of collaborative trust. The term comes from the word 'wikiwiki,' which means 'fast' in the Hawaiian language" (Sloan 2005). Chawner and Lewis point out six kinds of wikis that were originally identified by Leuf and Cunningham (Chawner and Lewis 2006). These have varying levels of openness: fully open, meaning that anyone has full access to the Wiki; lockable, with restricted editing for some or all pages; gated, with some public pages (that may be locked), but other pages restricted to authorized users; members-only, where access is limited to registered users; firewalled, where access is restricted to a range of specific IP addresses; and personal, where access is limited to a specific computer or private site.

Wikipedia, the popular encyclopedia whose entries are collaboratively created and revised by people worldwide, is an example of the fully open wiki. Wikis are popular social software tools because of the ease of creating and editing text without having to have extensive knowledge of HTML and automatic linking of pages. So, wikis can be used for facilitating various types of group work, collaborative information-sharing, tracking projects with organization or academic members spread throughout the country, and more. Spam, problems with standards, and different types of architecture for wikis present disadvantages. However, the wiki is a relatively easy and inexpensive tool for enhancing the e-learning environment.

Social writing tools such as wikis and weblogs used effectively in e-learning can provide rich opportunities to help students improve writing and critical thinking skills. At the Teaching Wiki site, Prof. Joe Moxley expounds on advantages of teaching writing using wikis: they "promote close reading, revision and tracking of drafts" . . . discourage "product oriented writing," and facilitate "writing as prose" (Lamb 2004, 44). The hallmarks of wikis are the collaboration and peer-enabled activities (e.g., peer editing, peer mentoring), support for distance learning, functionality, and ease of use, which facilitate the learning process for students with physical or learning disabilities, and, potentially, a more engaging learning space (Sloan 2005). WikiFish at Auburn University is an example of a student-run site. Schwartz et al. provide a case study of student interaction with wikis; they "test the wiki platform as a means of online collaboration in the tertiary education environment" (Schwartz et al. 2004)

RSS

RSS stands for either Rich Site Summary or Really Simple Syndication. "RSS is a format for syndicating news and the content of news-like sites, including major news sites like Wired, news-oriented community sites like Slashdot, and personal weblogs. But it's not just for news. Pretty much anything that can be broken down into discrete items can be syndicated via RSS: the 'recent changes' page of a wiki, a changelog of CVS checkins, even the revision history of a book" (Pilgrim 2002). An RSS file or "feed" is conveyed using XML (Extensible Markup Language), which allows users to "subscribe" to news and website content. RSS feeds are used commonly to access content from websites, news articles, weblog posts (blogs), vlogs, podcasts, vcasts, and bookmarking classification services like del.icio.us or Furl. RSS feeds can be accessed by using an aggregator, software used to collect feeds. A user subscribes to feeds, and the aggregator checks those feeds on a continual basis and alerts users when new information is available. Some aggregators are Web-based, while others require a software installation on a computer. A popular Web-based aggregator is Bloglines. Many websites now have a link to their RSS feed on their website that can be entered into an aggregator. Typically, Web sources will have an icon that says RSS or XML.

RSS feeds, which capture and push website content to the subscriber, have been used in creative ways to forward instruction goals. Will Richardson proclaims: "RSS lets us read and connect with what others write" (Richardson 2006, 91). Presented below are three instructional situations that exemplify the effective use of RSS.

First, consider this type of scenario: an instructor is teaching about the political and economical impact of 9/11. He or she has identified ten to fifteen websites, blogs, and podcasts that regularly feature pertinent information relating to the course topic. Mining these sites on a regular basis, in a timely manner, is an arduous task. RSS solves this instructional dilemma, collecting all of these feeds into an aggregator. Second, RSS feeds can be incorporated into student assignments involving weblogs. Third, RSS feeds can be utilized along with weblogs to facilitate collaborative student projects and as an information management tool for instructors. Students are creating their own weblogs with RSS feeds that continually collect new information. With Blogdigger.com, students working in groups are able to develop "groups of feeds" into one cohesive set. Blogdigger.com provides a unique address for the new feed, which can then be incorporated into a blog (Richardson 2006, 76, 85).

Mobile Learning

Software vendors say that mobile learning is "the point at which mobile computing and e-learning intersect to produce an anytime, anywhere learning experience" (Harris 2001). What comprises the m-learning environment? Personal digital assistants (PDAs), PC tablets, mp3 players, cell phones, handheld gaming tools, and Bluetooth-enabled devices (Alexander 2005; Wagner 2005).

Some consider podcasting, a term combining the words *iPod* and *broadcasting*, to be a part of the mobile learning arena, in that its content can be transferred via an mp3 player, Pocket PC, or cell phone with audio-play capabilities. Podcasts are audio files that can be accessed via a computer or an mp3 player. Users can also subscribe to and download them using RSS feeds to an mp3 player.

Creating podcasts is straightforward; a computer, a microphone and recording software, such as Audacity, an open source software and its companion LAME encoding software are the only components necessary to produce a basic podcast. Podcasts are gaining momentum both in academic settings and in corporate training. Their ease of use, low cost for development, and portability make them viable e-learning candidates.

Similar to RSS and blogs, podcasts have aggregators and search engines to facilitate discovery of relevant podcasts. Podcast aggregators include Juice, iTunes Music Store, iPodderX, Doppler Radio, and Yahoo! podcasts. Podcast.com, Podcast Alley, PodcastPickle, and Podcast 411 directory of directories are search engines that can be used to locate podcasts.

Naismith, Lonsdale, and Sharples provide exemplary cases of teaching and learning using mobile learning devices: mobile phones being used for language acquisition; a mathematics video game accessed from a Nintendo Game Boy Advance to teach addition and subtraction; and "classroom response systems" loaded onto mobile devices.

A number of faculty throughout the country have embraced podcasting as a supplement to classroom and e-learning activities. Many record lectures in order to provide an additional channel for students to review course material. Podcasts address the needs of aural learners. These audio recordings can be of great benefit to non-English-language learners. Margaret Maag, professor at the University of San Francisco School of Learning, also uses podcasts to provide feedback to her students and to provide self-assessment of course lectures to improve her teaching (Kaplan-Leiserson 2005). Podcasts provide supplementary content in a regular or blended learning situation. For example, libraries have begun to produce podcasts on various aspects of the research process to help students find this information at the point of need. Then, it can be uploaded into a CMS or LMS.

CD-ROM-based audio files have been used prevalently in the corporate arena. However, as Anders Gronstedt, president of Gronstedt Group, points out, podcasts are less expensive to produce than compact discs. The portability of audio files via mp3 players—which are reasonably priced—contributes to a continuous learning environment, where individuals can learn at their own pace. A cautionary note: the learning is "linear and one-way." Gronstedt suggests incorporating podcasts within blogs or other interactive media. This caveat notwithstanding, he sees this as a superb, cost-effective method for training employees without interrupting productivity (Kaplan-Leiserson 2005).

Social Classification Tools: Bookmarks and Folksonomies

Social bookmarking tools are basically hyperlinks that are "managed, tagged, commented upon and published onto the Web" (Hammond et al. 2005). Wikipedia describes them as: "a web-based service that allows users to save and categorize . . . a personal collection of bookmarks and share them with others." Users may also take bookmarks saved by others and add them to their own collection, as well as subscribe to the lists of others. It is the collaborative nature of bookmarking that makes it ripe for enhanced social networking opportunities. It utilizes user-created tags. This process of creating "open tagging" or "free tagging," in which users assign their own labels, is called "folksonomy."

Del.icio.us and Furl, along with Connotea, a tool for scientists, and others hold promise for instructors in e-learning. The ability to bring relevant links from multiple sources, provided by groups of people, makes for a potentially rich collection of information sources.

Game-Based Learning

A definition: "Learning that takes place in an artificial environment with rewards for choices or motor skills." Games typically provide specific win/loss criteria, random generation of questions, and often hidden prizes or surprises. The goal of the game is for the learner to win, although learning can be a by-product of this experience. The literature is rich with resources that talk about the benefits and drawbacks of digital game-based learning, simulations, videogames, and other types of gaming products that promote learning in higher education, government, and business sectors. Consult the further reading section for additional information.

It is an exciting time for e-learning. Web 2.0 applications have the potential to transform e-learning into a rewarding learning experience for users and a pedagogical goldmine for educators. As e-learning specialists proclaim, the learner should be the focal point of efforts to develop e-learning tools for academic and business markets. Social-software instructional examples abound from early adoptors, providing guideposts for those interested in applying these emerging tools to e-learning situations or integrating current tools with Web 2.0 tools. The e-learning possibilities are endless!

FURTHER READING AND RESOURCES

Learning Objects and LTAs

- For an overview of the process of creating data and multimedia learning objects, see Stephen Downes's essay at http://www.downes.ca/files/Learning_Objects_whole.htm.
- For excellent examples of learning objects, visit Merlot at http://www.merlot.org/.
- For examples of LTAs, see Steve Gilbert's page at http://www.tltgroup.org/ltas.htm and from University of Maryland's University College, http://www.umuc.edu/virtualteaching/module1/media.html.

Web 2.0

- For in-depth coverage of Web 2.0, along with a Web 2.0 meme map outlining its components, see http://www.oreillynet.com/pub/a/oreilly/tim/news/2005/09/30/what-is-web-20.html.

Wikis

- For those interested in creating wikis, see these projects: QwikWiki (http://www.qwikiwiki.com), PMWiki (http://www.pmwiki.org), and TikiWiki (http://tikiwiki.org).

RSS

- For a detailed listing of RSS aggregators, visit http://www.newsonfeeds.com/faq/aggregators.
- Fagan Finder's "All about RSS," http://www.faganfinder.com/search/rss.shtml#agg.
- Stephen Downes's "How to Create an RSS Feed with Notepad, a Web Server, and a Beer," http://www.downes.ca/cgi-bin/page.cgi?db=post&q=crdate=1059503386&format=full.
- Mary Harrsch's "RSS: The Next Killer App for Education," http://technologysource.org/article/rss/.
- Will Richardson's "RSS: A Quick Start Guide for Educators," http://weblogg-ed.com/wp-content/uploads/2006/05/RSSFAQ4.pdf.
- Steven Cohen's "RSS for Non-Techie Librarians," LLRX, June 2, 2002, http://www.llrx.com/features/rssforlibrarians.htm.

Podcasts

- Greg Schwartz's Podcasting 101, http://podcasting101.pbwiki.com.
- Podcast 411 resources, http://www.podcast411.com/page5.html.

Social Bookmarking

- For a comprehensive examination of social bookmarking tools, consult: Tony Hammond et al., "Social Bookmarking Tools: A General Review." *D-Lib Magazine*, April 2005, 11 (4). http://www.dlib.org/dlib/april05/hammond/04hammond.html.
- Tonkin, Emma. "Folksonomies: The fall and rise of plain-text tagging." *Ariadne*, April 2006, 47. http://www.ariadne.ac.uk/issue47/tonkin/.

Game-Based Learning

- Prensky, Mark. *Digital game-based learning*. McGraw Hill, 2004.
- Van Eck, Richard. "Digital game-based learning: It's not just the digital natives who are restless." *EDUCAUSE Review* 41, no. 2 (March/April 2006), 16–30. http://www.educause.edu/apps/er/erm06/erm0620.asp.

- Foreman, Joel, et al. "Game-based learning: How to delight and instruct in the 21st century." *EDUCAUSE Review* 39, no. 5 (September/October 2004), 50–66. http://www.educause.edu/pub/er/erm04/erm0454.asp.
- Squire, Kurt. "Game-based learning: An X Learn perspective paper." (2005). http://www.masie.com/xlearn/GameBased_Learning.pdf#search='game%20based%20learning%20squire%20perspective.

REFERENCES

Abram, Stephen. "Web 2.0—Huh?! Library 2.0, Librarian 2.0." *Info Outlook* 9, no. 12 (December 2005). http://www.sirsi.com/Pdfs/Company/Abram/InfoTech_Dec2005.pdf.

Alexander, Bryan. "Going Nomadic: Mobile Learning in Higher Education." *EDUCAUSE Review* 39, no. 5 (September/October 2004), 29–35. http://www.educause.edu/ir/library/pdf/erm0451.pdf (August 2, 2006).

Blood, Rebecca. "Weblogs: A History and Perspective." Rebecca's Pocket. September 7, 2000. http://www.rebeccablood.net/essays/weblog_history.html (July 30, 2006).

Carvin, Andy. "Tim Berners-Lee: Weaving a Wemantic Web." Digital Divide Web. 2005. http://www.digitaldivide.net/articles/view.php?ArticleID=20 (July 30, 2006).

Chawner, Brenda, and Paul H. Lewis. "WikiWikiWebs: New Ways to Communicate in a Web Environment." *Information Technology and Libraries* 25, no. 1 (2006), 33–43.

Downes, Stephen. "E-learning 2.0." *eLearn Magazine*. October 2005. http://www.elearnmag.org/subpage.cfm?section=articles&article=29-1 (July 30, 2006).

———. "Educational Blogging." *Educause Review* 39, no. 5 (September/October 2004), 14–26.

EduTech Wiki "Learning Management System." http://edutechwiki.unige.ch/en/LMS#List_of_Free_.2F_Open_Source_Softwares (August 6, 2006).

Farrell, Henry. "The Street Finds Its Own Use for Things." Crooked Timber, September 15, 2003. http://crookedtimber.org/2003/09/15/the-street-finds-its-own-use-for-things/.

Gilbert, Steven. "The Beauty of Low Threshold Applications." *Campus Technology (Syllabus)* (2002). http://www.campus-technology.com/print.asp?ID=6080 (July 24, 2006).

———. "TLT/Collaborative Change: Low Threshold Applications (LTAs)." http://www.tltgroup.org/resources/rltas.html (February 16, 2006).

Hammond, Tony, Timo Hannay, Ben Lund, and Johanna Scott. "Social Bookmarking Tools (I): A General Review." *D-Lib Magazine* 11, no. 4 (April 2005). http://www.dlib.org/dlib/april05/hammond/04hammond.html.

Harris, Paul. "Goin' mobile." *Learning Circuits,* July 2001. http://www.learningcircuits.org/2001/jul2001/harris.html (June 25, 2006).

Kaplan-Leiserson, Eva. "Trends: Podcasting in Academic and Corporate Learning." *Learning Circuits* (June 2005), http://www.learningcircuits.org/2005/jun2005/0506_trends (August 12, 2005).

Kasman Valenza, Joyce. "Blogs and Wikis in the Classroom." *Information Searcher* 16, no. 1 (2006), p. 1.

Lenhart, Amanda, John Horrigan, and Deborah Fallows. "Content Creation On-line." *Pew Internet and American Life Project.* February 29, 2004. http://www.pewinternet.org/pdfs/PIP_Content_Creation_Report.pdf (August 6, 2006).

Leuf, Bo, and Ward Cunningham. 2001. *The Wiki Way: Quick Collaboration on the Web.* Boston: Addison-Wesley.

Long, Phillip D. "Learning Management Systems (LMS)." In *Encyclopedia of Distributed Learning.* Thousand Oaks, Calif.: Sage, 2004.

Longmire, Warren. "A Primer on Learning Objects." *Learning Circuits,* March 2000. http://www.learningcircuits.org/2000/mar2000/Longmire.htm (July 30, 2006).

McGreal, Rory. "Learning Objects: A Practical Definition." *International Journal of Instructional Technology and Distance Learning,* September 2004, vol. 1, no. 9.

Meerts, John. "Course Management Systems." EDUCAUSE Evolving Technologies Committee, October 20, 2003. http://www.educause.edu/ir/library/pdf/DEC0302.pdf#search='meerts%20evolving%20course%20management%20systems' (August 8, 2006).

Naismith, Laura, et al. "Literature Review in Mobile Technologies and Learning," 11–12. 2005 *Report* 11. http://www.futurelab.org.uk/research/reviews/reviews_11_and12/11_01.htm (August 1, 2005).

Neal, Lisa. "Predictions for 2006: E-Learning Experts Map the Road Ahead." *E-Learn Magazine,* January 2006. http://www.elearnmag.org/subpage.cfm?section=articles&article=31-1 (July 9, 2006).

O'Reilly, Tim. "What Is Web 2.0?: Design Patterns and Business Models for the Next Generation of Software," September 2005. http://www.oreillynet.com/pub/a/oreilly/tim/news/2005/09/30/what-is-web-20.html (July 28, 2006).

Rainie, Lee. "Data Memo: The State of Blogging." *Pew Internet and American Life Project,* January 2, 2005. http://www.pewinternet.org/pdfs/PIP_blogging_data.pdf (August 3, 2006).

Pilgrim, Mark. "What Is RSS?" December 2002. http://www.xml.com/lpt/a/2002/12/18/dive-into-xml.html (August 10, 2005).

Richardson, Will. 2006. *Blogs, Wikis, Podcasts, and Other Powerful Web Tools for Classrooms.* Thousand Oaks, Calif.: Corwin Press.

Schwartz, Linda, et al. "Educational Wikis: Features and Selection Criteria." *International Review of Research in Open and Distance Learning* 5, no. 1 (2004). http://www.irrodl.org/index.php/irrodl/article/view/163/244 (August 10, 2006).

Sloan, Steve. "Emerging Technology: Wiki." November 2005. weblog.edupodder.com/2005/04/session-on-wikis-and-emerging.html (June 28, 2006).

Wagner, Ellen D. "Enabling Mobile Learning." *EDUCAUSE Review* 40, no. 3 (May/June 2005), 40–53. http://www.educause.edu/apps/er/erm05/erm0532.asp (June 26, 2006).

Wiley, David A. "Connecting Learning Objects to Instructional Design Theory: A Definition, a Metaphor, and a Taxonomy." In *The Instructional Use of Learning Objects: Online Version.* http://reusability.org/read/chapters/wiley.doc (January 10, 2005).

4

Business Planning 101

Starting a New Business Venture

Elaina Norlin, Manager, New Initiatives and Outreach, OCLC, Washington, D.C.

Why Write a Business Plan?

Whether you work for a small business, a corporation, or an organization, you have heard about the importance of a good business plan. Management experts consistently remind you that having a comprehensive, thorough, heavily researched business plan is an absolute necessity in running a successful business. This chapter focuses on an existing business starting a new venture. However, the same concepts can easily be applied if this is your first attempt at a business plan.

The typical business plan is at least 15 pages, with a cover page, an executive summary, a table of contents, a company profile, goals, objectives, a competitive analysis, a marketing plan, and an extensive financial plan. Many people don't want to spend that kind of time writing business plans, because, frankly, planning is not much fun. Imagine being at work when a creative idea hits you like a thunderbolt. For most projects, there is nothing more exciting than running with a great idea. Time is of the essence—who knows? someone else might be moving on your idea already. And you may think you don't *need* a plan. You do, but you also want to avoid allowing the planning to become so complicated and tedious that you lose the big picture.

Over 50% of all new projects fail.[1] A common saying is that most people don't plan to fail, most people fail to plan. Business planning, if done well, should help companies or organizations take more calculated, better-informed risks and eliminate pitfalls that could guarantee failure. In financial terms, even a simple business plan that outlines your goals and objectives, marketing strategies, and financial resources will make your presentations to investors more polished and professional.

The key to a business plan that can be applied whether you are starting a new company or developing a new but potentially large-scale product or service is simplicity. The business plan ultimately should be a living document that can be easily read and modified, not a static document in a beautiful binder next to the magazines in the boss's office. The following sections go over some of the traditional steps of the business plan. In addition, a fictional example, Educational Solutions, is provided to show how each concept can be applied.

Initial Preparation

According to the United States Small Business Administration, a business plan is a tool with three basic purposes: communication, management, and planning. As a communication tool, it is used to attract and raise money for your business venture. As a management tool, the business plan helps you track and monitor your plan. As a planning tool, a simple business plan will guide you through different phases of your idea and potentially identify complications and difficulties that might arise and help you to prepare accordingly.[2] Before designing the plan, you should ask yourself these important questions:

- What service or product does your business provide, and what needs does it fill?
- Who are the potential customers for your product or service, and why will they purchase it from you?
- How will you reach your potential customers?
- Where will you get the financial resources to start your business?[3]

These questions are very important because the answers can provide a framework for other business planning sections. So take some time to answer these questions as honestly and concisely as you can. In most cases the answers will change slightly as you go through the other sections, so it's important to remain open-minded and flexible.

Another crucial step before writing a plan is to decide who is working on the document. If it's just one person who will get input from others, then congratulations! This task is done. However, unless you work for a small organization or as a sole proprietor, the organization will usually want a variety of people working together to make sure a multitude of opinions and ideas are captured in the business plan. If forming a team is the approach of choice, here are some guidelines to consider.

- Make sure the team is comprised of people who are committed to the job. The more important part of this step is to make sure that the people on the team are committed to completing the task. The last thing the team needs is a person sabotaging progress and playing "devil's advocate" to the point where nothing gets done. Although it's not realistic to expect that everyone will be excited to be part of a business plan team, you do want people who are committed to the idea and want to be part of the solution.

- Make sure the team works around each person's skills and talents. Teams usually work more smoothly when team members know why they have been picked and what special talents they bring to the job. Make sure people work to their strengths, but encourage them to stay flexible enough to see this as a learning experience. For example, many business plans will need an accountant or someone with a financial background to work on the financial feasibility section. However, ensure that this person also knows that his or her financial or accounting background will help shape all the sections. Keeping everyone engaged and utilizing their talents yields a richer product.

- Appoint a team leader. This advice seems obvious, but selecting a team leader is sometimes overlooked in the haste of getting things off the ground. The team leader should not be the reluctant person who was not quick enough to look at the floor. Nor should it be the process person who keeps the team so far off course that everyone wants to jump ship. The team leader must be someone who will keep everyone on track and has the big picture in mind. The team leader should be skilled at soliciting input from all of the members but clearly has the authority to make final decisions to complete the plan.[4]

Practical Example: Educational Solutions (Profile)

For a practical example, let's say your organization, Educational Solutions, has a great idea for developing a series of worldwide conferences and workshops on literacy and learning. Before the organization launches a call for papers, a group has been assigned to develop a business plan. The new team appoints a team leader. One of its first tasks is to answer the questions discussed above. As you can see from the following answers, taking some time to address these simple questions helps give a better big-picture view as the group approaches writing the business plan.

What service or product does your business provide, and what needs does it fill? Educational Solutions is a nonprofit organization that provides interactive multimedia software. The software is designed for children (ages 10–17) who attend public, private, and charter schools. Educational Solutions' patented software has been tailored for and critiqued by children to make learning fun and exploratory. Educational Solutions has an 80% satisfaction rating and numerous success stories. The organization hopes that the conferences and workshops will not only bring scholars, teachers, and educators together to talk about literacy and education, but also attract new customers from its target market.

Who are the potential customers for your product or service, and why will they purchase it from you? Educational Solutions' potential customer base includes teachers, school library media specialists, librarians, and home-school parents.

How will you reach your potential customers? Educational Solutions usually reaches its customers through a combination of mass marketing, direct cold calls, and attending relevant conferences and workshops. Sponsoring a conference will be the company's first attempt at taking a leadership role in designing and implementing conferences on a variety of significant topics.

Where will you get the financial resources to start your business? To begin with, Educational Solutions will just finance on a cost-recovery basis and eventually make a profit. The company will offset the costs of the advisory board and the conferences with the revenue from software subscriptions.

CURRENT SITUATION ANALYSIS

Before your company or organization launches into the heart of the plan, it should take some time out to do a current situational analysis. The current situational analysis (CSA) is another method that can provide your organization with a big-picture view of what's going on before the goals and objectives are written.

A very useful tool to measure the current situation is the SWOT (strengths, weaknesses, opportunities, and threats) analysis. The SWOT analysis is one of the cornerstone planning tools for any organization. Strengths and weaknesses refer to what's happening *within* your organization. For example, a strength could be an aspect of your business that adds value to your product or service. A weakness could be a lack of marketing expertise or your inability to distinguish your product or service from the competition. Opportunities and threats are *external* factors. For example, an opportunity could be a new international market or a potential to expand your customer base. A threat could be a new direct competitor in your home market or an unexpected taxation or additional fees on your product or service.[5]

The CSA should be written with input from the whole organization. The quickest way to accomplish this is for the team or the principal person creating the document to make a draft document (no more than one page) and a timeline for people to respond. A quick tip is to tell the organization that you *know* you have not captured everything and request that people list things that are missing. Otherwise, you might not get any responses until the business planning document is complete.

Below is a practical example of a SWOT analysis. Notice that the document is short (ideally, one page), with some targeted key points. A conversation with your board, supervisor, and other employees can be used to check the validity of the comments. Use this instrument to highlight key issues within your current market that are relevant to your business plan.

Practical Example: Educational Solutions (CSA)

Strengths (Looking Inward at the Organization)

- Educational Solutions has experienced phenomenal growth in the last two years. The company has increased its client base by 20% and has a 60% return-customer rate.
- Educational Solutions has conducted two extensive user studies and found an 80% overall satisfaction rate, with a 70% "excellent" rating for software usability and design.

Weaknesses (Looking Inward at the Organization)

- Educational Solutions does not have depth in its sales department. Right now, the company has a sales manager and an inside salesperson.
- Educational Solutions has not decided whether to focus on a few quality software products and increase its customer base or to produce multiple software products and sell them to repeat customers.
- Educational Solutions does not have an identifiable unique selling position.

Opportunities

- Educational Solutions has enough customers and brand recognition to sponsor an international conference.
- Educational Solutions is in the process of putting together an international advisory board, which will consist of an influential group of current and potential customers.

Threats

- Educational Solutions' top competitor has been contemplating a premier user conference that would reach a subscription base of 85,000 clients.
- Three of Educational Solutions' top competitors have been considering a plan to combine their expertise to form a larger, more dynamic company.

GOALS AND OBJECTIVES

The next step of the business plan is to develop the goals and objectives. If this is the company's first business plan, the goals and objectives should tie in directly to the mission. The goals and objectives should clearly state the business plan's overall intention and a timetable for getting things accomplished. For the purpose of this business plan, the goals and objectives will also serve as the evaluation plan. By monitoring the goals and objectives and developing internal milestones, it will keep the business on track for success.

Business Goals

Goals are the broader business outcomes that your company wants to achieve. Goals are where you want to be once everything is accomplished. Some things to keep in mind as the team or work group begins to develop your goals:

- Determine who to involve in setting your company's goals. Because goals are the core of your company's business, the group members should include the people who are responsible for major business activities. If your business is a solo business, develop a group of advisers who can provide input as you develop the goals.
- Confirm that the company's goals will provide a clear outline of the business's broader intentions.
- Rely on the goals to communicate your business intentions not only to people outside the company but within your organization.[6]

Objectives

Measurable objectives are the quantifiable factors used to determine whether or not the organization has been successful in achieving its goal. Some things to keep in mind as the team or work group begins to sketch out the objectives:

- The objectives should be operational. In other words, they should spell out the specific things that you will accomplish in your project.
- The objectives should clearly advance the goal statements.
- Objectives should be measurable.
- For the business plan, the objectives will also name the person or department that will be responsible for getting the work done. This way, if the project manager resigns, another person could easily turn to the goals and objectives section and be able to ask the right questions.

Practical Example: Educational Solutions (Goals and Objectives)

The overall goal for Educational Solutions is to strengthen its market share in the educational multimedia software industry. In terms of the competition, Educational Solutions is in the top 50 but would like to be in the top 25 in the next three years. The specific business plan is just one of the strategies the company is using to increase its customer base. As you look at the following examples, the goals are in order, and one goal has to be completed before proceeding to the next. In addition, the objectives are simple and are easier to accomplish than ambiguous objectives. Another tip is to assign milestones or due dates to each objective.

Goal #1. To recruit 25 influential members for our newly created advisory board who will become advocates and conference speakers.

Objective 1.1. Research the educational literature and conferences and identify 40 people who have not used the Educational Solutions software. Responsibility: Research Team.

Objective 1.2. Identify 20 people from the user survey who expressed *excellent* or *surpasses my expectations*. Responsibility: Research Team.

Objective 1.3. Create a list of targeted questions that the company agrees are essential for committee members. Responsibility: Project Manager.

Objective 1.4. Conduct phone interviews. Responsibility: Project Manager.

Objective 1.5. Recommend 25 names and rank the other names as alternates. Responsibility: Project Manager.

Objective 1.6. Personally contact potential advisory board members. Responsibility: President.

Goal #2. To sponsor biannual conferences on important educational topics that will have an average attendance of 300 people.

Objective 2.1. Recruit the independent contractors. Responsibility: Marketing and Sales Team.

Objective 2.2. Organize a planning committee with members using advisory board members and Educational Solutions employees. Responsibility: Project Manager.

Objective 2.3. The planning committee will identify a location and hotel for the meeting. Responsibility: Conference Planning Committee.

Objective 2.4. Educational Solutions will identify a conference/event planner and get an estimate of the costs. Responsibility: Project Manager.

Objective 2.5. The planning committee will select keynote speakers, call for papers, and organize the outline for the conference. Responsibility: Conference Planning Committee.

Objective 2.6. The accounting manager will determine the appropriate amount to charge participants. Responsibility: Accounting Department.

Objective 2.7. The marketing manager will develop an inexpensive publicity campaign. Responsibility: Marketing Manager.

Objective 2.8. After the conference, send a follow-up survey. Responsibility: Research Team.

Goal #3. At the biannual conference, have at least 200 people sign up at the yearly subscription rates.

Objective 3.1. Offer a free luncheon for 50 conference attendees to preview the product. Responsibility: Marketing and Sales Department.

Objective 3.2. Offer two promotional drawings for attendees to sign up for a free trial. Responsibility: Marketing and Sales Department.

Objective 3.3. Educational Solutions Marketing Department and members from the planning committee will have three focus groups at the conference. Responsibility: Marketing and Sales Department.

Objective 3.4. Follow up with the free-trial members, introduce them to yearly subscription rates, and offer incentives to sign up. Responsibility: Marketing and Sales Department.

Objective 3.5. Reassess and revise sales strategy; set new target goals. Responsibility: Marketing and Sales Department.

PERSONNEL AND MANAGEMENT

Identifying the appropriate people to work on the business plan is essential. The strength of the management's commitment to the plan and how well people work together build confidence that the goals can be achieved. So, as you write this section, make sure you put down who is in charge of what responsibilities and their level of expertise. You also want to include how the specific personnel will contribute to the overall success of the business plan. If this is the company's first business plan, it's better to show a formal organizational structure that could aid in raising capital and investment interests.

Some areas that might need to be covered in your formal organizational structure as you write this section could include:

- President
- Vice president(s)
- Marketing/Advertising
- Sales
- Operation
- Distribution
- Human resources
- Accountant/finance controller
- Computer technology
- Legal

Although your business or organization might not be this big, it will still be helpful to show who will be taking on these responsibilities and how they are qualified. The descriptions will need to be verified before they can be incorporated into the business plan (no one likes surprises). If you are a solo business, this is where you would list the law firm, accountant, or human resource firm you have hired to help make the business successful.[7]

Practical Example: Educational Solutions (Management and Personnel)

Since the company is writing a specific business plan for some strategic initiatives, it will list any relevant personnel and management team members who are essential to completing the project. The goals and objectives statements from the previous section have made writing this section easier. For the management and personnel, the activities naturally follow who needs to do what to accomplish the goals. The descriptions are somewhat detailed and specific; however, the rule of thumb is that the more explicit the business plan is, the less confusion people will have about their roles in implementing it.

President. The president is responsible for chairing the advisory board nomination committee and eventually sending formal invitations to potential members. The president is also responsible for delivering all conference welcome addresses and approving the final budgetary figures.

Accounting manager. The accounting manager will work with the business planning committee to develop a budget and break-even scenarios for the creation of the advisory board and the biannual conferences. The accounting manager will determine how much the company can invest and break even and eventually make a profit from this business venture. The accounting manager will work with the legal department to determine what is a corporate tax write-off and how this factors into the overall budget.

Legal. The legal department will go over all of the documents to make sure that the company is in compliance with state and federal guidelines and regulations. As above, legal will work with the accounting manager to determine what a corporate tax write-off is and how this factors into the overall budget.

Sales. The sales department will be in charge of following up with conference attendees who signed up for the free trial offer. The department will work closely with the accounting manager to develop sale targets on what percentage of attendees should become long-term customers. A member of the sales department will be on the planning committee and will help organize the luncheon.

Marketing. The marketing department is in charge of all publicity materials and promotional campaigns for the conferences. A person from the marketing team will be on the conference planning committee and will help organize the focus groups for the conference. Marketing will also make sure the organization makes its recruitment goals for the conference each year by securing a desirable location and generating potential and confirmed conference attendee lists.

Program manager. The program manager will be in charge of making sure the business plan is implemented. The program manager will be an active member of the advisory board nomination committee and will make sure that the committee reaches its final goal. This person will review and work closely with everyone involved in the business plan to make sure the goals and objectives are met and that everything stays on track.

Research team. Two researchers will be members of the advisory board nomination committee. They will conduct the initial research for potential user group names based on criteria decided by the nomination committee. The research team will also be responsible for designing the assessment instrument, tabulating the findings for the conferences, and reporting the findings to the program manager and the president.

Technology team. The technology team will be responsible for handling all the computer technical functions for the conference and setting up the free trials for conference attendees. Two members from the technology team will be a part of all conference focus groups, to provide and receive feedback for our multimedia software products.

MARKETING PLAN

The next step is to develop a marketing plan. Developing a marketing plan can be overwhelming, because initially it takes a certain amount of persistence and diligence. However, businesses have closed or been severely downsized because they failed to take time to develop a comprehensive market strategy. Developing the marketing plan does not have to break the bank if your business spends some time understanding its product or service. For this marketing plan, the focus will be on market research, developing a marketing message, and promotion and placement.

Market Research

The first step in developing your marketing strategy is to briefly describe your market. The business should research the market enough to have a good grasp of the current and future trends in order to make some timely decisions. Any supporting documentation should be included in the appendix. Supporting documentation can include reputable Internet articles, newspaper and magazine articles, trade reports, government information, and formal and informal surveys. Most of these items can be found at your local library, or the librarian can refer you to where they can be found. A great article on how and where to find this information is "How to Get Started on Your Marketing Plan" by Bobette Kyle.[8]

How to get started with market research? Here is a list of questions to ask yourself as you research this section:

- What is the background information?
- What are the current trends?
- What are the long-term projections?
- Is there market stability?
- What are the market strengths, weaknesses, and potential opportunities?
- Where does your company fit in terms of market share with the competition?

Target Audience (Customer Profile)

- Who are your primary customers? What are their demographics?
- Who are your secondary customers? What are their demographics?
- Why would your primary or secondary customers want to buy your product/service?
- Who are your repeat customers? What percentage of your customers are repeat customers?

Competition

- Who is your competition?
- How does your top competition market its product or service?
- What are your competitors' strengths and weaknesses?
- How long has your top competition been in business?
- Have you lost any deals to your competitors?
- Where do you fit in with the competition?[9]

Define Market Strategy: Marketing Message

What is a marketing message? If someone approached you and asked you what makes your business/company/organization stand out from the competition, what would you say? That is not the time to rattle off your mission statement or vision, but instead to confidently communicate your marketing message. Keep in mind how your product or service solves problems. Identify what your target market perceives as a problem; communicate your proposed solution and how your business produces results. A good example of this is a 30-minute weight-loss infomercial. First the company shows you that people are overweight and discusses the health dangers; then it introduces its product or service as the optimal solution. The remaining time is spent reinforcing the message with proven testimonials and expert opinions. Infomercials may be corny, but they work. If your business is new and does not quite have satisfied customers or expert opinions, this could be easily accomplished by conducting some focus groups or assessment tools about the business potential for producing results. However, as you develop a marketing message, do not get caught in a common trap of stressing what you have to offer instead of what you can do for your customers. Always keep your message solution-oriented, with a simple way to solve problems.[10]

Promotion and Placement

Marketing is all about developing strategies to increase sales and visibility of your product or service. Many companies sink all of their dollars into promotion, when a more successful campaign considers all four Ps of marketing—price, place, promotion, and product. The more targeted and focused your message is, the stronger the impact it will have on your market. If you have done your market analysis, you should know what pricing you need to stay competitive. The marketing message is all about understanding your product and what makes it special. Promotion and placement allow you to strategize where to communicate your marketing message for the best impact. A key mistake in promoting and determining placement is spending too much time with the "creativity" of the fancy glossy brochure or the traditional pens, T-shirts, and other marketing gimmicks. These techniques are fine as long as you keep your marketing message in the forefront. Because after all is said and done, people want to know how you are helping them solve problems and making their lives less complicated.

If you don't know how to get started, here are some ideas to spark your creativity. If you would like a more extensive list of additional promotional ideas, take a look at the website Easy Marketing Ideas That Make (Common) Sense.[11]

- Send a targeted press release to a few trade magazines or local radio and television shows that might be willing to interview you about your product or service.
- Offer to give free speeches or workshops to local or national organizations (check the Yellow Pages).
- Capitalize on your business cards. For example, your business card could feature a 10% discount on your product or service, or a free gift. People tend to keep the card if you offer some kind of deal. This could also serve as a nice icebreaker.
- Cross-promote with a complementary business.

- Contact a list of your most valued customers to see if they would be willing to be a reference for your product. Place their testimonials on your website, business cards, and other promotional materials, with their contact information.
- Target your promotions around calendar holidays. People usually expect special deals, parties, and giveaways at that time. For example, for Halloween, offer to give away a free pumpkin; for Christmas, a free wreath; for Valentine's Day, a free box of chocolates, etc.

Practical Example: Educational Solutions (Marketing Plan)

Since this is a new initiative for Educational Solutions, the company spent a fair amount of time developing a comprehensive marketing plan. For this section, each person on the business planning team made a commitment to take one section of the research, and to work with experts in their area (marketing, technology, accounting) to develop a draft. This seemed to work better than everyone trying to tackle every section together. If your organization is a solo business, this is where you engage with experts in your community, especially libraries, which have access or who know how to find access to competitive analysis information.

MARKETING PLAN

Market Analysis

Educational Solutions is a nonprofit organization that provides interactive multimedia software to middle- and high-school children who attend public, private, and charter schools or are home-schooled. Educational Solutions software allows students to learn critical thinking skills through active learning and problem-solving exercises. Most of its software is designed to complement and enhance basic school curriculum subjects instead of replacing them. Educational Solutions' customers are school library media specialists, public libraries, teachers, and parents who provide home schooling for their children. According to the business literature, the current market rating for interactive multimedia software is saturated. The experts' prediction is that many smaller companies will be bought out over the next few years, with only 25% of the top companies flourishing by 2010. Currently, there are over 1,500 companies that provide interactive multimedia software, with 138 companies providing the exact same service as Educational Solutions. The company that has the biggest market share in the educational multimedia software business market is Weblearn. It has conquered the market because it expanded its customer base to include international clients, higher education, and government contracts. Weblearn's extra cash flow has been invested in an aggressive R&D plan. In addition, its prices are the lowest in the market, but its customer satisfaction rating is less than 70 percent. We see this as an opportunity to introduce our products that are more expensive but have a better "quality rating" than Weblearn's. In terms of market share, Educational Solutions is in the top 50% of its direct competition (138 companies). The company's goal is to move within the top 25% in the next three years.

Marketing Strategy

Educational Solutions' marketing strategy is to become a leader of valuable international information on literacy and learning. Currently, all multimedia software companies attend national and international conferences as either a sponsor or a vendor. Many of these conferences center around academic and professional experts providing updates on the newest trends and research. Educational Solutions would like to provide a space for networking and professional development for its customer base. This conference will be a space for teachers, librarians, school library media specialists, and parents to get together in "learning clusters" to exchange ideas and develop action plans. From these, Educational Solutions will have lunch and dinner receptions that will showcase recent innovations in literacy and learning. The speakers and facilitators at the conference will be the advisory board members.

Educational Solutions will have biannual conferences for two years to increase software subscriptions and increase brand recognition. The marketing money will be spent in two tiers. The first promotional tier is to reach potential conference participants through hiring temporary independent contractors who have a background in teaching or education. The independent contractors will be assigned different regions both nationally and internationally. The contractors will work with the marketing and sales department to develop a direct sales plan toward recruiting attendees for the conference. The independent contractors will be paid based on how many confirmed conference registrations meet the target market criteria. Educational Solutions has used independent contractors before and finds that direct-contact sales is the best method to reach its target market. The second tier for the marketing promotional dollars will be the traditional trade and news advertisements, website presence, and radio announcements, which will be used solely to enhance and complement the existing work of the contractors.

FINANCIAL FEASIBILITY

Financial projections are one of the last sections in any business plan; however, it's one of the hardest sections to write. For many businesses the development of the ideas is the easy and exciting part; making sure your idea doesn't send you spiraling into bankruptcy is the hard part. The main things that every financial projection should have are a break-even analysis, projected profit and loss statements, cash flow, and balance sheets. If you are accounting or mathematically challenged and do not have a financial person on your staff, invest in some accounting software or contract with an accounting firm to make sure the finances are in order. The costs of making sure the financial projections are sound, measurable, and obtainable will save your company money in the long run.

Your break-even point is the level of sales that produces neither a profit nor a loss. For example, if you generate $300 in sales but your variable costs are $150, you have a margin of $150 ($300 − $150), or 50% ($150/$300). But if you have $50 in fixed overhead, it's really $100 ($150 − $50). To determine your break-even point, divide your fixed overhead margin percentage $50/100 = $50. This means that if you generate less than $50 dollars in sales, you will lose money instead of make money.[12]

Projected profit and loss statements can be extracted from your marketing plan and any expenses from your goals and objectives section. Remember that these projections can become outdated very quickly and need to be reassessed on a consistent basis. The next step is to calculate the costs of the goods and services sold as well as your anticipated fixed overhead costs. The costs of goods and/or services sold will fluctuate with revenue volume, while fixed overhead cost will be static. The net difference of total revenues less total costs will determine the profit or loss of your business.

The balance sheet provides a profile of the worth of your company's assets (cash, accounts receivable) and its liabilities (accounts payable, wages payable, etc.). The difference between the assets and liabilities provides the company with its current net worth.

The cash flow statement contains any projections of your expected revenues, expenses, assets, liabilities, and equity to determine the level of cash flow. Keep in mind that if you are looking for money from investors, an accurate estimate of your current and projected cash flow can be a deal maker or breaker, so take time out to make a conservative but accurate estimate.[13]

Practical Example: Educational Solutions (Financial Projections)

For this section, the business planning team is relying very heavily on the accounting team member. However, since this is a new venture to an existing business, fleshing out the goals and objectives section along with the marketing plan has given the accountant a clear way of asking the right questions. Some of the variable costs anticipated for this new venture are included below (not in any order). Remember that these variable costs need to be checked on a regular basis to make sure the estimates are accurate. This example is pretty simplistic, but it provides the basics of how to get started.

As you work through the initial calculations, if you suspect any unforeseen costs, make sure you have a contingency plan to redo the costs. A good accountant or software package should be used to produce balance sheets, profit and loss statements, and cash flow. This example is geared toward showing how you can use the structure of your business plan to help you develop some estimated costs and projected revenues.

Variable Costs

- Independent contractors. From previous experience, the company already has a good estimate of how much it will cost for this temporary assignment. Estimated cost: $24,000/year.
- Promotional materials: This includes traditional advertising venues. Estimated cost: $12,000/year.
- Advisory board members: Recruitment, two board meetings per year (housing, airfare, per diem). Estimated cost: $10,000.
- Conference expenses (favorable location, exhibition planners, lunches, dinners, focus group sessions, keynote speakers). Estimated cost from planners after registration expenses: $80,000 per conference.
- Employee time (work outside regular responsibilities). Estimated cost: $15,000/year.
- Assessment materials/updates on technology. Estimated costs: $20,000/year.
- Cost for the employees and advisory board members to present and attend the conference. Estimated costs: $20,000/year.
- Initial projected variable costs: $181,000 per year.

Projected Expected Revenues

From the conference, the company plans to sign 200 people for the free trial. From there it needs to have 75 people sign up for the yearly contract of $1,000 for complete software access, and 75 people sign up for the $500 limited access. This estimate equals $112,500 potential revenue per conference and $225,000 for the year. However, this is a very progressive estimate, requiring a strong follow-through effort from the marketing department.

So for the purpose of this example, the break-even analysis would be $225,000 − $181,000 = $44,000. The fixed overhead costs are estimated at $18,000, for a real total of $26,000. From this cursory look at the financial projections, the sales from conference participants will justify the costs of this new business venture. However, this company is looking more at increasing the customer base and then working toward quality customer service and maintaining existing customers.

EXECUTIVE SUMMARY

The executive summary is the first part of your business plan but should be written last. It is the highlight of your business plan. You will never get a second chance to make a first impression, and many people will read only the executive summary, not the entire plan. The executive summary should be short and persuasive, providing a preview of the main points of your business plan. It should function as a standalone document.

Take some time to figure out which readers will read only the executive summary and who will read the entire business plan. From there, go back over your document and highlight the key sections that you consider important. The main goal is to edit the summary down to the point where the final product is concise and the reader feels like he or she understands the key highlighted points of the business plan. If you have a business plan team, this is the time to identify your best writers and editors to fine-tune the document. Some questions to ask that can come directly from the initial preparation:

Communication tool: Will your business plan be used to attract and raise money for your business venture?

Management tool: Will your business plan be used to track and monitor your business plan?

Planning tool: Will your business plan guide you through the different phases of your idea to identify roadblocks and complications that might occur?

Practical Example: Educational Solutions (Executive Summary)

At initial glance, the purpose of Educational Solutions' business plan is to serve as a management and planning tool. Currently, the company is using its own financial resources and does not need any outside investors or bank loans, so using the plan as a communication tool does not apply. After some discussion, though, the most important part of the business plan is to monitor and track the plan as the goals and objectives are accomplished. Educational Solutions' plan touches almost every department in the company. If one group is not on board, it could hamper the success of the entire venture. Therefore, these are the things that will be highlighted for the executive summary. Notice that the general background of the company and its competitive analysis have been eliminated as crucial points because it's currently an internal document. The people within the organization will probably not read the business plan from cover to cover but will likely read the the document as it pertains to their responsibilities.

COMPONENTS OF THE
EDUCATIONAL SOLUTIONS BUSINESS PLAN

- A summary of the main goals and objectives (the main goals and objectives here are the creation of the advisory committee along with the biannual conferences)
- A brief highlight of the marketing message along with the promotional strategies (currently they have an opportunity to be the first multimedia software company to sponsor a conference on literacy and learning)
- A review of the personnel and how they fit into the goals and objectives
- A review of the financial goals and objectives

NOTES

1. Paul Tiffany and Steven Peterson. *Business Plans for Dummies*, 2nd ed. For Dummies, 2004.

2. *Using Your Plan*, United States Small Business Association, http://www.sba.gov/starting_business/planning/usingplan.html.

3. *Business Plan Basics*, Small Business Association, http://www.sba.gov/starting_business/planning/basic.html.

4. Tiffany, *Business Plans for Dummies*, 16.

5. "SWOT Analysis: Lesson." Marketing Teacher, http://www.marketingteacher.com/Lessons/lesson_swot.htm.

6. "Project Details: Goals and Objectives." Guide for Writing a Funding Proposal, http://www.learnerassociates.net/proposal/index.htm.

7. Joseph Covello and Brian Hazelgren. *Your First Business Plan: A Simple Question and Answer Format Designed to Help You Write Your Own Plan*, 4th ed. Naperville, Ill.: Sourcebooks, 2002, p. 38.

8. Bobette Kyle. "How to Get Started with Your Marketing Plan," PowerHomeBiz.com, http://www.powerhomebiz.com/vol115/marketplan.htm.

9. Covello, *Your First Business Plan*, 40–48.

10. David Frey. "The Five Step Formula for Creating Your Marketing Message," PowerHomeBiz.com, http://www.powerhomebiz.com/vol129/marketing.htm.

11. Alf Nucifora. *Easy Marketing Ideas That Make (Common) Sense*, http://www.nucifora.com/art_197.html.

12. "Financial Management: Cash Flow, Frequently Asked Questions," CFO-Pro. http://www.cfo-pro.com/ask.htm.

13. Covello, *Your First Business Plan*, 68–71.

PART TWO

CASE STUDIES

5

The Importance of Planning and Vision in an E-Learning Environment

Christina Goff, Golden Gate University, San Francisco

Every project begins with an idea. As the idea is explored and discussed, it becomes a vision. This vision acts as the project's foundation, and how completely it is defined and developed sets the tone for the entire project. Having a clear and definite vision affects the development process, which begins with planning and ends with the launch of the product or deliverable. Taking the time in those beginning stages of your project to explore your vision and create a detailed project plan saves time and energy, much like in research, where deliberate preparation helps target energy and effort, and results in a more thorough and complete search.

Developing a project for an online environment adds another dimension to the project development process. Much of the project is developed in the abstract, with ideas and theories taking the place of more traditional or tangible components. When preparing to create or build a product that will be used online, the vision or plan for that end product lays an important groundwork. In an e-learning situation, where the goal of the project is to create a teaching tool, the vision of that project is especially helpful both in anticipating challenges specific to the online environment and in planning your response to these challenges. Moving instruction from an in-person or face-to-face setting to an e-learning platform not only requires the design team to decide what subject matter to include, but also adds the obstacle of creating the visual framework that will deliver the content.

In the case of the Golden Gate University Library, the idea was to expand the reach of the library and its instruction program by creating an online research skills course. This chapter describes the steps taken to develop the course, with an emphasis on how the library's vision and plan played an important role in the successful design and launch of the course. The chapter also discusses steps to take for developing your own project vision.

BACKGROUND

Golden Gate University (GGU) is a professional practice institution located in San Francisco. Founded in 1901, it is the largest nonprofit private university serving adult students in the San Francisco Bay area.[1] The university offers undergraduate and graduate degree and certificate programs in tax, law, business, and information technology. Its main campus is in San Francisco, with additional locations for the tax program in Los Angeles and Seattle, as well as additional locations for the business and information technology programs in San Jose, Sacramento, Monterey, and Walnut Creek. GGU also has a well-developed CyberCampus, offering degree and certificate programs in business, tax, and technology completely online. Of the 6,115 students that make up the population of GGU, 81% of those are in graduate programs, and 87% attend the school part-time. With an average age of 36, working adult students make up the majority of the student body.[2]

The Golden Gate University Library serves the Schools of Business and Information Technology at all locations. While there are small libraries at the Sacramento, Walnut Creek, Monterey, and San Jose sites, the majority of the library's resources and all the librarians are located at the San Francisco campus. In response to the growing number of regional and CyberCampus students, the library has incorporated the idea of being borderless into its mission, aiming to link students to its resources and services regardless of student location. In fact, the vision statement for the library reads, "To establish a borderless Library which would provide equal opportunity access to appropriate resources and services for all members of the Golden Gate University community."[3] The first three steps listed in the library's mission statement are:

1. Provide access to relevant, quality, and value-added collections of recorded information and knowledge, regardless of format or location.
2. Ensure timely and equitable access to the library's resources and services to meet the needs of our clientele, irrespective of their location.
3. Develop and maintain an educational program for the Library's clientele for maximum utilization of resources and services.[4]

The language of the mission is carefully chosen to reflect the changing needs of a growing and diverse student population. This mission affects the different library departments in different ways. For the Information Services Department, whose responsibilities include reference support, library website development, collection development, and research instruction, the mission to be a borderless library creates unique challenges for the librarians.

One response to this challenge is met with a focused collection development practice of discovering resources available online so that all students can take advantage of the collection. These online resources, including the library catalog, databases, and librarian-authored research guides, can be accessed through the library website and are consistently reviewed for relevance and ease of use. The library catalog, GOLDPAC, has been expanded to include access to full-text electronic books from online vendors Ebrary and Netlibrary. The addition of full-text material that can be accessed through the online catalog adds value to a traditional search tool and opens the library collection up to those who cannot physically access the book collection. Some of the online databases the library subscribes to added material traditionally available only in print. Such is the case of some Gale publications, like the *Market Share Reporter* or *Encyclopedia of American Industries*, now available through Infotrac's Business and Company Resource Center. This allows the library's collection to be accessed from any location at the time of need, instead of limiting use of these resources to the reference section in San Francisco. The librarian-authored research guides, called research roadmaps, were the first attempt at moving the research instruction online. These guides offer step-by-step examples of how to use the library collection to do research for a particular class or on a specific topic. When the guides moved onto the library website, they were fully linked to the catalog or databases mentioned in the research strategy. The online guides were used in instruction sections and distributed as handouts. With all the tools and resources available online, the new challenge lay in making the distance learners aware of what is available to them.

The main challenge in providing library service, including reference assistance and library instruction, is reaching those students who do not have immediate access to the main campus. For reference assistance, librarians are available by phone, by email, and by appointment, but the patron's access is limited by the library's hours of operation. For the instruction program, the real challenge is making the workshops or in-class sessions available in the regions or online in a cyber-course.

In the past, there had been a regional campus librarian whose responsibility was to deliver service to the main regional sites around San Francisco. The regional librarian was able to travel to the regional sites each term for class visits and collection maintenance. When that position was eliminated, existing staff within the Information Services Department absorbed the responsibility of regional support. Due to budget and time constraints, the service to the regions was reduced. Although support by phone and email continued unchanged, the regional site visits for collection maintenance and research instruction were unable to continue on a regular schedule. Visits to the regions relied on faculty invitation, so newer faculty or students were becoming less familiar with the library and what it had to offer.

Students who were taking courses through the university's CyberCampus had challenges similar to those of the regional students and had the additional problem of not being in a physical classroom anywhere in the GGU system. Many of the courses are taught fully online. For those unfamiliar with online learning or the online class structure, this can be difficult to visualize. The courses are built on the e-learning platform, and all course content is made available through this portal. The classes are generally arranged with weekly topics and assignments, and lectures can be posted as text, PowerPoint, or even video. The interaction between students and instructor takes the form of asynchronous chat and discussion sections. Much of the time, students post their assignments for the entire class to read and receive feedback in the same way. The course platform also has built-in course management capabilities, including a grade book and testing mechanism. Because students are not required to meet at any of the site locations, unless faculty included a description of the library, students were unaware of its resources and services. Many students are introduced to the library and its resources through in-class instruction sessions, and although librarians attempted to re-create these sessions in cyber-courses, this relied on faculty invitation, and contact varied from term to term.

FINDING A SOLUTION

The goal of the library's instruction program is to help create lifelong learners that have the research skills needed to be successful in the scholastic environment as well as the business environment. With the student population spread across many different locations, the challenge is to reach students who need assistance at the time and place they need it. The majority of the students who attend GGU work full-time, come to campus only to go to class, and prefer to do their research online. The main delivery for the research instruction sessions is in the form of one-time in-class instruction sessions. These sessions last one to two hours and introduce the students to resources and services available to them. Most instruction sessions are overviews of the library collections, but many of the upper-division sessions focus on a specific topic or assignment. The library's in-class instruction sessions reach a percentage of the student population but rely on faculty request. The library also offers subject-specific workshops that are open to anyone in the GGU community. The topics vary during the term and can range from a general library orientation at the beginning of the month to a workshop on researching companies and industries or finding country data. In addition to the library-sponsored workshops, the research instruction librarian had partnered with other university departments to deliver workshops on library resources and how they related to the functions of other departments. For example, the university's Career Services Department sponsors a workshop on using the library resources when preparing for a job search or interview. While these are valuable topics, and are well received by attendees, they are generally available only on the San Francisco campus. Workshops can also be made available to the regional sites by a video conferencing system, but this again requires students to work around the library's schedule. There was a need for the library to meet the students where they were, and not wait for the student to find the library.

This challenge could be met by the creation of a stand-alone course that could be taken where and when it was needed. The Information Services team decided to create an online library research skills course that could be used by all students, regardless of their site affiliation. The main goal of the course was to facilitate the development of key research skills needed to be successful in the courses offered at GGU, and to move beyond the academic setting to help users become lifelong learners and successful business professionals. The content of the course would be the same as that currently taught in class and through the online research guides: the research process. The difference would be that it did not rely on librarian-led instruction, and could be used by students independently and at the time they needed it.

Once the decision to create a course was made, the planning process began. The first step was to create the vision of the course. While the librarians had an idea of what the purpose or goal of the course was, creating the vision of what the course would be was a more challenging exercise. It included deciding what the librarian wanted to include in the course, what it would look like, and what would it accomplish. This vision needed to be fully developed before moving forward with the planning process. To aid in the course development, the Information Services librarians met with the university's CyberCampus dean and one of the in-house instructional designers to discuss the needs and ideas for this new course. It was decided that the library could build the course on the e-learning platform currently in use by the university, and that the instructional designer would assist the librarian with the development. Once these decisions were made, many of the questions about course structure were answered.

The university was currently using the eCollege learning platform for the delivery of its CyberCampus programs. The benefit of using an existing course platform was that the library would not have to create a tutorial from scratch, through HTML or another Web tool. The e-learning platform allowed for editorial control by the professor or, in this case, librarians. They would be in control of the content and organization of the lessons. The other benefit is that using this platform kept the structure in line with the courses being taught through CyberCampus, making the library's course familiar to a good portion of the targeted audience.

DEVELOPING THE VISION

Once the decision to work with the CyberCampus team was made, the library team could focus more closely on what content was to be included in the course. There are many approaches to library instruction, and much has been learned about what makes this type of instruction successful. Before deciding what to include in the course, the librarians looked at successful online research courses offered at other institutions, paying special attention to the format, content, graphics, ease of use, and audience for each of the projects. The team compared other course strategy and content to what would work best for their own students, and this process allowed them to see what was missing from other tutorials that needed to be included in this one. For example, much of what was already available at other institutions was aimed at an incoming freshman audience or was part of an information literacy requirement. The course that would best serve the students at GGU would be aimed at an adult learner, and could not be required for graduation. Reviewing the existing courses helped to clarify the vision for the course and made the team aware that the course would have to be attractive enough for students to do on their own time. The course that they were building would appeal to students who have very little extra time and need to get targeted information in a user-friendly way.

In addition to viewing existing online courses, a literature review was performed, both to gather case studies of similar projects and to see what pedagogical best practices on online instruction were available. There were two questions that drove this early research: What were the experiences of libraries that had developed online research instruction, and how did teaching online differ from teaching an in-person course? These were important issues to explore before the course was created. It would benefit the team to see what had worked, or not worked, at other institutions, and would also help to review the standards for traditional library instruction and compare those to what was possible online. Part of developing that early vision was not to limit the course to what might be possible, but to explore the options completely so one could get a better sense of what was definitely possible.

The librarians looked at case studies for online instruction programs or courses at Emmanuel College in Boston,[5] California State University at Chico,[6] California State University at Hayward,[7] and the University of Nebraska in Lincoln.[8] Although the details for each e-learning project differed, the overall process of moving from a traditional in-person instruction format to one where the teaching was done online was the same. Each institution described the development process they went through, including technology used, what was most challenging, and what success they had. Libraries at both the University of Nebraska and California State University, Hayward, had developed semester-length courses, so while the development process was similar, the end result was very different from what GGU hoped to accomplish with its library course. More similar was the case from Emmanuel College, where an online tutorial for the school's nursing program was being created. The nursing tutorial was aimed at adult learners and intended to help develop skills for lifelong learning and professional development. This was in line with the mission of GGU, and the description of the college's own course development further clarified the vision for the GGU library course.

While case studies of the online instruction process were helpful, it was important to make sure that the type of course that the librarians were envisioning would be successful at meeting the professionally accepted learning objectives set forth by library instruction, specifically information literacy skills. In a 1999 article, Nancy H. Dewald not only explores the criteria for good library instruction, but surveys existing online tutorials to see whether they meet that criteria. She also discusses whether it is even possible to duplicate these characteristics in an online environment. Good library instruction, as discussed by Dewald:[9]

- is course- or assignment-related
- encourages active learning
- is collaborative among participants
- is delivered in more than one medium
- contains clear educational objectives
- focuses on concepts over mechanics

In her survey of existing online tutorials, Dewald finds that while many include certain of these characteristics, such as clear learning objectives or active learning principles, the online setting makes other characteristics difficult to reproduce. Two of these, for example, are a mixed medium for delivery and collaboration between course participants.[10]

The approach of this article and analysis helped the GGU librarians decide what type of information they wanted to include in the course. One of the main ideas to come from this was the focus on concepts instead of mechanics. The librarians felt that to best serve their goal of introducing the students to the research process, the focus should be on how to do research, not on how to use the tools available in the library. This again goes back to the main vision of creating a lifelong learner who is well prepared for the demands of his or her professional and academic life.

COMMUNICATING THE VISION

After reviewing the different courses and the literature, the library team met with the instructional designer who would be working on the project. The instructional designers at GGU work with faculty who are teaching on the CyberCampus platform. They help faculty move content online, suggest interactive tools or exercises, and assist with the transition to teaching in an online environment. The designer's role in the library course project was to act as consultant and help the librarians create effective instruction in the e-learning platform. The first step in working with the designer was to explain the purpose of the course and introduce the designer to the ideas of information literacy and research instruction. It is important when working with others from different professions to be prepared to share your own professional standards or practices in a clear, concise manner. Having a well-developed vision of the course and its content was thus a crucial component in this first step of communicating the library's needs and expectations for the course. In planning the course content the team decided that the learning objectives would be aligned with the information literacy (IL) standards developed by the Association of College and Research Libraries.[11] Once the IL standards were reviewed in their entirety, they were translated by the librarians into learning objectives that would form the backbone of the course content. An example of this translation process is below:

Standard One: The information-literate student determines the nature and extent of the information needed.

Learning objective: Identify the scope and type of information needed.

The learning objective is a simpler version of the IL standard and can be easily woven into course content. This translation serves to create learning objectives in a language that is easily understood by all, and does not rely on professional jargon that can be off-putting to the user. This process was repeated for all the standards.

Through the process of reviewing the IL standards, the vision and plan for the course changed slightly. The library team decided to divide the course into two parts and focus on creating course content to support four of the learning objectives. The chosen objectives were:

1. Identify the scope and type of research information needed.
2. Select the best resources for your research project.
3. Critically evaluate the research information and its suitability for the project.
4. Introduce and position these findings in your own words.

Mapping the objectives allowed the team to view the outline for the course and to focus on skills that are best suited for online instruction. One of the major roles of the instructional designer was to analyze the information and skills that the library wanted students to learn, and to make sure these learning objectives were attainable through online instruction.

Once the objectives were chosen, the designer led the library team in developing a plan for designing the course. At this point, no content had been created, and all preparation was still offline. The designer instructed the library team on the development process and explained that the library course would be developed using the ADDIE model of instructional design. ADDIE stands for Assessment, Design, Development, Implementation, and Evaluation. Following these steps keeps project development on course, and attempts each section in order. This process formed the basic outline for the course development and allowed the project to be broken down into smaller steps.

The library team felt that their course would serve the student population and help to support a need that was not currently being met. In order to gain support from the university faculty, it was important next to make sure the goals of the course were in line with what the actual student needs were. The goal was to instruct users on the importance of research and what the research process consisted of, and librarians felt that there was a definite need for students to acquire these skills. The designer helped the library team perform a needs assessment to judge how the proposed course objectives aligned with the overall mission of the university. To get the best sense of what students needed to know about research, a faculty survey was conducted, asking faculty to first rate the importance of different skills needed in research, and then rate how well the students completed these tasks. The results of the survey showed that skills covered in the research course were highly valued by faculty, but there was a discrepancy between the importance of the skill and the level of skill the students had. In other words, the faculty felt it was very important for students to be able to conduct research, evaluate their findings, and incorporate their findings into their existing knowledge base. The survey also showed that faculty perceived these skills as problematic for the students they taught. This reinforced the perceived need for a stand-alone research course that could be used by students to become reacquainted with the research process. The survey also helped garner interest from faculty about the possibility of an online research course they could direct students to when needed. Feedback about desired content was taken into consideration and added to the project plan. The librarians now had a well-developed vision of the course, as well as outside interest from the university. The next step was to design the course content and structure.

OUTLINING YOUR PLAN

Through the beginning stages of the project, the team took time to develop a clear vision that could be used to pave the way for the actual development of the course. Once the needs assessment was done, it was time to begin outlining the plan. Led by the instructional designer, the library team was introduced to the concept of a design document that would serve as the blueprint for the project. The design document is created by the instructional designer to show the client or project team they are working with what the project entails from start to finish. Every step of the project was outlined and described in detail so that it was clear what needed to happen, when it would happen, and who would be responsible for that portion of the project. Using a design document forces the detailed planning to happen at the beginning of the process and helps to keep the team on track and focused on the upcoming tasks. It also lets the team get a complete view of the project, and it shows how all the different pieces fit together.

The design document for the library's cyber-course project included six different sections, each addressing a different step in the course development process. The first section, Course Impact/Goals, gives a short overview of the project vision and explains what the course aims to achieve. The next section, Course Objectives, details the four objectives that had been developed by the library team based on the ACRL IL standards. In the third section of the design document, Instructional Strategy, the instructional designer details the learning theory that will be used for this course. Section four, Course Deliverables, lists expectations for course content, including the use of any technologies and descriptions of exercises that will be used. The next section, Project Plan, is a timeline for the project with the action steps for the project, when they are to be completed, and who is responsible. The last section, Roles and Responsibilities, defines the role that the team members play and details what is expected from each.[12] For example, the librarians are the subject matter experts in this project and provide instructional content to the designer. Using a design document need not be limited to people working with an instructional designer. The basic format of the document and its contents are easily adaptable by anyone beginning a new project and can save valuable time and energy. Below are some excerpts from the design document used in this project.

Section One: Course Impact/Goals

To design an online course that provides students with the library skills to achieve the information literacy proficiency standards as recommended by the Association of Colleges and Research Libraries (ACRL) and GGU faculty. Available to GGU students, alumni, and the online community.

Section Four: Course Deliverables

1. An opening flash or animated .gif (in eCollege) showing the benefits of research skills. Introductory concept site design option (http://

www.ecollege.com). We need to answer: "So what?" Maybe combine #3 info with this?

2. Exercises on identifying the scope/type of information needed. (Suggest choosing a topic for the course and using this topic throughout the lessons.)

Section Five: Project Plan

Refer to table 5.1, an outline of the project plan.

EXECUTING THE PLAN

Having already decided on the learning objectives for the course, and having outlined the course plan, it was time for the team to begin the actual development of the course content. The structure of the course was discussed during this phase. The course would be made of four modules that each addressed a different learning objective. Each module would contain different sections that each addressed a skill needed for successful research and closely related to the learning objective stated at the beginning of the module. Each module would also include an introduction explaining what would be found in the lesson, and a discussion section where students could post questions about the course or their own research topics. In developing content, focus again moved back to the criteria for successful instruction from both the Dewald article and recommendations from the instructional designer. Each module was to include clearly stated objectives, have an obvious navigation, and make use of interactive exercises or content that would engage the learner.

Table 5.1.   Project Plan

Action Steps	Completion Date	Owner
Needs assessment	7/7/03	Kim and Library Team
Design template	7/2/03	Kim and Library Team
HTML session content		
Pages posted	7/21/03	Christina, Session 1
	7/28/03	Christina, Session 2
	8/4/03	Elizabeth, Session 3
	8/15/03	Kim and Library Team, Session 4
Games/exercises	8/15/03	Kim and Library Team
User testing (students)	8/18–8/24	Janice and Library Team
Modifications/show class	8/25–9/10	Kim and Library Team
Final project	9/10/03	Kim and Library Team

The four instructional modules, plus the course introduction, were divided among the library team. The modules were to be developed in order and one at a time so that the librarian responsible for the "active" module could focus on that development without distraction. This is one area where additional planning would have been beneficial to the team. Before dividing any work among team members, it is important to be realistic about how much time can be devoted to a new project. This is especially true for an e-learning project, where there can be the added struggle of learning a new technology along with a new style of teaching. When planning the timeline for an e-learning project, keep in mind the learning curve for people who have never taught online, as this is very different from face-to-face instruction. Dewald asserts that one of the most important components of successful online instruction is the learner's motivation for taking the course. Building in content that is not only instantly attractive to the learner, but also can sustain their interest, is very different from doing the same in person. Transferring personality into the online world is much harder than it seems, and those who rely on energy and delivery in an in-person setting would be surprised to find how difficult it is to re-create that same atmosphere online.

Developing the module content proved to be the lengthiest part of the course development process. The library team had to become familiar with the learning theory being used in the course, a theory called reception-based learning. As described by the designer in the design document, reception-based learning theory explains new information as it relates to existing ideas and asks the learner to connect the smaller detail back to the big picture. As this was, for all the librarians, a new way to think about teaching, it added yet another level of challenge to the process. Librarians were to create content incorporating the learning theory and also had to make sure that the content was engaging, informative, and relevant to the students using it. Any student coming into the course could immediately see what was in it for them, and the module content had to relate directly back to the learning objective for that module. Because the students were working adults who wanted the shortest path to the best information, it was in the library's best interest to design the content to be quickly utilized and extremely relevant. Any exercise or interactive tool included in the module should also directly relate to the skill set that was being taught. Both discussion section and introduction needed to directly support the learning objectives, while still being attractive to the students. This is an area where advanced planning and vision played a large role in the successful development of the different modules. Even though the workload had been spilt among team members, all involved knew what the end result would look like. There were a shared vision and a shared plan that enabled the team to act independently while still moving toward that shared goal.

KEEPING CONSISTENT

Having a clear vision helped to keep all the librarians on track, but it was necessary to continuously review content and course development to make sure everything was staying in line with the initial plans. One person on the library team, the research instruction librarian, had the responsibility of reviewing submitted content and keeping the language, exercises, and message consistent. With different people working on the project, you will have different writing styles and different approaches to instruction all trying to blend together. Electing one person to have final editorial oversight can help with this and make sure that the course appears seamless to the user.

One tool to keep the different modules working with each other was to employ the use of a metaphor that the team incorporated throughout the entire project. The metaphor also serves as a learning tool in that it helps the learner relate a new idea or concept back to existing knowledge and helps to make a new idea more familiar. A lot of time was spent at the beginning of the project to develop a metaphor that would be useful and interesting while not overshadowing the message of the course. The cyber-course used the metaphor of travel to introduce the research process. By comparing research with traveling, the librarians were able to explain the process of research as something that benefits from preparation and is more involved than just searching the database. Again, the focus here is on the research concept and less on the mechanics of searching. The metaphor was woven into both text and graphics, and helped not only to pull the ideas together, but to keep the course together. Once the travel metaphor was chosen, the course vision was further solidified and enabled planning to move ahead. See below how the metaphor was woven into the learning objectives for the course:

1. Charting Your Course: Choosing a Research Topic
2. Getting from Here to There: Finding Appropriate Sources
3. Upon Your Arrival: Evaluating the Source
4. Bringing It Home: Applying the Information

As course modules were completed and added to the course structure, the research instruction librarian acting as main editor reviewed all course content to make sure the metaphor was consistently used, and all content successfully related back to the stated course objectives.

IMPLEMENTATION AND EVALUATION

To test the course before its official launch, the library invited both students and faculty to user-test the course. This user testing was a way to make sure that the course could be used by its intended audience, and that any problems with format, content, or technology could be caught before the major launch of the project. Participants were given a pretest, and then asked to complete one of the four course modules. After completing the module, participants were given a posttest with the same questions. Test answers were compared, and results of the testing showed that 90% of the testers were able to achieve the session objectives after taking the course. In addition to the testing, participants were encouraged to give feedback on the course itself. Comments ranged from suggestions about the usability of the course platform, to usefulness of the intended skill set, to visual appeal. From feedback received at the user testing, the library team and the instructional designer were able to make changes to the course. Technical changes were made to some of the planned exercises that didn't work during the testing. One of the most important edits made was to add instruction on how to navigate through the course. The course platform is set up in a way that all modules can be accessed from a permanent toolbar on the screen, but some testers were unaware that this was how to begin the tutorial. A section was added to the introduction to fully explain how to use the course platform, and how the format affected the use of the course. Because the vision for the course was that it would support the idea of just-in-time learning, it was important that the course's independent modular format be obvious to users. Students could come into the class and work on the section that was most relevant to their research needs at the time, and were not required to complete the entire course. The time needed for user testing and revision was built into the original project timeline and served as an excellent way to test the course with the target audience. It also served as a reminder that even the most well planned projects need to remain flexible and adaptable to users' needs.

THE COMPLETED PROJECT

The course, Competitive Core Research Skills, was officially launched in the beginning of the 2003 Fall term. The course was advertised through the library website, the university email newsletter, on the CyberCampus website, and in email blasts sent to all students and faculty. Courses in CyberCampus are normally available for students currently taking a course online. The librarians felt strongly that the research skills course should be accessible to any student, so it was also made available using the free demo username and password.

Usage of the course was tracked within the course management platform, and the minutes a student spent in the course were measured. Every cyber-student was listed separately, but anyone accessing the course through the free demo log-in was grouped as "Cyberstudent." Even with

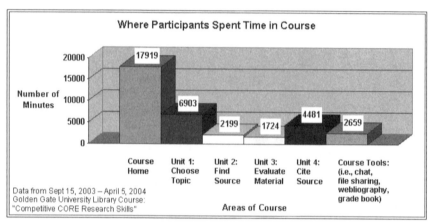

Figure 5.1. Where participants spent time in course.

that challenge, it was relatively easy for the librarians to view usage statistics and see where students were spending time within the course. Statistics were broken down by course module, so librarians could see which modules were seeing the most students. Above is a graphic (fig. 5.1) created by one of the designers at CyberCampus, representing the number of minutes spent by students in the first six months of the course, with a breakdown of which modules were visited.

In reviewing the usage statistics from those beginning months, it was clear that the modules for Choosing a Topic and Citing Sources were attracting the most students. The popularity of those two sections was aligned with the type of reference questions that are most frequently asked.

EXPANDING THE VISION

The Competitive Core Research Skills course, designed by librarians to be used by students interested in learning more about the research process and developing their skills, has found another use as well. Librarians are using the course in some in-person instruction sessions and workshops. The course introduces the learner to the course content and serves as an outlining tool for workshop content. Using the course in this way was an unforeseen benefit of creating the cyber-course.

The next step for the Information Services Department and the research instruction librarians is the creation of the second part of the research skills course. This will require the planning to begin again from the vision development stages, for while the delivery format is the same, the content and goal of the second section of the course will have a different focus.

The first part of the course successfully addresses the different components and needs of the research process. The second section will give additional detail on the mechanics of the search. Possible content could include the difference between keyword and subject searching, specifics on researching companies and industries, and examples and demonstrations of database searches. As the development process repeats itself, the librarians build on what was learned from the first design experience.

DEVELOPING YOUR OWN VISION

Much of the successful planning and vision development experienced by the library team at Golden Gate University relied on the guidance of the instructional designer they were working with. The designer acted as consultant, guide, instructor, and mentor to the team, and helped them find a voice for the online course. What can you do if your department or organization doesn't have access to such an in-house expert?

Most books on project management will detail the planning process and offer suggestions as to what steps to take and which tools to use. In his book *Mastering Project Management*, James P. Lewis devotes an entire section to explaining and exploring the planning process. In this section, he reviews the process of developing a vision. According to Lewis, "having a vision for the desired end state creates a driving force that pulls or drives the team toward the final result,"[13] and the importance of the vision should not be underestimated. Understanding the role that the vision plays in the planning process can influence the team's desire to complete this first step.

The steps taken by the team at Golden Gate University can be followed and adapted by anyone embarking on the creation of an e-learning tool:

1. Understand the role vision will play.
2. Develop your vision so that it clearly reflects the goals of the project.
3. Use the vision to create a detailed plan the project team can use to keep on track.
4. Review the project as it develops, and compare it to your original vision, making sure your team is being consistent.
5. Adapt your plan as your project encounters obstacles or feedback from influencing sources.
6. Evaluate the project before making it available to the public, and review its effectiveness through user testing.

CONCLUSION

Vision and planning are important first steps in any project development process. In the e-learning environment, this initial effort can set the tone for the entire project and allow the developers to anticipate obstacles or challenges and take a proactive approach in dealing with them. For the design team at the Golden Gate University Library, having a clearly defined vision that was reviewed throughout the development of the course allowed for the successful creation and launch of an online research skills course.

NOTES

1. Golden Gate University, "Fast Facts about Golden Gate University," Golden Gate University homepage. http://www.ggu.edu/about/FastFacts.

2. Ibid.

3. Joshua Adarkwa, "GGU Library Mission Statement," Golden Gate University Library homepage. http://www.ggu.edu/university_library/about (accessed February 10, 2005).

4. Ibid.

5. Mary Ann Tricarico, Susan von Daum Tholl, and Elena O'Malley, "Interactive Online Instruction for Library Research: The Small Academic Library Experience," *Journal of Academic Librarianship* 27, no. 3 (2001): 220–223.

6. Sarah Blakeslee and Kristin Johnson, "Using Horizon Live to Deliver Library Instruction to Distance and Online Students," *Reference Services Review* 30, no. 4 (2002): 324–329.

7. Kate Manuel, "Teaching an Online Information Literacy Course," *Reference Services Review* 29, no. 3 (2001): 219–229.

8. Paul S. Hoffman, "The Development and Evolution of a University-Based Online Library Instruction Course," *Reference Services Review* 30, no. 3 (2002): 198–211.

9. Nancy H. Dewald, "Transporting Good Library Instruction Practices into the Web Environment: An Analysis of Online Tutorials," *Journal of Academic Librarianship* 25, no. 1 (1999): 26–31.

10. Ibid.

11. Association of College and Research Libraries, "Information Literacy Competency Standards for Higher Education," American Library Association. http://www.ala.org/ala/acrl/acrlstandards/informationliteracycompetency.htm.

12. Kim Barber, "CyberCampus Design Document" (unpublished internal document produced for Cybercampus, Golden Gate University, July 1, 2003).

13. James P. Lewis, *Mastering Project Management: Applying Advanced Concepts of Project Planning, Control and Evaluation* (Blacklick, Ohio: McGraw-Hill Trade, 1998), 140.

BIBLIOGRAPHY

Adarkwa, Joshua. "GGU Library Mission Statement." Golden Gate University Library homepage. http://www.ggu.edu/university_library/about (accessed February 10, 2005).

Association of College and Research Libraries. "Information Literacy Competency Standards for Higher Education." American Library Association. http://www.ala.org/ala/acrl/acrlstandards/informationliteracycompetency.htm.

Barber, Kim. "CyberCampus Design Document" (Cybercampus, Golden Gate University, July 1, 2003).

Blakeslee, Sarah, and Kristin Johnson. "Using Horizon Live to Deliver Library Instruction to Distance and Online Students." *Reference Services Review* 30, no. 4 (2002): 324–329.

Dewald, Nancy H. "Transporting Good Library Instruction Practices into the Web Environment: An Analysis of Online Tutorials." *Journal of Academic Librarianship* 25, no. 1 (1999): 26–31.

Golden Gate University. "Fast Facts about Golden Gate University." Golden Gate University homepage. http://www.ggu.edu/about/FastFacts.

Hoffman, Paul S. "The Development and Evolution of a University-Based Online Library Instruction Course." *Reference Services Review* 30, no. 3 (2002): 198–211.

Lewis, James P. *Mastering Project Management: Applying Advanced Concepts of Project Planning, Control and Evaluation.* Blacklick, Ohio: McGraw-Hill Trade, 1998.

Manuel, Kate. "Teaching an Online Information Literacy Course." *Reference Services Review* 29, no. 3 (2001): 219–229.

Tricarico, Mary Ann, Susan von Daum Tholl, and Elena O'Malley. "Interactive Online Instruction for Library Research: The Small Academic Library Experience." *Journal of Academic Librarianship* 27, no. 3 (2001): 220–223.

6

Building and Managing Personnel

Implementing an E-Learning Development Cycle at the Criminal Justice Team, University of Hertfordshire, UK

Stella Lee, University of Hertfordshire, Hatfield Campus, UK

The Criminal Justice Team (CJT) is a professional academic group that resides within the Department of Social, Community and Health Studies at the University of Hertfordshire in Hatfield, England (http://www.herts.ac.uk). Founded in 1997, the CJT was among the first to deliver the face-to-face BSc (Hons) degree program, as well as a certificate program in criminal justice, the newly structured professional qualification to train probation officer trainees throughout the UK. In 2003, the UK Home Office, the department that is responsible for setting standards and training probation officers nationally, declared that the university's traditional classroom teaching style was no longer cost-effective and that they were interested in the new online learning approach. As a result of this change, the university was contracted to transform both its aforementioned programs into a 50% e-learning/50% face-to-face program, that is, a "blended" learning environment.

For the purpose of illustration, this chapter will focus on the CJT E-Learning Team's case study of the development of the BSc (Hons) degree program and the building and managing of personnel.

STRUCTURE OF THE PROGRAM

The BSc (Hons) in Criminal Justice is the professional qualification that confers probation officer status on successful students. The BSc (Hons) in Criminal Justice is an integrated program of education and training that combines on-the-job experience and university-based studies. The degree is completed within 24 months and is divided into two phases:

Phase 1 consists of six modules that will be completed in six months, and covers foundational knowledge, skills and values, and assessed performance at a foundation level of practice.

Phase 2 consists of nine modules and is completed within 18 months. This phase has developing effective practice as its key overall theme.

The development of this program was the direct result of the decision announced by the Home Secretary on 29 July 1997 to implement a new qualification for probation officers. This decision made it clear that the new qualification of the BSc (Hons) in Criminal Justice was to be an employment-led provision, commissioned through designated probation consortia, and developed in partnership with higher education partners. Over 500 graduates have now successfully completed the degree.

According to the *Program Handbook* for 2004, the program's aims are:

- To provide an integrated honors-degree-level education in the academic disciplines and practice learning which will equip students/ trainee probation officers to play their full part in Probation's top-priority role of protecting the public and reducing crime through correctional work with offenders.
- To enable students to be eligible for the professional qualification, which confers probation officer status on successful trainees subject to employment by a probation board.
- To enable students to develop an awareness of their strengths and weaknesses as accountable practitioners and to develop skills of critical reflection and analysis for continuing professional development.
- To equip students with the knowledge, skills, and values to be effective practitioners in a diverse, multicultural, and multiracial society.

OUR TARGET AUDIENCE

The e-learning program targeted students who are full-time probation officer trainees working at the London Probation Area, which is a branch of the National Probation Service in England. The CJT strives to deliver a program that combines theory with practice. Students work three days a week on-site at various London probation offices for on-the-job probation experiences. The remaining two days are e-learning days and are somewhat flexible in terms of time and location. Students can spend this e-learning time to access Web-based materials, read e-journals, conduct research, attend seminars, and go to the libraries. Demographically, the students are very diverse in terms of age (from 21 to over 50), ethnic background (fewer than

50% are classified as white Caucasian), and level of education (range from secondary school graduates to master's degree holders). One consistent element was that none of them had any previous e-learning experience.

At the start of each phase, the students will travel from their base location in London to undergo an intensive one-week residential teaching at the University of Hertfordshire and subsequently a once-a-month seminar by the CJT instructors in an arranged venue in London, usually a classroom rented from a nearby college. The rest of the time, students are expected to complete their coursework over the Internet using the university portal—StudyNet.

STUDYNET: THE VIRTUAL LEARNING ENVIRONMENT (VLE)

StudyNet, which was established in the summer of 2000 by the Learning Technology Development Unit, is the university's home-grown VLE. It is similar to other course management systems such as Blackboard and WebCT in the way that students access their module material and general information about the university, including student services, campus facilities, learning resources, and program-specific information. In addition, users can interact via e-mail; post comments in discussion forums; work on multimedia exercises; take quizzes; and submit assessments online. It is accessible both on- and off-campus.

It was decided to use StudyNet as the e-learning platform to deliver modules within the criminal justice program. The obvious advantage of using StudyNet is that the team would not have to create module websites from scratch, and the university has been providing integrated support and training on StudyNet for incoming students as well as for staff. As a result, the team can focus their effort on developing e-learning material rather than learning the technologies involved. In addition, due to the structural control and layout limitation within StudyNet, each module in the program will be consistent with the rest of the university's modules.

Amounts of information and material vary from website to website, but for all the modules being taught by the CJT, the team follows a standard guideline for content and presentation developed by the instructional designer.

WHO'S WHO IN AN E-LEARNING TEAM

Before starting any project, it is essential to spell out what roles and skills are required to structure an e-learning development team. This section outlines the personnel in CJT involved in each stage of the e-learning development cycle. Please note that *a role* doesn't equal one role per person; rather, it is more likely that one person will take on more than one role. For example, in the CJT, the project manager wears many hats by doing project planning, technology management, and curriculum development. So, when planning for your project, think in terms of roles, not just individuals.

Once the e-learning project for the degree program is confirmed, the CJT begins its work by developing the following roles: subject matter experts, project manager, instructional designer, multimedia developer, trainer, learning technologist, instructor, information consultants, and learning disability specialist.

Subject matter experts are responsible for the creating, editing, and managing of content. They are usually highly knowledgeable about a particular subject and are in charge of the accuracy of the e-learning materials. On the CJT, they are members from the academic staff who have extensive experience working as probation officers or had been teaching in the field of criminal justice with another institution before joining the university. In addition, these experts help guide other staff on the team on module content and subject-specific jargon, locating learning resources, and chunking content into learning objects. The experts work closely with the instructional designer to establish what is included in each unit of each module, and together they develop a structure for the program. In CJT, they also take on a dual role as instructors, who deliver the modules to the students.

The project manager is the planner of the CJT. She defines the project scope, conducts needs assessments, overlooks the daily operation, allocates resources, manages the processes, and communicates to the team about the e-learning development cycle. In addition, the project manager builds collaboration, encourages feedback, embraces diversity, and involves everyone from the team.

The instructional designer in the CJT works closely with subject matter experts on mapping out the structure of the e-learning modules. Being well versed in curriculum design and adult learning theories, the instructional designer lays out a framework and navigation structure for modules in each phase, organizes material into a presentable and meaningful format, and converts theories and ideas into learning exercises and practices. The instructional designer also collaborates with the multimedia developer in developing reusable learning objects in StudyNet such as interactive exercises, quizzes, video/audio lecture clips, and animations.

The multimedia developer takes on the task of transforming learning concepts into actual finished e-learning objects. In addition, the multimedia developer stays abreast with changing technologies. In order to integrate more with the student development program at the university, the CJT takes part in the student internship program and has recruited a full-time, one-year post of a multimedia developer to work with the team. This intern's responsibilities include the production of engaging learning objects; work with the instructors and the instructional designer on translating raw materials into interactive exercises and learning tools; brainstorming possible in-class games and case studies to convert into e-learning format.

The trainer provides technical as well as pedagogical training for the CJT. Initially, the trainer in the team performs a needs analysis to determine knowledge gaps and training needs. As a result of the needs analysis, she gets the team up to speed on e-learning by setting up hands-on workshops and seminars; providing individual consulting, and supplying additional resources to support the team in the delivery of the modules.

The technology support officer in the CJT is a half-time post, and her tasks include the support and maintenance of the general computing environment. She deals with software and hardware issues, irons out any glitches in the system, and provides StudyNet support when needed. Depending on the technical needs of the project, sometimes various levels of technical expertise are needed to support the team. Outside the CJT, there is a wider departmental-level general technical support staff available. Furthermore, the technical support officer educates the team on the front-end as well as back-end technologies involved in e-learning environments, the different types of learning technologies available, and the appropriate use of each one.

Instructors in the team deliver the e-learning material; interact with students online via e-mail, discussion forums, etc.; grade assignments; and deal with any subject- and student-related issues, online and face-to-face. Currently, the CJT has eight instructors working full-time and four as part-timers.

Information consultants are essentially librarians. They provide advice on locating learning resources, obtaining e-journals, utilizing the library's online catalog, etc. For the past two years, the University of Hertfordshire has assigned one information consultant who specifically liaises with the CJT on subject related research and resources. The consultant also advises on copyright issues on the Web, and intellectual property rights.

The learning disability specialist works with the team on any special learning needs students may have in an e-learning environment. Issues relating to visual impairment, hearing impairment, dyslexia, color-blindness, etc. are addressed and dealt with by this specialist. In the CJT, the learning disability specialist is also a part-time instructor. She takes on a dual role of supporting learning-disability-related issues as well as delivering modules. Furthermore, she educates the team on current governmental and institutional policies on disability and learning technologies, as the team has limited understanding of how learning disabilities affect students in an e-learning environment.

SETTING A PROJECT PLAN AND DEVELOPMENT STAGES

It is imperative for the entire team, and everyone else involved in the e-learning development cycle to know what the project plan is and what the stages of the development cycle will be. For the CJT, it was the first time such a project was being developed. Therefore, the use of the development cycle not only gives the team an overview of the project, but also acts as a benchmark to follow.

The diagram below illustrates the four stages of development that were employed in the e-learning project. This process worked for the CJT, but it may not suit everyone. The stages should be modified according to a particular team and project's needs. The stages as indicated in figure 6.1 emphasize the iterative nature of the development process.

STAGE ONE: GETTING STARTED

At the Getting Started stage, the most important step is to define your project scope, that is, the proposed definition of project boundaries. This process involves setting goals and objectives, needs analysis, assigning roles, scheduling, technical needs analysis, and overall project size.

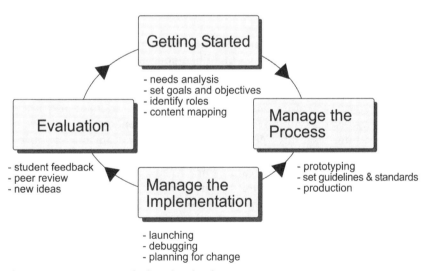

Figure 6.1.   Four stages of e-learning development.

Needs Analysis

Start by gathering and analyzing the information, asking a lot of questions related to the project. Get a sense of the target audience, and spend as much time as you can to get the big picture of the e-learning project.

The CJT's first step was to define the project. The team gathered as much information as possible and set the scope of the entire project from day one. Fortunately for the team, the target audience was predetermined by the Home Office. In addition, demographic and technical information about the target audience was collected during the initial student survey.

Set Goals and Objectives

After all the information is gathered, you can determine what the overall goals and objectives are and prepare documents for your project scope.

In the CJT's case, the project manager prepared a project plan that spelled out the scope of the project in minute detail. In the project plan, she detailed the goals and objectives of the project, outlined the technical requirements, and created a schedule for module delivery. In addition, she met with the university administrators as well as the London Probation Office liaison to set clear expectations of the e-learning project.

Identify the Roles

Once you assess the needs of the project and the skills of your staff, you can start assigning roles to the project team. While on this task, keep in mind that people often wear multiple hats, so you need to set expectations and clarify each role and responsibility for the team members.

Concomitant to setting goals and objectives, the CJT's project manager started assembling the project team. With the available team members, the roles needed to be explicitly spelled out, so everyone understood what they were supposed to do at each stage. Due to budget limitations, each CJT member took on two or more roles. For example, the team's technology support officer also led the training for staff. Being realistic is one thing the project manager needs to embrace early on. You can't overload your team members with too many roles without risking productivity, due to burnout.

Documentation

This stage is the key for repeatability. Document everything, such as project plan, schedule, roles and responsibilities of the team, and information gathered and results of information analysis. This will help manage the project and settle any doubts and issues that arise later on.

For the CJT, the project manager created and managed the documentation. And there was plenty to be documented: the needs assessment form, the project plan, results of the student survey, the maintenance form, and the roles and responsibilities list. All these documents were posted in the staff area in StudyNet as well as printed as hard copy at the team office for all to view. For a sample of the CJT project plan, please see Appendix 6.1.

STAGE TWO: MANAGING THE PROCESS

This is the stage where design and development of modules take place. During this stage, guidelines and standards are set for developing the e-learning modules, planning the sequences of the module material, managing the production process, and in general, making sure all the pieces for the module coalesce.

Content Development and Management

Determine how to organize module material so that students can access it easily and quickly. Create a content outline and delivery plan. Establish deadlines for content delivery. Not having content on time is a major reason for project delay. You need to be firm about due dates and manage the process tightly. Having a backup plan is essential in case part of the content is delayed.

To overcome the challenge of delayed content, the CJT's project manager worked together with everyone to reinforce the deadlines. One way to address this issue is displaying an oversized printout of the project plan at the CJT office. Everyone, including the supervisor, could clearly see what was being done on time and what was lagging. This approach works well, as it reminds the team what their responsibilities are and motivates them to get things done.

Prototyping

Developing module structure, planning navigation, and defining key learning objects are all part of module prototyping. Storyboarding is one good technique to use for developing prototypes. You can visually lay out what sequence of events takes place and how events fit together as a module.

Within the CJT, the instructional designer and the multimedia developer worked together to brainstorm storylines, created the look and feel of each module, set up prototypes for new modules, and documented everything in the development guide. For an example of a development guide, see Appendix 6.2.

Production

This is where all the pieces are put together and made to work. Guidelines need to be established for the module such as font size, type, color scheme, writing style, naming convention, etc. In production, conduct quality assurance and testing of the modules, including hyperlinks, animation, audio, cross-browser compatibility, network bandwidth, etc.

Everyone at the CJT is busy with this process. The instructional designer, the multimedia developer and the technology support officer are all busy doing their share of production work, with constant collaboration with the subject matter experts (in this team's case, the instructors) on adapting the materials on the Web.

STAGE THREE: MANAGE THE IMPLEMENTATION

Actual delivery of modules occurs at this stage. In order to manage this stage seamlessly, the following workflow must take place:

Launching the Modules

Make sure to meet deadlines for various elements. Are all the materials and objects in place for each module? Do you have a backup plan to replace missing materials? What about error checking? Who is responsible for edits and updates of module information? All these elements need to be in place to prepare for the final launch. Often, material is not delivered until the last minute. To manage this process, you need to be firm about deadlines and deliverables.

At this stage, the CJT's project manager referred to the project checklist and made sure who had done what for a particular module. Hopefully, the project manager had a moment to breathe and follow up on any lingering issues, such as incomplete content, and to address any delays in launching the modules.

Debugging

Double-check for errors of fact, typographical errors, spelling, hyperlinks, interactive elements, and all the scripts, animations, and audio across computer platforms. Fix bugs that are detected at this stage. Distinguish between "showstoppers" and minor bugs. Prioritize, develop, and schedule maintenance plan.

CJT's instructional designer and the support officer took over at this point to conduct a final check. Working with the module instructors, the duo prioritized and decided what needed to be fixed right away. Items that needed attention immediately were the glaring errors: broken links, interactive exercises not working properly, etc. The list of errors consisted of high-priority, medium-priority, and low-priority items.

Planning for Change and Growth

Launching the module is a major milestone. However, in e-learning, change and growth are inevitable. Build in room for future expansion when developing an e-learning program. The development and availability of new technologies also means that the material needs to be adaptable and reusable in new ways.

Maintenance is built in as part of the iterative process in the CJT. All the team members meet and conduct a post-launch assessment. At this meeting, the team reflects on the module as a whole and decides on which area to improve and expand on next. The document that comes out of this meeting goes into the next CJT's project plan for the next cycle of the e-learning development process.

STAGE FOUR: EVALUATION

This stage measures and evaluates what works in the whole development process. Evaluation should be continuous, and feedback should be collected at every stage of your e-learning development process. Here are some of the metrics the CJT used:

Student Feedback

Gather and evaluate student feedback to ascertain whether effective learning occurred. Online surveys, one-on-one interviews, and focus groups are all effective ways of getting students to comment on their e-learning experience.

Two types of student feedback were gathered by the CJT: focus groups and online surveys. The instructional designer and the project manager conducted a focus group once per semester. Group sizes ranged from 5 to 10 people, and students were asked to participate as volunteers. The idea of the focus group is to generate consensus, detect overall trends, and gain feedback regarding the students' online learning experience. Online surveys are set up and sent out at the end of each module by the instructors. These surveys ask about module-specific e-learning experiences, such as the amount of materials available in StudyNet and the feedback on the accessing of interactive exercises for a particular module.

Peer Assessment and Review

Equally important is to get your peers to assess how well your e-learning works. Evaluate each other's modules, instructional design methods, and students' learning outcomes. It is easy to overlook the simplest thing in a module when you have already spent hours working on it.

With the CJT, a simple peer-review system is set up for each module. With StudyNet, everyone in the team already has read-only access to all the modules available. Each instructor will then take turns reviewing a module other than their own, using a two-page review sheet. Questions such as "Is the content relevant to the module's aim and objective?" and "Are the amount and the type of tasks appropriate to a particular module?" will be addressed in the review sheet. For a sample of a peer review sheet, see Appendix 6.3.

External Feedback

Generate ideas and suggestions within the institution, and across departments and disciplines. Invite other faculty and staff to browse your modules and critique them. To a greater extent, if resources and the means are available, get external feedback. Set up a "guest visit" to the online modules, and allow people outside the university community, such as working professionals, writers, other subject matter experts, etc., to review the modules.

Since StudyNet does not allow guest access (at least not external to the university), the feedback for the team is limited to internal, cross-departmental suggestions. However, the team managed to overcome this challenge by inviting external examiners and visitors to come to the team's office and view the modules there. This way, the team can log in as themselves, and external feedback can be gathered on site.

HERDING CATS: FACULTY TRAINING AND SUPPORT

One of the biggest challenges for the CJT while setting up the e-learning program was to support and train a group of very experienced, old-school faculty members with a limited understanding of e-learning and very basic computer skills. Complicating this, the CJT does not share the same office and often are not at the same location at the same time. To promote a team-building culture, and provide faculty training and timely support, the following strategies were employed by the team:

Embrace Diversity

Not everyone is comfortable with technology from the beginning of the program. People come from all kinds of background and experiences, so make sure you acknowledge this diversity and use it to your advantage. For example, faculty who are new to learning technologies such as e-learning can offer tremendous insight into usability and accessibility issues. In the CJT, faculty members who are novice users offer the most insight to the e-learning usability issues. For example, they are the people who will point out certain navigational links or icons that do not make sense in StudyNet. When testing new module icons, the CJT's instructional designer always runs the ideas by one of the instructors who is unfamiliar with standard computer icons to see if they get the meaning behind those icons.

Allow Play Time

Time was set aside for each training session to allow people to play with the technology before they had to use it. The CJT tried to introduce each technology-and-training session as a fun activity and not a boring exercise. Instructors were encouraged to spend time trying out new ideas, and to explore new, interesting, more workable technologies. For example, for each training session the CJT's trainer conducts, she sets aside at least 45 minutes for exploration time for the faculty members. In addition, when new technology is acquired, try-out time, space, and help are allocated in the office.

Promote a Sharing Culture

Share lessons learned and what works. During team meetings, ask staff to reflect on their own experience and create a peer support group to share their knowledge and a place to ask for help. For the CJT, the peer review system allows time for reflection and learning from one another. Once a month, during team meetings, 20 minutes are allocated for instructors to summarize and share their peer review results. Additional time is available for the team to contribute suggestions and comments for the module highlighted.

Keep It Simple

Know the technical competency level and ability of the faculty members involved. Use vocabulary they are familiar with, and break the technical training into small segments. The last thing you want is to overwhelm the staff and turn them off with complex technical jargon. An example is the word "lurking" (as in lurking in the discussion board). To the faculty in Criminal Justice, the term has negative connotations (as in criminals lurking in the shadows), so the trainer was sensitive to their background and has subsequently adjusted the use of terminology.

Pair Experts with Novices

Traditionally, teamwork has been part of the university's teaching philosophy. Since the inception of the e-learning program, each novice CJT member was paired with another who was more techno-savvy, for developing module content. So, each module had two lead instructors, with at least one instructor competent with editing materials in StudyNet and authoring basic HTML. This approach to curriculum design and development helps promote a peer support system and encourages team members to learn from one another.

Provide Access to the Technology Expert

Make sure your team has access to at least one technology expert. CJT has a half-time technology support officer who supports the team's technical needs. She meets with the instructors and trains them on general computing issues, such as how to update virus definition files, back up files, copy module material onto CD-ROMs, etc. Having access to the technology support officer on site makes the faculty feel "secure" and can free up their time to focus on content development. As the instructors gain confidence in using technology, they are more likely to try out new ideas in their modules.

Individual Consultation

Providing individual consulting is very time-consuming but is an effective way of supporting the faculty. Often, in the case of the CJT, instructors are too busy to attend any planned training sessions or too averse to ask questions in a group setting. In addition, the CJT's instructors are unlikely to be at the team's office at the same time (most of them travel to and from London for teaching sessions and site visits). A one-on-one meeting can eliminate this barrier and provide direct assistance. At least once a week, both the instructional designer and the technology support officer meet with the instructors individually to assist with any aspect of e-learning development they found challenging.

Conduct Training Surveys

Twice a semester, the trainer in the CJT sets up an online survey asking faculty questions about their satisfaction with learning technology support.

The survey is in a one-page multiple-choice format. Each consists of fewer than 10 questions asking faculty about their e-learning experiences so far, their support needs, other issues that need attention, and any suggestions they may have. This survey is a great tool for gathering ideas and can be used to determine needs for further training and fine-tuning the content.

TRAIN THE TRAINER: LEARNING TECHNOLOGISTS SUPPORT

Learning technologists, by definition, are professional practitioners supporting the effective use of learning technologies in institutions. Until recently, it has been unclear as to what is required to fulfill the role of a learning technologist. E-learning projects demand many different skills, usually more than what one person can take on. Generally speaking, learning technologists should strike a balance among three core knowledge areas: technical, pedagogical, and creative. *Technical* refers to the computer software and hardware know-how; *pedagogical* concerns the area of education research and learning theories; and *creative* concerns the aesthetic presentation and layout of the e-learning programs. Integrating these three core knowledge areas requires dedicated support and ongoing professional development.

In the CJT, the instructional designer, the multimedia developer, and the technology support officer all share the role of learning technologist. They are the trio who create, design, and develop e-learning projects. Here are some of the activities they take part in for their ongoing support and professional development:

Conferences and Research

Due to the ever-changing nature of technology, learning technologists should keep current with the latest research findings by reading journals, and by attending and participating at professional conferences. It is not always easy to find time to conduct research and related activities; however, in an emerging field, keeping abreast with current trends will help turn theories into practice. At present, the learning technologist trio in the team plan to attend and present at the StudyNet conference held by the university.

Membership in Professional Organizations/Interest Groups

The field of e-learning technology is still in its seminal stage; therefore, it is important to establish some credibility and common ground within the field. As a result, a number of organizations and interest groups have been established for practitioners and for those who take an active part in developing learning technologies. Being a member of these organizations serves a valuable purpose in helping learning technologists to network and exchange notes and stay current. In the CJT, a special-interest group for e-learning was set up with a listserv and a face-to-face meeting quarterly. The team invited all the interested parties within the university to participate in the interest group and also to share ideas across the institution.

Skills Development

To integrate the many skills required in the profession, learning technologists must continue to receive training in the three core knowledge areas: technical, pedagogical, and creative. The instructional designer on the CJT was required to participate in the university's teaching certificate program to gain some pedagogical knowledge and an understanding of adult learning theories.

Networking

Because learning technologists usually function across many communities and departments, they are expected to engage in dialogues with these communities and sometimes bridge the knowledge gap among these communities; and they visit area meetings or associations for learning technologists and e-learning committees. It is important that learning technologists are able to manage the relationship among different communities and act as "evangelists" in promoting the e-learning culture. In the CJT, many networking opportunities are available. For example, the instructional designer has visited the e-learning team at University of Birmingham, University of Southampton, and University of Portsmouth to share e-learning development ideas. Both the Technology Support Office and the multimedia designer take part in departmental meetings across the university to promote e-learning.

MANAGING YOUR BOSS

Of managing various personnel in the e-learning project, one of the most neglected aspects is learning to manage your boss, otherwise termed managing-up. Often, people are under the impression that their bosses manage them, and not the other way around. However, in my experience, this is a two-way street. You need to manage your boss effectively in order for the project to operate smoothly and for your boss to be effective in managing the project.

Here are some of the successful team practices for managing the boss.

Educate Your Boss

In many universities and institutions, e-learning project supervisors and managers are often not trained with people skills or technical know-how. Sometimes, they are first-time managers and do not have a good idea of what an e-learning development cycle entails. This is where your role, as a guide and teacher of management principles and practices, comes in. You should be ready to explain all the technical terms, the jargon, and the project management methodologies to your boss, and have additional information available for his or her reference.

One of the steps the CJT took was to create an A–Z glossary of e-learning terms/definitions, along with some Frequently Asked Question (FAQ) sheets. This is a quick reference guide not only useful for the boss but also available freely for anyone within the community to use.

Keep Your Boss Informed

It is critical to keep your boss informed about the status of the e-learning development process at each stage. Do not assume that your boss will automatically find out what your team is up to and where you are in the development cycle. Remember that the boss is usually very busy managing other projects, so the CJT's project manager provides monthly project updates and a summary in a Microsoft Excel spreadsheet so that the boss can get the big-picture view. It is important to let the boss know about the negatives, as well as the positives, of the project development cycle. Don't hide your failures. It will only make you less credible if your boss finds out later from someone else or, worse yet, too late in the process to take corrective action.

Get Your Boss to Be Part of the Process

Do not consider the project as "your" project. Instead, make your boss a part of the team, part of the project, and thereby create a stakeholder of the boss. It is not enough to have your boss supporting the project; get him to be part of the process.

The CJT involve the boss in all the curriculum planning meetings and team meetings, as well as taking part in the team training days. For some of the e-learning modules, the boss was enrolled as an additional tutor so he could participate in some of the interactions and activities online with the students.

Let Your Boss Know What You Need

Do not be afraid of asking your boss for what you need in terms of resources, support, and training for the project. With the CJT team e-learning
project, regular meetings are held twice a month with the boss, and he is
supplied with all meeting minutes and progress reports.

SUSTAINING AN E-LEARNING CULTURE

It takes time to build effective team relationships. As with any team, it
takes time to learn, develop, and grow. By nature the e-learning process
and related technologies are ever changing. Does your team know where
you are headed? It is important to have a structure in place to encourage,
sustain, and stay on course with an e-learning environment. In this section,
some of the ideas and ways of maintaining the team's e-learning culture
are shared.

The following are some highlights of what the CJT did to foster a sense
of teamwork and to create a sustainable e-learning culture.

What Is in It for Us

To achieve "buy-in" from your staff, you need to spell out why developing
e-learning modules is a beneficial collaboration for them. Establish a stakeholder in everyone. The staff needs to know that they are part of the process
and that something positive will come out of the development cycle.

In the CJT, staff promotion and performance evaluation is directly linked
to the progress of the respective modules. As a team, the existence and the
continuation of the Criminal Justice degree program is also largely dependent on the renewal of the contract in 2008 with the London Probation
Area. Having that as an incentive, everyone in the CJT is committed to the
development and ongoing improvement of the e-learning program.

Establishing a Reward System

Reward and praise team members who have done a good job contributing to the e-learning process. Staff should be positively reinforced by best
practices and share their successes with the rest of the team.

Once a month at the CJT team meeting, a "Champion of the Month" is
named. This person has done an outstanding job at shaping his/her module. The champion is voted by the members of the staff, and he or she gets
recognized publicly within the department.

Ongoing Research and Development

Set aside research time and encourage ongoing exploration of new e-learning practices and developments in the field. Develop staff interest in e-learning by encouraging attendance at conferences, joining special interest groups, subscribing to relevant journals and reading material, and circulating e-learning topics of interests.

At the CJT, faculty are encouraged to present at international conferences on e-learning, and are granted release time for e-learning related research. At the time of this writing, two of the team members are scheduled to go to Beijing to present at the 4th International Conference on Technology in Teaching and Learning in Higher Education. Two additional CJT members are conducting concurrent research on the students' motivational factors in e-learning and are expected to present their findings in another conference within the university later on this year.

APPENDIX 6.1: CJT E-LEARNING PROJECT PLAN

See table 6.1.

APPENDIX 6.2: MODULE DEVELOPMENT GUIDE

UNIVERSITY OF HERTFORDSHIRE: CRIMINAL JUSTICE TEAM E-LEARNING DEVELOPMENT GUIDELINES FOR STUDYNET

This is a guideline for all module tutors who are inputting materials into StudyNet for all CJ modules. We need to have a consistent writing and development style across board.

Planning Your Module

- The first step is to set up a meeting with the e-learning team at least two and a half months in advance and discuss your project plan for your module. At the end of the meeting, you should be able to draw an outline of what your aims for the module are (a form will be provided for you to fill out), how many materials will go into the module, how many units (and what the unit titles are) you will have and the general timeline for completing and sharing the module work among the teaching staff.
- You need to produce the materials in all units. This may include, or wholly consist of, sections from a textbook. You should produce the

Table 6.1. CJT E-Learning Project Plan by Module, February to July 2005

Module name: Introduction to Psychology
Module leader: Maria
Module start date: March 7, 2005
Timeline: Feb. 1–March 1

Tasks to work on:

Date	Task
By Feb. 15	Review and edit existing content (tutors + Stella)
	Need to add content in Unit 6 (currently there is an empty folder)
	Add e-journals and other resources (tutors + Ann)
By Feb. 25	Hand over completed units in Word to e-learning team (tutors)
	Convert this Word document into PDF file (Gill)
	Tutors to post discussions on discussion area

Module Name: Penal Studies (brand new module)
Module Leaders: Wendy and Devinder
Module Start Date: April 11, 2005
Timeline: Feb. 1–April 1

Tasks to work on:

Date	Task
By March 1	Develop new content (tutors + Stella)
	Meet with the e-learning team to go over content and structure
	Add "learning outcomes" for each unit (tutors)
	Create one interactive quiz (David)
By March 15	Add e-journals and other resources (tutors + Gill)
	Hand over completed units in Word to e-learning team (tutors)
	Convert this Word document into PDF file (Gill)
	Provide information on guest lecturers (tutors)
By April 1	E-learning team make final edit with lecturers

raw material in Word. Please provide both soft and hard copy (soft copy on a CD-ROM).

- Proofread your material. It is YOUR responsibility to make sure your material is error-free and has no typos.
- Put all your module information—the entire unit lectures—into ONE Word document, unit by unit. (That is, one Word document per unit.) This way, you can easily check spelling, grammar and other mistakes. All materials will be developed unit by unit. You can also easily convert the file into PDF format for students to download. (If you don't know how to convert to a PDF document, you need to identify which

documents need to be converted.) Remember, students always want to print pages out, so you should have one complete document for them to print out easily.

- You then need to set up a meeting with the Learning Consultant for Criminal Justice if you need to learn about the online catalog, searching e-journals and how to link that to StudyNet. Please do that as early as you can.

Module Structure

All folders are divided into units. Each module should have 7–14 unit folders under "teaching resources." For example:

Unit One: Introduction to Criminal Justice
Unit Two: Terminology
Unit Three: How the Criminal Justice System Works

Each unit folder should have the unit number, followed by a colon and the unit title. Please use a descriptive unit title if possible.

Each unit starts with "Unit Aims." They are the learning outcomes of the unit. They must be in bullet form and enclosed in a table, for example, Unit Aims. When you have completed this unit, you will:

- begin to understand the roots of your own values in relation to drugs
- begin to consider the ways in which values influence action

For each unit, there are sections. For example:

Unit Two: Concepts of Justice and Sentencing
Section 1: Overview of Criminal Justice System in the UK
Section 2: Structure of Sentencing

Use of Web Links

Please use some Web links if possible. Spell out what the site is, not just the Web address. For example, don't just have the links like this:

http://www.drugs.gov.uk/Search/SearchResults?SearchableText=tackling
+drugs+to+build+a+better+britain

Instead, say something like, "This is a link to the Tackling Drugs website. You see, you can click on the blue text and it will link directly to the website." This way, your students know ahead of time where and what they are linking/clicking.

If you want, you can always provide the full URL as an alternative, but at least give a descriptive link title so your students know what they are linking to. For example: "I want you to go take a look at the Tackling Drugs website: http://www.drugs.gov.uk/."

Tasks and Exercises

- Each unit should have *one* task but no more than *two*. A quiz counts as a task.
- Tasks should be embedded in the sections. There will not be separate folders for tasks and resources.
- All tasks should be put at the end of each unit and be consecutively numbered throughout *all* units.
- A task should be clearly marked by a colored table (in this example, a grey table) and with a set guideline as to what you want the students to do.
- Suggested answers need to be provided for each task.

Use of Module Information

In this area, you should add information such as:

- Module guide
- Definitive Document Module (DMD); it is the syllabus of your module (automatically appears in every module under this area)
- Information on how to write essays, referencing, using the Harvard System, etc.
- Some information about yourself
- Other information that is more administrative/logistical.

Use of Module News

Please make announcements and other updates in this area. Useful things to post here are:

- New information that relates to the module (news articles that just come out), radio programs, TV programs, etc.
- Any corrections/mistakes in the module
- Room changes, seminar cancellations, etc.
- Reminder to students about essay deadlines, etc.

- Reminder to students about your leaves, any changes in your teaching, etc.
- Any post-seminar follow-up

Notes on the proposed structure:

1. The units, which are at module level, are used to place lecture notes, seminar information, interactive exercises and tasks in a given module.
2. There will be one discussion forum per module where students can discuss general topics to do with the module. StudyNet currently has only one discussion forum per module.
3. To enable unit discussion forums on StudyNet, each module tutor needs to create one discussion per unit.
4. Tasks and exercises must be consecutively numbered throughout each unit. The numbering follows the convention: unit number followed by task number.
5. Each module will have its own mailbox, which module tutors will service. Students will use this to email tutors.

APPENDIX 6.3: PEER REVIEW SHEET

UNIVERSITY OF HERTFORDSHIRE: PEER REVIEW, BSC CRIMINAL JUSTICE E-MODULES

Module Code and Title: _____

Reviewed by: _____

Date reviewed: _____

For each item please circle the number as appropriate, and add any comments you wish in the space provided below each item.

1. Do the e-learning materials reflect the DMD learning outcomes?

No   Yes
1   2   3   4   5   6   7   8   9   10

2. Is there an appropriate amount of material to study (i.e., appropriate to a 15-credit module)?

No   Yes
1   2   3   4   5   6   7   8   9   10

3. Is it clear how the material is "blended" (i.e., a clear linkage or references between the StudyNet materials and the face-to-face teaching)?

No   Yes

1   2   3   4   5   6   7   8   9   10

4. Are the resources accessible electronically (i.e., available Web links, e-journals, PDF files, or do the students have to borrow actual books and journals from libraries)?

No   Yes

1   2   3   4   5   6   7   8   9   10

5. Is the material user-friendly and pedagogically sound for e-learning (i.e., are students guided through the material, is there a clear link between resources and tasks, are the materials well written for Web format, do students know what to do with tasks, are they provided with suggested answers, etc.)?

No   Yes

1   2   3   4   5   6   7   8   9   10

6. Is the material made interactive and interesting (i.e., makes use of graphics, charts, video, audio and quiz features)?

No   Yes

1   2   3   4   5   6   7   8   9   10

7. Is there a consistency of style within the module (i.e., consistent writing style, states unit aims and learning outcomes, summary at the end, highlights area for reference materials and tasks)?

No   Yes

1   2   3   4   5   6   7   8   9   10

7

Marketing Specialist Technology Information Services

EEVL's Experience of Promoting OneStep Industry News and OneStep Jobs

Roderick MacLeod, Heriot-Watt University, Edinburgh, UK

EEVL (now part of Intute: Science, Engineering and Technology) was a freely available virtual library. Its official full name was the Enhanced and Evaluated Virtual Library. Up until 2001, when it dealt with only engineering, its title was the Edinburgh Engineering Virtual Library, but it became widely known as "EEVL, the Internet guide to engineering, mathematics, and computing." Originally one of several Access to Network Resources (ANR) projects established as part of the Electronic Libraries Programme (eLib), it became part of the Resource Discovery Network (RDN), a cooperative network of subject gateways that provide access to high-quality online resources. The RDN was funded by the Joint Information Systems Committee (JISC), on behalf of the UK Higher and Further Education Funding Councils.

EEVL was available as a free service on the Web from 1996 at www.eevl .ac.uk. It was led by Heriot-Watt University Library, with technical support provided by the Institute for Computer Based Learning (ICBL). Cranfield University, the University of Birmingham, and specialists at other universities and institutions also had input into the service.

EEVL's mission was to provide access to quality networked engineering, mathematics, and computing resources, and to be the national focal point for online access to information in these subjects. In addition to Internet resource catalogues, which fulfill the core gateway function of the service, EEVL provided a number of additional services, such as subject-focused search engines, e-journal search engines, virtual training suite (VTS) tutorials, bibliographic databases, including Recent Advances in Manufacturing (RAM), Hot Topic in-depth reports on technology issues, and Internet resources booklets. New services were regularly added to EEVL's portfolio, and each one was marketed in an appropriate way. In some instances, for example when new features of fairly minor importance were added, a press release sufficed. In other cases, as with the OneStep services, which are the focus of this study, a fully fledged promotional campaign was conducted. Some previous marketing exercises by EEVL have already been documented.[1,2] These have involved press coverage in LIS publications, coverage in the national, educational, and Internet press, exposure in trade publications, the distribution of promotional items such as pens, posters, sticky notes, and unusually designed triangular leaflets and calendars, papers and presentations at seminars and conferences in the UK, and three widely promoted marketing campaigns.

The first large-scale marketing campaign involved a Web-based competition in 2000 entitled The EEVL Challenge and was sponsored by a number of companies and institutions. The second campaign, in 2001, involved a promotion to give away £5,000 worth of engineering books to those who visited the EEVL website. It was run in conjunction with the publishers Springer, Kluwer, Academic Press, and Palgrave, and also with *Engineering* magazine. The campaign was very successful, resulting in nearly 5,000 registered entries, the distribution of 70,000 fliers, and an increase in usage and awareness of the EEVL service. This campaign was commended in the Library Association & Emerald PR & Publicity Awards 2001, in the "Joint promotion between a publicly funded service and commercial organisations" category. The third campaign, run in 2002, was essentially a rerun of the free-books idea, except that more books (£7,500 worth) were given away to entrants, and more publishers and institutions participated, including Kluwer, Wiley, Pearson Education, Springer, Butterworth Heinemann, Taylor & Francis, *Engineering* magazine, E2, the British Computer Society, and the Institute of Mathematics and Its Applications.

EEVL always attempted to maintain a strong visual image for marketing purposes. The EEVL eye graphic, which is a representation of the ancient Egyptian eye of Horus, was featured prominently on the EEVL website and was incorporated into all printed promotional items. In addition, from the beginning, EEVL energetically marketed its service in the knowledge that, in a very busy Internet world, it is not enough to provide a Web-based service and expect online traffic to magically appear. As Stephen Arnold wrote, "The catchphrase 'If you build it, they will come' is flannel."[3] Along with technical competence and relevant high-quality content, marketing is a vital component in the management and success of an online service.

THE ONESTEP MARKETING CAMPAIGN

On November 12, 2004, EEVL, the Internet guide to engineering, mathematics, and computing, was commended in the "Public Relations Campaign over £500" category of the Chartered Institute of Library and Information Professionals (CILIP) PR & Publicity Awards, for its OneStep Promotional Campaign. The comments of the judges were: "EEVL has always had high standards of presentation, and it is good to see that these have been maintained. Their entry demonstrates the use of print-based and online promotion complementing each other to publicise engineering industry news and jobs, which is now part of EEVL. This was a well-executed campaign with well-documented evaluation which we are pleased to commend."

The new, free services in question had been launched the previous November. Whilst being useful and important additions to EEVL's portfolio, the new services were aimed at a relatively small niche market, mainly within the UK higher and further education (HE/FE) community. Being based in practical and applied subjects, it is fair to say that this community is not particularly renowned for its awareness of, or enthusiasm for, information retrieval tools. At an early stage, therefore, it was decided that something a little different was needed in order to promote the two rather specialized services.

One of the biggest restraints on the marketing campaign was the small level of funding available for the effort. EEVL's marketing budget was in any case small (about 2.5% of its overall budget), and other marketing commitments (for the service in general) meant that only a proportion of this amount could be used to promote non-core services such as OneStep. A limit of £2,400 was placed on the marketing budget for the OneStep services, and income was sought from publishers to offset the cost to EEVL.

The marketing campaign described below contains several elements of traditional promotional activity. As the services in question were electronic and delivered via the Web, it was also vital to promote them electronically by all means available, including email lists, Web groups, and the relatively new medium of weblogs. At all stages in the process, the effectiveness of each promotional activity was monitored using various methods. These included analyses of referrer logs, statistical software that measured hits and visits to the website, search engines, and weblog indexing sites. Ongoing evaluation was regarded as an important part of the exercise and resulted in developments that were not anticipated when the promotional campaign began. The overall result was, it is believed, an innovative and effective campaign that was conducted with an element of humor.

The campaign can be divided into several distinct processes, and, amusingly, horticultural terminology fits these processes. These processes are, however, firmly grounded in the main principles that underpin good marketing practise. Commonly known as the "four Ps" framework of the marketing mix (product, price, place, promotion), attention to all of these is essential for successful marketing. Also important for a successful outcome is ongoing evaluation of each process.

FERTILIZATION OF THE IDEA:
PRODUCT, AUDIENCE, AND PRODUCT PLACEMENT

A description of the technical elements that make up the OneStep services was originally provided by the EEVL technical officer. This is an application for displaying an aggregation of RSS feeds on a Web page. The back end gathers XML-formatted feeds from publishers every hour. The gathered XML data are parsed and stored in an SQL table. The front end queries this table by "feed type" (jobs, news, etc.) and "subject type" (engineering, mathematics, computing). The results are displayed to the end-user on CSS-formatted XHTML pages.

Although accurate, this is plainly not a "user-friendly" description and as such would almost certainly cause confusion if publicized to a nontechnical audience. Early in the marketing exercise, therefore, a clearer explanation was required. In addition, memorable and appropriate names for the services were needed.

The "eureka" naming moment came while the EEVL manager was on vacation in a remote part of Scotland. Whilst walking through a village, he noticed some footsteps painted on a pathway leading to a school. The footsteps were designed as a humorous guide for schoolchildren, but their purpose was instantly recognizable. Why not incorporate the same concept in the services being planned for guiding people to online information? The services in question were very simple to use, and relevant information could be retrieved normally within one click of the mouse. Putting these elements together resulted in the following: These two new, free services make it much easier to scan the latest industry news and jobs announcements from top sources in engineering, mathematics, and computing. The services are so easy to use that they have been named OneStep Industry News and OneStep Jobs.

As will be shown below, the footstep concept was incorporated into various aspects of graphical representations of the OneStep services.

The Product

One of the first rules of successful marketing is to understand, as much as possible, the product and its potential audience.

The OneStep services used RSS technology. RSS stands for "RDF Site Summary," but a more widely accepted expansion is "Really Simple Syndication."[4] RSS is an XML format that facilitates syndication of data and allows potential users to see some (essentially snippets, such as headlines and brief descriptions) of a publisher's content at other, completely separate, websites, with links back to the original source where the full content can be viewed. Although obviously important for the delivery of the OneStep services, end-users have little or no interest in such technicalities. RSS does, however, have considerable potential for the delivery of information products.[5]

EEVL's OneStep Industry News and OneStep Jobs services (which are now delivered through the TechXtra service) gather together, or *aggregate,* RSS content from a number of top sector-specific trade publishers and recruitment agencies. Instead of having to visit a number of different sites, therefore, the OneStep services make it possible to scan the latest industry news and jobs information in engineering, mathematics, and computing at one site.

The original concept for OneStep Industry News was a service that would aggregate news content from the top four UK-based engineering trade journals: *The Engineer, Engineering* magazine, *Eureka,* and *Industrial Technology.* These titles are all widely read by engineering academics and practicing engineers, yet no print or online indexing service provides good coverage of their content. Therefore, an online service that facilitated access to their combined news content at one site was identified as being potentially very useful. In the initial planning stages, mathematics was not regarded as a subject likely to specifically produce *industry* news. Again, in the initial planning stages, no particular sources were identified as providing comprehensive industry news for computing.

As the development of the beta OneStep Industry News service took shape, it was found that only one of the original four targeted publications was interested in, or at that time capable of, producing an RSS news feed—*The Engineer* (via the e4engineering.com website). However, not only were several completely different potentially useful RSS feeds identified that covered engineering news, but numerous feeds covering computing, and to a lesser extent mathematics, were also discovered. The OneStep Industry News service, which was subsequently launched in November 2003, was therefore a quite different product from that originally planned. Feeds (content) from e4engineering.com, Pro-Talk Ltd (a distributor of product press releases and online newsletters in various engineering subjects), the Institute of Physics Publishing, scenta (a gateway for the science, engineering, and technology community), Nature—Materials Update, and LTSN (Learning and Teaching Subject Network) Engineering, LTSN Materials, and LTSN Maths were included in OneStep Industry News. Also added just before the launch were feeds containing computing news from The Register, Slashdot, and Nanodot, plus two well-known general technology feeds from BBC Tech News and CNN Technology. The result was a news aggregator with less specific subject focus than the one originally planned. At the time of the launch, it was not known whether this broader coverage would be an advantage or a disadvantage.

The OneStep Jobs service took shape much more according to expectations. When launched it included feeds from Jobsite (a large UK-based recruitment agency), jobs.ac.uk (a recruitment agency aimed specifically at the academic market), theengineerjobs.co.uk (a recruitment arm of Centaur Publications Ltd, who also publish *The Engineer* and e4engineering.com), the Institute of Physics, and, specifically for computing, Perl Jobs. Though the service contained content from a number of popular recruitment agencies, at the time of launch it was recognized that there were numerous agencies that were not providing RSS feeds and could not, therefore, be included. Nevertheless, the content available provided reasonable coverage of a proportion of new jobs in the three subjects covered.

The Audience

The main target audience for the OneStep services consists of students, staff, and researchers in UK further and higher education. However, anyone else looking for news and jobs in the subjects covered should also find the services useful. In terms of size, there are over 210,000 students, staff, and researchers in engineering, mathematics, and computing in UK higher education (roughly 11% of the total student population),[6] and more than half a million studying those subjects in UK further education. This audience is based at several hundred different institutions (colleges and universities).

Although EEVL was specifically funded to serve UK academics, there are numerous benefits of promoting online services outside of this audience. UK academics do not restrict their online activities to only the ac.uk domain and therefore may well follow links from sites in other domains to the OneStep sites. In addition, links from any site, in any domain, will improve the OneStep search engine rankings. In a similar way, UK academics do not restrict their reading to only academic journals and therefore may notice items mentioning the OneStep services in any relevant publication. At an early stage in the planning process, therefore, it was decided that while promotional materials (fliers, etc.) would be distributed only to UK academics, other marketing efforts would not be restricted to this sector.

While the target users were academics, information intermediaries (librarians and other information professionals) have an important role to play in the successful marketing of any information product. They were recognized early in the planning stage as being vital targets for the promotional efforts, as distributors of fliers and information about the two services.

Early challenges facing the EEVL designers were to decide on URLs and to create logos and a set of Web pages for the OneStep services that would make the process of finding relevant information easy, thereby living up to their "OneStep" names. As with all elements described below, the OneStep home pages and logos were seen as an integral part of the marketing process, and were concerned with the placement aspect of the marketing process.

ONESTEP URLS, LOGOS, AND HOME PAGES

All EEVL services had the root URL www.eevl.ac.uk, and it was therefore a simple decision to make the URLs for the new services:

http://www.eevl.ac.uk/onestepnews/
http://www.eevl.ac.uk/onestepjobs/

In addition, and in case anyone keyed in the names of the services exactly as used on promotional materials, redirect addresses were made from:

http://www.eevl.ac.uk/OneStepNews
http://www.eevl.ac.uk/OneStepJobs

The OneStep home pages were designed to be as simple to use as possible, so that their various features could be identified with minimum effort and minimum textual explanation. They have four main elements, which essentially lead the user from left to right across the page and subsequently down the page to where the real content is revealed.

1. *"About" Scrollbox.* The About scrollbox, shown toward the top left of figure 7.1, features a welcoming message and, subsequently, the logos of participating source feeds, along with a brief description of that feed. The prominent visual representation of the source logos was regarded as being important by the content providers, and helped to gain their cooperation and involvement.

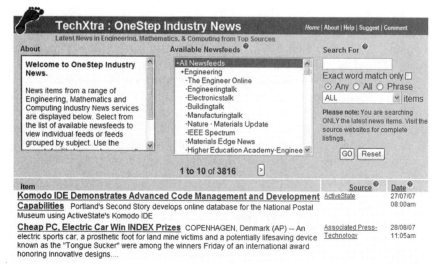

Figure 7.1.   The OneStep industry news home page (www.techxtra.ac.uk/onestepnews/).

2. Available Newsfeeds scrollbox. This is a text list of available feeds under appropriate subject headings. When a feed title is selected, items from that source will appear below.

3. Search box. A simple search box allows the input of search terms. Although the main purpose of the OneStep services is to allow browsing of news items or job announcements, a search facility was added to increase functionality. The size of the database serving each OneStep service is not large, as only the very latest news items and job announcements are included from each source, and therefore a warning note was added alerting users to this fact, underneath the search box.

4. Items. Individual news items, consisting of title and brief description, appear below the main console. These are intermingled according to source (thus allowing each source equal exposure), with the most recent item from each source appearing first. Clicking on the title of any item takes the user, in one step, to the full story/job announcement at the source site. Source titles are noted to the right of the item headlines, and the time and date that the item was added to the database completes the item section. Items are automatically harvested from the content providers every hour.

In addition to the four main elements, a foot graphic and bylines were added: "Latest News from Top Sources" in the case of OneStep Industry News, and "Latest Jobs from Top Sources" in the case of OneStep Jobs. Finally, a total number of items (appearing below "Available Newsfeeds") was automatically generated, to show users the extent of what they were viewing. This number varies according to how many items have been gathered, and which subject heading or feed is being viewed. The maximum number of items is a few thousand.

Links were made in the title bar to detailed "About" and "Help" pages, plus "Comment" and "Suggest" facilities. The "Suggest" facility allowed users or content suppliers to alert EEVL to potentially useful new feeds. Finally, the logos of funders and some of the participating content providers with whom EEVL had been working were included at the bottom of the website.

The OneStep logos were designed to be small, yet eye-catching, and featured the footstep graphic. These logos were featured on the EEVL home page and main subject section home pages, and linked to the OneStep services. Evaluation of the logos has subsequently shown that while being eye-catching, they cause confusion among some users, who mistake them for advertisements for commercial services. As a result they were later reviewed.

SOWING THE SEED: PREPARING THE PROMOTIONAL PROCESS

Having designed simple and user-friendly Web pages, the next steps were to write a press release, announce the availability of the services through its distribution, and have a public launch. These efforts were the beginning of the promotion process.

Press Release

The press release was entitled "New, free, OneStep Industry News and OneStep Jobs News services from EEVL."

Thought was given to the wording of the press release. The word "free" was included in the title to attract attention, and also so that where quoted electronically it would be discovered by those looking in search engines for free sites and services. Terminology used in the body of the press release was kept as simple as possible. Jargon was avoided on the whole, though it was felt that RSS should at least be mentioned somewhere in the body of the text, as it is a protocol that is attracting considerable interest in information circles. Early in the press release, the purpose of the services was explained.

It was important, for their continued support, to acknowledge all of the contributing publishers in the press release, and also to mention that the services were based on development work which had previously been funded by the JISC. As soon as some feedback was received about the services, a couple of positive quotations from users and intermediaries were added to give the release a more personal feeling. The name of a contact person was given at the end, along with the date of publication.

The press release, shown below, was first made available on the EEVL website and included in EEVL's own RSS news feed and then distributed as described in sections below.

New, free, OneStep Industry News and OneStep Jobs News services from EEVL: www.eevl.ac.uk/onestepnews/ and www.eevl.ac.uk/onestepjobs/

November 2003: Two new, free services which make it much easier to scan the latest industry news and jobs announcements from top sources in engineering, mathematics and computing are available from EEVL: the Internet guide to engineering, mathematics and computing. The new services are so easy to use that they have been named OneStep Industry News and OneStep Jobs.

The OneStep services aggregate the very latest headlines and announcements from top sources and present them in an easily accessible format. Only the very latest industry news and news headlines are included in the OneStep services, and by following direct links, the complete full text is available from participating publishers' own websites, in "one step."

"The two new OneStep services fill several important gaps in information availability." Michael Breaks, the Heriot Watt University Librarian, and EEVL Director, stated. "Many people know and use general news sources such as CNN, BBC News, and so on, but there is a distinct lack of awareness of sector-specific news services. Not only that, but the various excellent sources of industry news that do exist are spread out on the Internet at various locations.

OneStep Industry News is an aggregator, or intermediation service, which gathers together in one place news items from a number of top sources, and makes them immediately available. OneStep Jobs provides a similar function for the latest job announcements. Instead of having to visit numerous recruitment sites at different locations, OneStep Jobs allows those looking for jobs in engineering, mathematics and computing to browse the latest vacancies from several top sources. If a job vacancy looks to be of interest, full details are only one click away at the source site."

"This is an excellent example of how RSS and World Wide Web sites can give the latest and most current information to the Internet community . . . great job."—Marcus P. Zillman, M.S., A.M.H.A., Happenings and Events

"I love the jobs idea."—Steven M. Cohen, Library Stuff

"I certainly plan on using the industry news one myself."—John Dupuis, Confessions of a Science Librarian

Included in OneStep Industry News are headlines from: e4engineering.com, Buildingtalk, Manufacturingtalk, Electronicstalk, Nature—Materials Update, Moreover, LTSN Engineering, LTSN Materials, the Institute of Physics (Optics .org News, Fibers.org News, Nanotechweb.org News, Compoundsemiconductor.net News), scenta, LTSN Maths, The Register, Slashdot, Nanodot, and general technology feeds such as BBC Tech News and CNN Technology. More will follow.

Included in OneStep Jobs News are announcements from Jobsite, theengineerjobs.co.uk, jobs.ac.uk, the Institute of Physics (Nanotechweb.org Jobs), and Perl Jobs. More will follow.

For more information, contact Roddy MacLeod, EEVL Manager, Heriot Watt University, R.A.MacLeod@hw.ac.uk, 0131 451 3576

The original press release also contained a fair amount of background information about EEVL, but this was edited from the distributed version in order to make the content briefer, and in the knowledge that such information was easily available elsewhere on the EEVL website.

THE LAUNCH

The venue for the launch was the JIBS User Group meeting held at York University on 13 November 2003. Although not a large meeting, it was chosen because the JIBS User Group is an influential collective of information professionals and end-users in HE/FE, and is therefore an excellent forum for initial dissemination.

As part of a presentation about EEVL services in general, the EEVL coordinator launched the OneSteps and gave a live demonstration of how to find the latest trade news and job announcements. To emphasize the event, hopefully making it stick in the minds of the audience, and add a touch of humor, envelopes were distributed to each of those present. In the envelopes was a copy of the OneStep press release and also, as a play on the One-Step concept, a foot-shaped sachet of "Feet Treats" conditioning lotion.

FEEDING THE ANNOUNCING SERVICES: BEGINNING THE PUBLICITY PUSH

See figure 7.2 for a press release announcing services. The press release was posted to three wire services: PRWeb, FreePint's VIP, and URLwire. Wire services are scanned by numerous journalists and commentators, who often pick interesting items for further discussion in other online and print publications. They can therefore be an important part of the promotional process. However, because the OneStep services are aimed at a specialist audience, no great expectation of further distribution was anticipated from these postings.

Weblogs

Weblogs are emerging as an important component of the marketing process. Nowadays, they are read by a large number of information professionals, commentators, and end-users. They are therefore an excellent medium through which to make early announcements about new networked

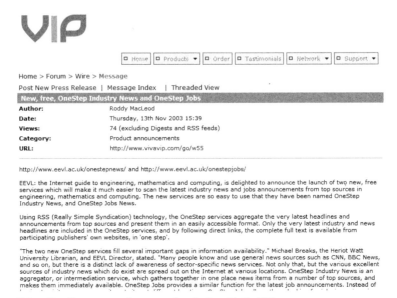

Figure 7.2.   OneStep press release posting to FreePint's VIP.

services, as they help to spread the word about online developments and news. Although there are millions of weblogs, relatively few deal with information issues. Some have a wide readership, and others have a very specialist clientele. For the OneStep marketing effort, EEVL identified and targeted weblogs written by information professionals, those with an interest in information retrieval, and educationalists.

In all cases, personalized email messages announcing the OneStep services, giving brief details of the services, and including a link to the press release, were sent to the authors of the selected weblogs. Though this approach is time-consuming for the marketer, authors of weblogs undoubtedly appreciate it, as it shows that the marketer has taken a particular interest in their efforts. It also makes the submission stand out from email spam. An email message with the subject line "Press release of interest to Happenings and Events" with content beginning "Dear Marcus . . ." is far more likely to attract the attention of a well-respected blogger such as Marcus P. Zillman, who authors the weblog Happenings and Events, than is a message with the subject line "New OneStep services" and content beginning "Dear Sir/Madam . . ." In an encouraging number of cases, authors subsequently featured the OneStep announcements in their weblogs. Figure 7.3 is a selection from the postings.

Figure 7.3.   The (sci-tech) library question blog, 9 November 2003.

Weblogs That Featured the OneStep Announcement

Successful weblog postings about the OneStep services were identified by monitoring individual weblogs, and through weblog indexes such as Bloglines and Technorati, as part of the evaluation of the marketing program. They included:

Happenings and Events. 7 November. http://zillman.blogspot.com/
The (sci-tech) Library Question. 9 November. http://stlq.info/
ResourceShelf. 10 November. http://www.resourceshelf.com/
EngLib. 10 November. http://englib.info/
Confessions of a Science Librarian. 10 November. http://jdupuis.blogspot
    .com/
Peter Scott's Library Blog. 10 November. http://blog.xrefer.com/
EdTechPost. 10 November. http://www.edtechpost.ca/
EduResources Weblog—Higher Education Resources Online. 10 November. http://radio.weblogs.com/0114870/
Roland Tanglao's Weblog. 10 November. http://www.rolandtanglao.com/
Library Stuff. 11 November. http://www.librarystuff.net/
LocalFeeds Vancouver. 11 November. http://www.localfeeds.com/near/
    ?city=113&dist=50
NHS eLibraries—Digital libraries in the NHS. 11 November. http://nelh
    .blogspot.com/
Edu_RSS. 11 November. Ben Hammersley's Weblog. 25 November. http://www.benhammersley.com/blogindex.html
Lockergnome. 1 January. http://rss.lockergnome.com/

NOURISHING THE "CROP": CONTINUING THE PUBLICITY CAMPAIGN

Email Lists, Discussion Groups, and Online Newsletters

To reach a wider audience of LIS professionals and end-users, details of the OneStep services, with a link to the press release Web page, were posted to email lists, including EEVL's own mailing list, eevl@jiscmail.ac.uk, and also the following: rdn-announce@jiscmail.ac.uk, lis-scitech@jiscmail.ac.uk, lis-link@jiscmail.ac.uk, business-information-all@jiscmail.ac.uk, lis-ukolug@jiscmail.ac.uk, uk-colleges@jiscmail.ac.uk, portals@jiscmail.ac.uk, web4lib.

Similar postings were made to the following Google Groups and Yahoo Groups, where they could be expected to have a wide and varied readership in the UK and elsewhere: Sci.engr.civil, sci.engr, sci.engre.mech, sci.materials, sci.misc, sci.math, comp.misc, aggregation, engineering_jobs.

A note was posted to the FreePint Bar, which is a popular bulletin board for LIS professionals. Contact was made with five Learning and Teaching Subject Networks (LTSN). This resulted in several mentions, for example, in the *LTSN Engineering e-bulletin* (14 November), on the LTSN Engineering website, and in the *LTSN-ICS News Sheet* (8 December). The UK Centre for Materials made the OneSteps their "Featured Resource" for November.

The editors of several online newsletters were contacted, once again through the medium of personalized emails. This resulted in the OneSteps being featured in *RLG ShelfLife*, no. 132, the NSF *SciTech Library Newsletter*, 26 November 2004, and *Tales from the Terminal Room*, January 2004. The press release was also included in *Internet Resources Newsletter*, no. 111.

Other Publications and Mentions in the Press

An article entitled "RSS Made easy by JISC and Publishers. What? How? Where? All revealed here," which mentioned the OneSteps, was featured on the JISC website.[7] An article written for *Ariadne* featured screen dumps of the OneStep logos.[8] *Engineeringtalk* posted a press release about the services on 9 February, as did the Scottish Further Education Unit (SFEU) on 5 February. Links to the OneStep services on other websites, such as that of Fife College, began to appear.

Print publications are still a very important medium for news about networked services. The press release was either faxed or emailed to several print publications, and of these, *ICLG News* included details of the OneSteps.

It was probably because the OneSteps are intended for a specialized audience that some of the more general print publications did not carry news of the services; however, they were featured in an article in *Library + Information Update*,[9] which looked at how weblogs could be used in library and information services and which included a screen dump of OneStep Jobs as an example of an RSS aggregator. *CEBE NewsUpdate* featured both the press release and a graphic of the OneStep Industry News.

Personal Contact

A coordinated marketing campaign has many different elements. The OneSteps were featured at the RDN stand at Online Information 2003, held in Olympia, London, in early December; at a Learning and Teaching Conference at Heriot Watt University in March 2004; and at the JISC Conference, Birmingham, in late March 2004.

Once more playing on the OneStep concept, novel foot-shaped sweeties on sticks were displayed on the conference stands. These unusual items proved very successful in attracting passers-by, and supplies quickly ran out.

The EEVL manager presented a paper featuring the services at Online Information 2003, Specialist Subject Focus Theatre. They were also mentioned several times in various presentations at Information and Access: Improving Communication between Publishers and Academic Users.[10]

Flyers

As previously mentioned, the potential users of the OneStep services consist of students, staff, and researchers in engineering, mathematics, and computing who are interested in industry and trade news and job announcements. Though a proportion of this audience, plus of course the LIS professionals who serve them, may occasionally read some of the printed and electronic publications in which the OneStep services were publicized, EEVL realized that other methods were needed to more directly reach a wider audience.

Ten thousand OneStep flyers were therefore printed and distributed in batches to libraries, engineering, mathematics and computing departments, and careers services at universities and colleges in the UK. Designed by Graphic Services, Heriot Watt University, the double-sided flyer once again played on the footstep concept. Its novelty appeal and bold design very much helped to attract attention to the new services when displayed or distributed to potential end-users. The effort of LIS professionals in distributing the flyers was very much appreciated.

Careful consideration was given to the wording used on the flyers. At the top, in as large a font as possible, was the URL. The title was prominent, and was followed by the subjects covered. Sources came next, and then a brief explanation of the purpose of the service. Finally, the fact that it was a free service was noted. Extraneous text was avoided.

REPOTTING NEEDED:
PRODUCT REEVALUATION AND ENHANCEMENT

As part of the evaluation exercise, by March 2004 it became apparent from an analysis of the usage logs that, while overall the two OneStep services were proving very popular, OneStep Jobs was becoming much more successful than the OneStep Industry News service.

As the promotion of both services had been almost identical, it was concluded that one probable reason for this was that the content included in the OneStep Industry News service (the RSS feeds) was not sufficiently comprehensive to attract and retain a sizeable audience. Another reason was undoubtedly that other general news aggregation services were competing for the news audience. However, there was nothing that could be done about this.

Additional content was therefore sought. Several potential content providers had submitted details of their services via the website's "Suggestions" facility, and these were followed up. Other feeds from the ever-growing number of publishers producing RSS feeds were identified using various weblog search engines. The end result was that a number of feeds from new sources were added, including Materials Edge, Yenra, impeller.net, OECD Nuclear Energy Agency, EurekaAlert!, *PC Magazine*, ActiveState, *New Scientist*, World Wide Web Consortium, Web Services—Network Consortium, and Reuters—Technology. New job announcement feeds were also negotiated from JimFinder, Materials Edge Recruitment, NES International, Constructor .co.uk, Machtech, The Career Engineer, and Jobs 4 Engineers. OneStep Industry News now includes 60 RSS feeds, and OneStep Jobs includes 25 feeds, with new potential sources being identified on a regular basis.

Some of the new sources were persuaded to contribute to the costs of printing 1,000 copies each of two large (A2 size) posters, once again using the foot concept and the same basic design as the flyers, which highlighted new feeds via the addition of a banner across the toes. The only other change to the design was an increase in the font size of the words "Industry News" and "Jobs" to give more emphasis to the subject of the content. These posters were then distributed throughout universities and colleges in the UK, using the same distribution lists that had been used for the OneStep flyers, and also via JISC Regional Support Centres. Press items detailing the new feeds were also added to the EEVL site and to EEVL's RSS news feed. Finally, on a regular basis, messages were posted to the email list engineering-all@jiscmail.ac.uk containing extracts from new items added to OneStep Industry News. These additional promotional efforts helped to reinforce the original message and, along with the improved content, have resulted in a steady increase in the usage of both services.

Some development work funded by JISC allowed several enhancements to be made to both services. Boolean and phrase searching was enabled, and a filter option allowing only breaking news and today's jobs to be displayed was added through a "New in Last 24 Hours" drop-down option. These enhancements were then publicized in an article in *Ariadne*.[11] Upgrading the website allowed a minor cosmetic change to be made to the by-lines, which were edited to include the subjects covered: "Latest Job Vacancies in Engineering, Mathematics and Computing from Top Sources" and "Latest News in Engineering, Mathematics and Computing from Top Sources."

THE SHOW: FEEDBACK

Testimonials

Testimonials were received from some of the original OneStep content providers. While these show an appreciation of the effectiveness of the services being provided, and are therefore welcome feedback, they have also been used in the marketing process. They have not been publicized to users, but instead have been quoted to new potential content providers, to help encourage them to produce RSS feeds for inclusion in the OneSteps. Promotion to stakeholders is also important for the continuation of publicly funded services, and the testimonials have therefore also been included in reports to the RDN and JISC, from which EEVL receives funding.

"Jobsite's partnership with EEVL and the OneStep recruitment service has proved to be highly successful. In 7 weeks we received 2,228 redirects from EEVL, which has resulted in 105 applications and 19 registrations for our personal career management service. The implementation of the partnership and the general day-to-day running of the service between ourselves and EEVL has been hugely professional and entirely problem free. The service is currently helping to provide both recruitment agency and corporate recruiter clients of Jobsite with a generally higher quality of application for the vacancies that they advertise through Jobsite. For Jobsite this translates into us being able to tap into a section of talent that we had previously struggled to reach through other marketing partnerships. In return the profile of Jobsite and its services are raised within the engineering community. Also through the excellent PR and offline marketing work undertaken by EEVL, Jobsite has benefited from additional exposure to create even more value to the partnership. Jobsite is very much looking forward to working more closely with EEVL in the future and building increasingly beneficial relationships within the engineering community." —Jamie Bodkin, Jobsite

"Here at Engineeringtalk we were pleased to be involved in the OneStep project from the start, and having an important end-user like EEVL proved to be invaluable in developing our RSS feeds, which in turn have been widely appreciated by our own readers. The encouragement and support from the EEVL team was instrumental in getting things under way. The traffic and branding we have received from participating in the project has been the icing on the cake!"—Chris Rand, Pro-Talk Ltd

Quotations and Feedback

Various quotations from feedback received by users and from mentions in weblogs and articles were gleaned, and were on occasion used in publicity materials for the OneStep services. Such quotations are particularly useful in the marketing process because they show the opinions of objective commentators and third parties. They were also included in reports to EEVL's funders. The following are some examples:

> This is an excellent example of how RSS and World Wide Web sites can give the latest and most current information to the Internet community . . . great job.—Marcus P. Zillman, M.S., A.M.H.A., Happenings and Events

I love the jobs idea.—Steven M Cohen, Library Stuff

I certainly plan on subscribing to the Industry News one myself. It's interesting that the name my fingers wanted to type was "OneStop," which, when you think about it, is also a pretty good description of the service.—John Dupuis, Confessions of a Science Librarian

This is definitely an approach that should be taken more often.—Mikel Maron, University of Sussex

Great service! I've already spotted a job that looks interesting and I will be visiting some of the sites included in your service for more info.—Anon.

I have a very attractive footprint promotional leaflet for OneStep—any chance I could have a few more to send to the engineering department?—K. Gardner, Worcester College of Technology

We received the EEVL calendars and fliers today and we really loved the OneStep fliers.—Janet Drake, Queen's University Belfast

JUDGING THE HARVEST: MARKETING EVALUATION

Evaluation

All stages of the OneStep promotional campaign were evaluated, and some examples of how evaluation had an effect on the development of the service and the marketing process have already been given.

The launch went well, and although the audience was small, enthusiasm for the new services was obvious, and the novelty foot balm had its desired effect. The number of weblog announcements was higher than anticipated. The flyers were very well received, and after the initial distribution EEVL received many requests for more copies. Exposure in online and print publications was good, and interest was generated through presentations and at conferences. One area that evaluation has shown could benefit from further attention is search engine optimization. Search engine optimization is a craft in itself and is very important for the long-term success of online services. This was later followed up. Another area identified for future work is the development of subject-based services similar to OneStep for other resource types, such as book announcements and journal tables of content.

Usage

Statistical logging software showed that by the end of May 2004, the OneStep press release had been viewed 2,326 times on the EEVL site. By the end of December 2004, the total views were 3,052.

The press release was distributed to 23 weblogs, of which 15 posted details. Three newswires published the press release. The OneStep services have been featured at seven conferences/workshops. Several online publications and three print publications have featured the services.

Ten thousand flyers were distributed to 630 libraries and academic departments, plus 163 careers services. Two thousand posters were distributed to the same locations. The day after the launch (13 November 2003), hits to the two OneStep home pages totalled:

OneStep Jobs	896
OneStep Industry News	1,206

The day after mention in the *Internet Resources Newsletter* (1 Dec 2003), hits totalled:

OneStep Jobs	3,310
OneStep Industry News	2,931

B the end of May 2004, hits totalled:

OneStep Jobs	38,067
OneStep Industry News	14,846

By the end of December 2004, hits totalled:

OneStep Jobs	73,091
OneStep Industry News	28,103

The number of hits to the Help/About/etc. pages by the end of 2004 were 5,967, and the total number of hits to all OneStep pages by then was 110,813. By February 2005, the OneStep Jobs homepage had risen to be the 12th-most-popular page on the EEVL service.

THE TEAM

Members of the EEVL team who contributed to the OneStep campaign are: Roddy MacLeod, Linda Kerr, Malcolm Moffat, Geir Granum, and Colin Gruber, the graphic designer.

THE BUDGET

100 foot-shaped sweets	£30
30 foot balm sachets	£14.70
Design and print OneStep flyers	£1,226.23
Distribution of OneStep flyers	£188.59
Design and print OneStep posters	£1,366
Distribution of OneStep posters	£375
Total	£3,200.52

Income from publishers who contributed to poster production costs was
£900. The total cost to EEVL was £2,300.52.

TIDYING UP

The essential elements of the OneStep marketing campaign included a
good knowledge of the product and its potential audience, some creative
ideas, a team that brought a variety of skills and enthusiasm to the table, a
determination to evaluate all aspects of the effort, and most importantly, a
flexible development plan.

Marketing is not an exact science. When promoting online services it is
impossible to anticipate all outcomes. Will a new service be accepted by
its target audience? Will the product stand up to scrutiny? Will authors of
online and print publications publish a press release? Will those at institutions who are asked to distribute promotional materials to their members
be motivated to do so? These are all unknown factors. Having too rigid a
marketing plan or sticking to a predetermined plan when unanticipated
opportunities arise can diminish the effectiveness of a promotional campaign. A flexible approach to marketing can help to make the most out of
any online service.

Yet at the same time, basing the overall marketing process around the
main principles that underpin good marketing practice—product, price,
place, and promotion—is just as important for successful marketing.
Ongoing evaluation of each process is also vital. EEVL's promotional
campaign for the OneStep services was by no means perfect, but given
restraints of funding and time, it helped to embed the new services in the
rest of the portfolio.

NOTES

1. Roderick A. MacLeod and Lesa Ng, "Shoestring marketing: examples from
EEVL," *Ariadne*, 27 (2001). http://www.ariadne.ac.uk/issue27/eevl/ (April 7, 2008).

2. Roderick A. MacLeod, "Promoting a subject gateway: a case study from EEVL,"
Online Information Review, 24, no. 1 (2000): 59–63.

3. Stephen Arnold, "Technology from Harrod's Creek," *Information World Review*,
May 2002. http://www.iwr.co.uk/ (April 7, 2008).

4. Malcolm Moffat, "RSS—a primer for publishers & content providers," EEVL.
http://www.eevl.ac.uk/rss_primer/ (April 7, 2008).

5. Roderick A. MacLeod, "RSS: Less hype, more action," *FreePint*, 161, 17 June
2004. http://www.freepint.com/issues/170604.htm (April 7, 2008).

6. Higher Education Statistics Agency, *Students in Higher Education Institutions,
2002/03* (Cheltenham: Higher Education Statistics Agency).

7. Helen Hockx-Yu, Roderick A. MacLeod, and T. Hannay, "RSS made easy by JISC and publishers. What? How? Where? All revealed here," *JISC Feature*, November 2003.

8. Roderick A. MacLeod, "What's in EEVL for further education," *Ariadne*, 38 (2004). http://www.ariadne.ac.uk/issue38/eevl (April 7, 2008).

9. Ian Winship, "Weblogs and RSS in information work," *Library + Information Update*, 3, no. 5 (2004): 30–31.

10. Information and Access: Improving Communication between Publishers and Academic Users, A Book Industry Communication, BIC/Publishers Association (PA), National Information Standards Organization (NISO) meeting, 4 December 2003, the Commonwealth Institute, London.

11. Roderick A. MacLeod and Agnes Guyon, "EEVL news: EEVL update," *Ariadne*, 41 (2004). http://www.ariadne.ac.uk/issue41/eevl/ (April 7, 2008).

8

Structuring Interdepartmental Collaborations in E-Learning Design, Delivery, and Support

Rose Roberto and Sue Abbott, University of Glamorgan, UK

The e-College Wales (ECW) project was an experiment combining a new educational e-learning paradigm of offering online business courses to local Welsh communities and founded on unprecedented collaboration between different UK education sectors and local Welsh government to serve the business community of Wales. As one of the largest e-learning projects in Europe, ECW consisted of the University of Glamorgan in partnership with six other colleges around Wales supported by the European Structural Funds[1] Objective One Program's[2] online business courses (see figure 8.1).

Developed by Glamorgan's Business School, its chief aim was to support the creation of a new generation of entrepreneurs through the use of new technology. The courses, or modules, were available totally online and supported on the university campus.

As the university manager of e-resources, the Learning Resource Centre (LRC) inevitably became involved with the university's e-learning programs and took a collaborative leadership role in ECW. In fact, many individuals involved learned that through team effort, rather than solo endeavor, the project work ran much more smoothly.

Participation in ECW required a major change in the thinking behind academic structure, services, and delivery by engendering a collaborative atmosphere. The ECW project is the case study for this chapter, which also provides an overview of the LRC at the University of Glamorgan and its history of providing online academic support. In addition, we look at the history of ECW during Phases I and II, how management structured different departments during both phases, and why that structure evolved. Issues we plan to investigate are collaboration as a project standard, challenges staff faced during ECW, and some of the lessons learned from the project.

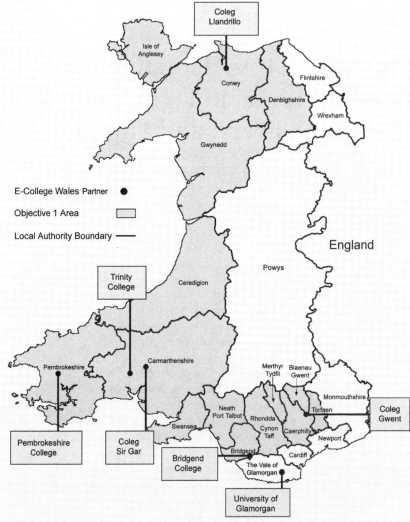

"Source: Welsh Assembly map taken from the Forestry Commission website. Crown copyright material is reproduced with permission of the Controller of HMSO and Queen's Printer for Scotland."

Figure 8.1.　ECW partnerships.

E-LEARNING AND COOPERATIVE WORKING

E-learning offers librarians a new way of working within their organization and, in some cases, a new direction for their careers (Allan, p. 249).[3] It has become increasingly important for the information specialist to understand other organizational perspectives and to successfully navigate through new creative methods when doing this type of collaborative work. What information specialists are discovering in this burgeoning field are new opportunities for outreach and teaching, as well as the need to provide new services and innovative resources for customers, all of which are presenting themselves as opportunities to enlarge or change current support services.

In the past, the different stages of creating a teachable module have been like a production line, with individuals contributing their parts without contact with one another. In ECW the production role was taken on not just by academics, but with the assistance of instructional designers, multimedia personnel, editors, and LRC staff. In the circular model depicted in figure 8.2, the two key areas that are identified as the most logical place for direct involvement of the production are the development stage and the evaluation stage. However, ensuring that the learner's needs are met and that there is a sound educational pedagogy, usability design, effective multimedia, and information support contributes significantly to the quality of the educational experience. In fact, ensuring that the learner's needs are met should be an integral part of the course's design from beginning to end. Alongside this effective e-learning, production needs to emphasize teamwork, rather than a solo direction from academic or managerial areas. The structure of the academic team (see figure 8.3) shows how it was hoped that academics would be part of a supported configuration that relied on others in the department.

The major shift between the first phase of ECW and the second was the realization that in order to make the new e-learning team model work, management would need to examine the teaching-learning cycle and see what needed to be adjusted to make e-learning just as effective as traditional learning.

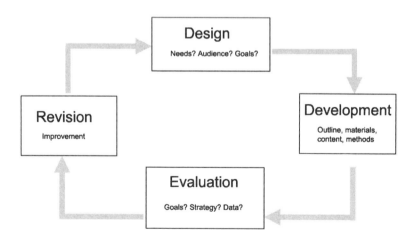

Figure 8.2.   E-learning production model.

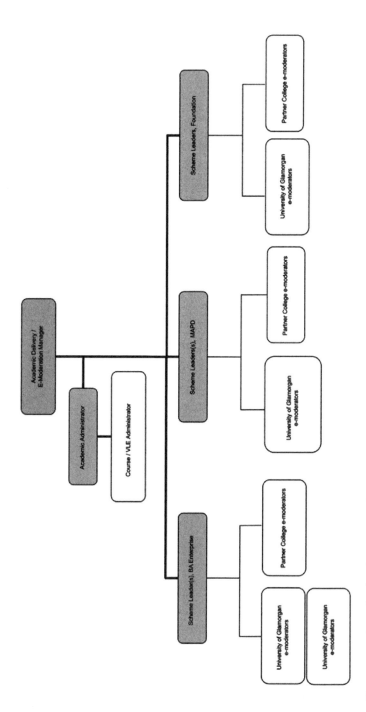

Figure 8.3. Organizational structure of academic team.

THE LEARNING RESOURCES CENTRE
AND ITS HISTORY OF ONLINE SUPPORT

In the valley north of Cardiff, the capital of Wales, lies the University of Glamorgan. This ever-growing university began in 1913 as the privately financed Monmouthshire School of Mines. In the 1930s it became known as the Glamorgan School of Technology, and after the 1970s, the Polytechnic of Wales. Since its incorporation as a "new" UK university in 1992, the student population has grown to more than 22,000. Of this number half are part-time, and many of them distance learners, creating a diverse and interesting group of students with varied needs.

One of the university's main goals in its mission statement is to "contribute to the creation of wealth and social regeneration in Wales." Its location in an old mining community offers a perfect opportunity to achieve this.

The LRC provides library, media, and research services to the University of Glamorgan. Its 70+ staff acquires, organizes, designs, produces, stores, and makes available resources to meet the teaching and learning needs of the students and faculties. LRC staff work closely with other departments to plan, implement, and provide support systems and services for specific client groups, researchers, part-time students, distance and e-learners, users with specific needs, and franchise college students.

The primary role of the LRC is to support the teaching mission of the University of Glamorgan. The students at Glamorgan are predominantly Wales-based, and over the years the university has shifted its teaching emphasis from engineering and technical disciplines to studies in business, law, humanities, and medical-based subjects such as nursing and chiropractic. It is important to note that 75% of funding for the university comes directly from student tuition. As with many "new" universities in the UK, management of the university is increasingly based on business models where demand creates a supply. In other words, departments with subjects that have high student enrollment get more institutional support and more resources available to them. These factors have greatly influenced what resources the LRC collects and manages. The university's involvement with ECW has meant that the LRC has expanded business collections to support the institutional interest.

The LRC was perhaps one of the few departments at the University of Glamorgan that had already moved into the area of online support in a major way before the advent of ECW. Because the university now included a lot more part-time, distance, and franchise college users, the LRC began to change its services to cater to those students' needs. The evolving nature of resources from hard copy to CD-ROM to online also reflects this growing trend across many institutions.

As one of the most extensive websites on campus, the LRC pages have an entire section devoted to information that can be obtained only online. This FINDit gateway, as it is known, is there to support students who cannot necessarily access hard-copy documentation. It also leads students into their own research that can be conducted 24/7, with full-text access to journals, newspapers, and books online. ECW presented some new issues, mainly to do with teaching students how to access these resources in a competent manner online.

During the transition from ECW1 to ECW2, LRC management advocated a more active role for the LRC, because they realized the initial module workload was underestimated. For example information librarians (subject specialists) in areas of business, care science, and law were supposed to allot 10% of their time to ECW modules on top of reference duties, collection management, and liaison work with different academic schools. What was needed was additional support—librarians who could be dedicated to ECW. They would get to know all the modules, academics, and instructional designers, and would understand ECW structures. They would ascertain the extent of partner college participation and support and be able to answer student inquiries and provide an adequate reference service for them and the ECW academics. It was also felt that the LRC needed more control over how students were taught information literacy skills and how these students were administered. The problem was that it would make a difference whether students were calling for assistance from a partner college like Coleg Llandrillo, located in north Wales, or on campus at Glamorgan (see figure 8.1).

LRC input in the area of copyright management was also paramount. Someone was needed who could manage intellectual property rights (IPR) and keep track of what academics and publishers wanted and to ensure that all materials required for online modules conformed with the law. Fair use of published materials for educational purposes in a classroom has different issues and implications when those materials are taken online.

INTRODUCTION TO E-COLLEGE WALES

On paper, ECW began in September 2001 delivering e-learning courses to hundreds of students throughout Wales. Students were officially enrolled either part-time or full-time in a local college participating in ECW, and they took one of six modules leading to the award of a BA Enterprise degree. Blackboard software would be used, as it was already a part of Glamorgan's virtual learning environment (VLE) and because it was simple to learn. An online Web-based method of delivery was chosen, because it was believed that the method of delivery would teach students IT skills and computer literacy.

The program had begun testing several months before the launch date, and the idea behind it was several years in fruition. The project began as the brainchild of Aldwyn Cooper, then pro vice chancellor of the university. Cooper not only believed that it was possible for higher education institutions to talk to local companies and ask what they need, but was excited by the opportunity to build a bridge between the University of Glamorgan and local business communities. He believed that by doing so Glamorgan could play a fundamental role in supporting growth of local economies and aiding individuals and communities to generate their own economic development solutions.[4] "The University of Glamorgan is keen to forge mutually beneficial links with a range of companies and encourage the economic development of Wales by taking training of technology out into the community,"he said.[5]

When one understands the geography of Wales, its history and current affairs suddenly make sense. For over a century Wales based its local economy on the mining industry. However, by the 1980s whole swaths of local UK economies disappeared with the decline of traditional coal, steel, and other manufacturing-based commerce. The areas hardest hit were northern England, Scotland, and Wales.[6] Wales heavily relied on its coal industry, but attempts to maintain the level of employment during the boom of coal-mining proved to be futile. Changes in the sources of fuel for energy and heat, especially the replacement of coal by oil and gas, led to the collapse of the coalfields' markets and, consequently, the coal industry, leading eventually to mass unemployment.[7]

Meanwhile in December 1999, the European Commission (EC) launched the e-European initiative, with the aim of accelerating the uptake of digital technologies across Europe and ensuring that all Europeans had the necessary skills to use them.[8] The priorities of the EC when it came to funding major projects[9] were:

- the development of small and medium-sized enterprise (SME) through capital investment, business, and training
- community economic development/regeneration
- human resources support
- infrastructure development
- rural economic diversification

Projects that could meet most of these criteria would be supported by the European Social Fund (ESF).

Although several unsuccessful partnerships were initiated by Glamorgan to get nontraditional students involved with further business training, the experience of working on other collaborative projects allowed the university to get leadership experience and fine-tuned the type of program they wanted to create. At the time the university was in the process of deciding where to proceed, news came from the university's European Office that there was an ESF opportunity to obtain funding. The idea to seek this for the type of project Glamorgan wanted to create anyway emerged. Initial funding was obtained by arguing that the program met the criteria for creating applied knowledge of business and newly emerging knowledge based on e-economy built around the Internet; thus, the stage was set for ECW.

It was decided initially to target SMEs with fewer than 10 employees who could take practical courses in different aspects of business administration, such as accounting or personnel management. However, the project was also aimed at budding entrepreneurs who wanted to develop a good business idea and needed relevant enterprise feedback from someone else with real experience in the business world. The program worked on the principle that everyone has the ability to be an entrepreneur but needs the right support, education, and guidance to have the confidence to realize their ambitions and start their own business. The original planners of the project thought that entrepreneurs with degree qualifications would have other options available to them if their small business went under, a common scenario in three out of five new businesses.

Completing the application was no simple task, as it required going through more than a thousand pages of project documentation. The bid process required partnerships between different education sectors, local government, and local businesses to be formed relatively quickly.[10] However, what made the University of Glamorgan and its partner colleges a good candidate for the ESF money was that the EC heavily stressed collaborative initiatives and Glamorgan already had some experience working with a few local companies and with the partner colleges. In addition, they were all located in the Objective One area of the 1999 map of Wales created by the newly devolved Welsh Assembly to bring to light the poorest communities in need of European funding.[11]

Finally, not only was ECW including partners geographically spread throughout Wales, it was made up of a combination of colleges classified as further education (FE) institutions. With the University of Glamorgan classified as a higher education (HE) institution, there was an added component of diversity to the project.[12] ECW students had the option of enrolling anywhere in the network of seven partner colleges. The partners (Evaluation Report, p. 6) were:

- Bridgend College
- Coleg Gwent
- Coleg Sir Gar
- Trinity College (students later became attached to Coleg Sir Gar)

- Llandrillo
- Pembrokeshire College
- Pontypridd College

HISTORY OF E-COLLEGE WALES, PHASE I

In the Objective One application bid, the project aimed to develop the foundation enterprise modules to deliver training, skill development, and business assistance with resources to increase company start-ups, enhance management skills, and raise the GDP of Wales. A high proportion of the project was based on the development of course materials, such as new modules, and promoting their use online. The bid stated clearly that the training element was to be purely the piloting of the project through 180 beneficiaries and that all modules developed during the pilot phase would be delivered with online tutorial support. Target dates for preparing the first 27 modules were set for the schedule as shown here in table 8.1.

The program was designed so its beneficiaries could complete six modules per year if studying full-time and three modules if studying part-time. All modules successfully completed would provide the beneficiaries with credits toward qualifications and were validated in accordance with the University of Glamorgan's accreditation scheme. The development and updating of material in the Blackboard system was scheduled to continue throughout the lifetime of the project so that none of the information would become obsolete.

ECW1 successfully recruited 190 participants for the first cohort of the BA Enterprise degree, and after the second and third cohorts joined in 2003, there were over 340 students. Two further qualifications, the MA in Professional Development (MAPD) and the Foundation Degree in Business Administration were also developed and recruited 54 and 55 students respectively. Therefore, the total of direct beneficiaries of the project was nearly 400.

Table 8.1. Schedule of Degree Programs Being Rolled Out

Target Dates	Modules
September 2002	BA Enterprise
October 2002	MA in Professional Development (MAPD) and Foundation Degree in Business Administration
January 2003	BA Enterprise, second-level modules
September 2003	BA Enterprise, third-level modules

Some of the statistics about these beneficiaries is very interesting in establishing the types of students who were recruited onto the 'courses. The demographic breakdown, types of employment, status, and gender of applicants seem to reflect traditionally underserved communities (Evaluation Report, pp. 21–23). (See tables 8.2 through 8.6.)

Table 8.2. Number of Beneficiaries inside the Objective One Area

Local Authority	Numbers of Beneficiaries
Blaenau Gwent	24
Bridgend	48
Cerdigion	17
Gwynedd	16
Neath Port Talbot	14
Rhondda Cynon Taff	70
Caerphilly	28
Conwy	33
Isle of Anglesey	9
Swansea	30
Denbighshire	15
Merthyr Tydfil	18
Pembrokeshire	37
Total	359

Table 8.3. Number of Beneficiaries outside the Objective One Area

Local Authority	Number of Beneficiaries
Cardiff	29
Flintshire	2
Monmouthshire	2
Vale of Glamorgan	5
Wrexham	1
Newport	7
Torfaen	12
Powys	3
Total	61

Table 8.4. Beneficiaries by Employment Status When Starting ECW

	Male	Female	Total
Employed	183	122	305
Unemployed	45	37	82
Not stated	5	5	10
Total	233	164	397

Figure 8.5. Type of Employment Beneficiaries Had before Starting Project

Age	In SMES/ Self Employed		In Large Enterprises		Not Stated	
	Male	*Female*	*Male*	*Female*	*Male*	*Female*
16–24	5	1	11	11		1
25–49	63	41	66	49	6	1
50+	22	11	9	7	1	

Table 8.6. Beneficiaries Categorized by Gender and Ethnic Origin

	Male	*Female*
White, British	186	118
White, Irish	2	1
White, other	3	8
Mixed, white and Asian	1	
Mixed, other	3	
South Asian or Asian British, Pakistani	2	
South Asian or Asian British, Bangladeshi	1	1
Black or black British, African	1	1
Chinese		1
Other	3	
Not known	32	34

The benefits of e-approach to the ECW project were that it merged a quality teaching opportunity with a high-level outreach opportunity. It also provided a focus for the development and promotion of management, entrepreneurial, and IT skills in Wales (Evaluation Report, p. 3). "E-Learning ticked all boxes because it brought training into the homes of the local community and sexily fit with University of Glamorgan's goals of being an applied university."[13]

Although the vision of e-learning is big and inspiring, the difficulty of it lies in the details of implementing the program. With this in mind, the organization of ECW gradually began to form (see figure 8.4). It was a fluid structure, and so Phase II of the project saw some major changes and additions because of certain problems.

Originally, it was thought that all colleges and areas would provide their students with the same level of technological support at the same time. Initially, British Telecom (one of the ECW business partners) promised that it could deliver ISDN lines, free of charge, to the first cohort of 190 students enrolled in the program. Unfortunately, however, many students, especially those in the most remote areas, were not hooked up in time for the beginning of the course. This was simply because there was no telecommunication infrastructure in their areas. What eventually happened was that the

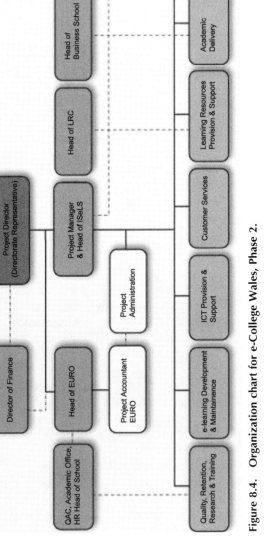

Figure 8.4. Organization chart for e-College Wales, Phase 2.

University of Glamorgan had to take the administrative initiative and hire technicians specifically to install cable in these remote areas.

Even for students who were connected at the right time, their IT skill levels were not uniform. According to an internal evaluation report of ECW1, "All students were interviewed and asked to complete a questionnaire . . . students who had rated themselves as computer literate were not!"[14]

Another unanticipated problem was how different types of students would cope in the online environment. For example, in traditional settings it is as easy for students to move from one lecture topic to another as it is to move from one physical space to another during the passing of the day. However, during ECW1, staff discovered that students came to feel overwhelmed by their course modules and were not confident in their choices. Coupled with this, they were encountering technical problems related to software navigation and were questioning their understanding of the coursework. In those instances, which were frequent as this project got off the ground, the learners needed to talk to mentors, counselors, or technical support. Instructional-designer skills were also necessary to create appropriate tasks to measure outcomes of coursework goals. They also needed to facilitate substitutes or simulations for classroom discussion, since it was not always a matter of opening a chat session, because other course takers had different schedules and different rates at which they progressed through a topic. For such reasons, extra staff were hired to support the e-learning on different levels.

At the beginning of ECW1, Gilly Salmon from the Open University in London was hired as a project consultant, as she is well known in the field of e-learning (Evaluation Report, p. 69). Much of her literature in this area indicates that she is an e-learning purist; that is, she thinks the e-moderators and e-learners should never meet face-to-face, because face-to-face meetings discourage development of online socialization. However, the program managers at the University of Glamorgan and its partner colleges decided when the program was piloted that all modules would have an initial face-to-face meeting. They thought, given the special circumstances of their beneficiaries, meeting in person was important to providing students in Objective One areas with greater service (Evaluation Report, p. 73). This was the beginning of a blended learning approach, an approach that the ECW partners strongly supported because it places less emphasis on technology for technology's sake and more on what can be done to encourage e-learning use as a tool for higher education. It is interesting that post-ECW the University of Glamorgan is moving to a blended learning pedagogy across all its faculties and hopes to have this implemented by 2008.

During the early days of ECW, the blended learning approach thus was born. According to this viewpoint, online socialization is better when students and e-moderators can match a real person to a virtual entity. It becomes important not only to meet in person but also to have the ability to communicate by other means, such as the telephone, if necessary.

You will notice in the original organizational structure (figure 8.4) that the only presence of the LRC is in multimedia development. Initially it was thought that the LRC's sole involvement would be in creating media, for example, taping a part of a lecture and then reformatting the lecture to work with Blackboard software. However, other issues related to student resources and intellectual property began to arise, questions such as "Should direct links to journal articles be created?" or "Should the university look into the possibility of hosting a copy of a .PDF document on a server and link to that to ensure that article was persistent?" In addition, there were also copyright questions if the academics writing module content wanted to refer students to diagrams, graphs, case studies, and large blocks of text. Alongside these production issues, it was decided to use some of the ECW money to purchase textbooks for students, since many of the local partner colleges didn't necessarily have 15 copies of a particular book that all students enrolled in a course could use. But again this solution posed more questions, such as "Who will administer this service?"

These issues directly impacted module production schedules. While it was possible to produce modules fairly quickly, it became apparent that the organizational structure didn't adequately support the way that academics and students were using Blackboard. The organization needed to be made more responsive, especially if they hoped to now focus on module delivery.

HISTORY OF E-COLLEGE WALES, PHASE II

The ECW2 bid was made just prior to the completion of ECW1. While the goals for ECW2 were still very much the same as those of ECW1 in a governmental sense—that is, "to make Wales' economy stronger through encouraging the creation and survival of new businesses and through the continued professional development of the people of Wales"—it was hoped that ECW2 could focus more on delivering the modules created as part of Phase I and providing the students with more staff support. "Whilst the first phase incurred significant development work, marketing and start up costs, and a 'trial delivery,' the project partners are now in a position to roll out the program to a larger cohort of beneficiaries."[15]

It was expected that the original pilot group of students from ECW1 would continue with the program for another two years at minimum, although many had switched to part-time status and would actually take longer. It was expected that a further 470 beneficiaries would be recruited, 200 on the BA Enterprise course, 240 on the Foundation Degree, and 50 onto the MAPD. The bid made to the Social Fund was to state that the recruitment and successful completion of credit for 870 beneficiaries was necessary for a successful conclusion to the project. "Following the recruitment of a further 490 beneficiaries onto the ECW program, the project will have demonstrated its value."[16]

The second bid stated that a new group of students could be drawn from the same Objective One area. There was much reason to believe there would be significant recruitment success, because during Phase I, ECW received in excess of 700 applications. ECW program managers felt that the demand for the program was still there, and there were about 2,000 potential-student inquiries about the course. Such overwhelming interest enabled careful selection of a cross section of individuals for the project. The project maintained some of the ICT features begun in ECW1. There were still to be free ISDN lines and laptops for those students eligible, but now paperwork increased because every potential student needed to provide written, documented proof of income and savings to qualify for a tuition-free slot. Ironically, this additional red tape and extra screening conflicted with the ECW mission of encouraging beneficiaries from peripheral areas to access the program. The provision had hoped to create a flexible approach to learning and the use of ICT to reduce barriers to further and higher education.[17] For many, especially tutors and moderators, this paperwork became a thing of contention, holding up applications and delaying students from beginning their modules while they waited for equipment.

STRUCTURE OF ECW PERSONNEL
AND CHANGES BETWEEN PHASE I AND II

A major break with ECW1 came in the form of an interim internal assessment of the practicality of ECW1 and its staffing levels. As mentioned earlier, the ECW1 organizational structure could not be maintained for the intended expansion of ECW2. After much internal discussion and further assessment, the general consensus was that while goodwill was a major part of ECW1, ECW2 should not be goodwill-reliant (Evaluation Report, p. 87).[18] A more professional approach was needed in Phase II, and management reasoned that it would be unable to deliver the 500 new e-learners with present resources and the present model (Evaluation Report, p. 9).[19]

As far back as 2001, it was known that more roles would be necessary to properly deliver the work that had been developed through ECW1. As the need for an exclusive and more extensive ECW team had been recognized, the JISC ECW Evaluation of 2003 praised the unique integrated team approach to the development, delivery, and quality assurance of online learning provision and stated that ECW was a leading example of innovative practice.

As recommendations were adapted, a new team structure was drawn up, which included the need for more student and administrative support and which also laid out the creation of various "teams" to deliver the modules and to develop more. It is from this beginning that a new bid was raised at the start of 2003, which would provide for these staff dedicated to ECW work. No longer were people creating, moderating, teaching, and resourcing "on the side." The impetus was also changed, as the new project would be 20% development and innovation, 80% concentration on extended delivery. Thus, the structure was devised to fit within this new remit of production and delivery. New sections were also set up, including customer services and quality and research, while existing teams were all enhanced—library, ICT support, and administration. The Business School was also to receive more funding to recruit new e-moderators and to deliver more extensive e-moderator training while continuing to utilize the adapted blended learning approach.

THE NEW DEPARTMENTS

The new departments that were created in ECW2 clearly demonstrate the collaborative nature of the project and illustrate to a great extent how the support of students had become the paramount feature of the project.

Customer Services Helpdesk

A customer services team was created both to provide pastoral care for students and to improve communication. The need for this specific type of support was highlighted by a couple of problems that arose during Phase I.

In the organization chart for ECW1, the desktop support officer was to work in relative isolation. His or her responsibility was to answer phone calls and e-mail inquiries. On paper, the officer worked traditional hours: Monday to Friday, 9:00 AM to 5:00 PM. However, the reality of the situation was that the officer was frequently working until 7:00 PM or 8:00 PM in the evening, because that was when ECW students were online and encountering problems. On average, 400 inquiries per week by phone and e-mail were being answered. On paper, eight or ten technicians backed up the support officer, but in reality the technicians' time was not wholly dedicated to ECW, since the technicians supported all university staff and devoted only around 20% of their time to ECW problems. The reality was that the support officer was overextended with work.

It was through this realization and the results of a thorough assessment at the end of ECW1 that the reality of student needs began to emerge. The second ESF bid specifically allocating funding for "a support service . . . available to troubleshoot and help beneficiaries"[20] and money from ECW2 was specifically budgeted for this particular team. This was a key part of the new department structure (see figure 8.5).

The customer services team was to consist of three or four staff moderately trained and managed by the original support officer as team leader, while a new post of manager would oversee the running of the team in conjunction with the university IT desk team. The direct relevance to student satisfaction with this type of support cannot be understated. According to the Evaluation Report, one student recruited during the ECW1 phase said, "I would have quit many times by if it weren't for that guy," indicating the support officer (Evaluation Report, p. 30). Naturally, ECW2 aimed to maintain that same level of personal service to students but without risking overwork for staff.

The customer services team was available from 9:00 AM to 9:00 PM five days a week, and they also ran a weekend service during crucial times of the academic year, such as after a new intake of students. There was a single phone number and e-mail address that centralized support but was also offered online, meaning that students had several alternatives, depending on their own preference of support method. In fact, the team was run much like a normal company call center, with calls being logged and a reference number being given. They devised a simple flow chart to show students how it worked (see figure 8.6), and they publicized this during induction.

It was felt that the system was far more professional and gave the support services a physical identity. To clarify and quantify this new degree of

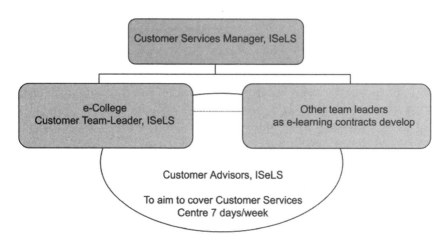

Figure 8.5.   Organization structure of customer service team.

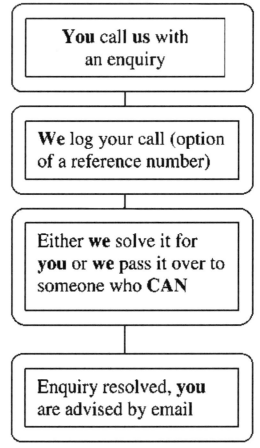

Figure 8.6. Customer service helpdesk procedures.

support, a service level agreement was drawn up by the manager, which laid out the services and expected level of response from the team. This created a uniformity of service that improved quality.

This team became the frontline of the e-learning team, and its role became integral for the support of students across all the colleges. From its inception, this team worked in close conjunction with the LRC and the ICT team.

In 2007, two years after the end of ECW, this team merged with the staff IT helpdesk, and the new team adopted many of the procedures and services of the customer support team. It was felt that the lessons learned from ECW were so valuable that they could be applied to helpdesk support for both staff and students of the whole university.

IT Team

The IT support department received the majority of ICT referrals from the customer services team. During ECW1, this team was originally just members of the university IT team whose time was partially given up to support online students. However, the amount of time taken to set up the accounts and sort out the ISDN problems was definitely disproportionate to the amount of time they had been allocated. This team was not allocated any dedicated staff for ECW1, a disadvantage that has been previously identified as a major drawback in services, so when the opportunity arose, a new section was created (see figure 8.7). The newly recruited staff members had an expanded role with clearer objectives[21] to:

- deal with technical issues raised by students and staff through customer services
- ensure the e-learning systems are available 24 hours a day, seven days a week
- perform regular planned maintenance and upgrades to the e-learning environment
- issue and support bursary laptops
- issue and support Internet access accounts
- provide technical advice

Internet connections were still free for eligible students, with ISDN being now efficiently set up. Reverse thinking would demonstrate the team's importance in the delivery of ECW services; if they were not there, then there could be a return to the unacceptable situation of ECW1 where students did not have the facilities to even begin and maintain their study on ECW courses and so dropped out in significant numbers. Improvement in the Blackboard (VLE) maintenance also became essential for the production process. Therefore, IT support's place in the e-learning team became essential, and their integration into the customer support structure meant that they too became integral to the retention of students.

Quality, Research, and Administration

This team was created to take advantage of the unique opportunity to conduct some research into a new area of teaching and learning. ECW was such an innovative project that there existed an opportunity to glean some interesting original research from it. During ECW1 the workload was so high that staff hadn't an opportunity to write up their experiences. Valuable data that could be passed on to others seemed to be slipping away, because nothing was being published or even recorded in any way. This was to be rectified with the creation of the team for Phase 2.

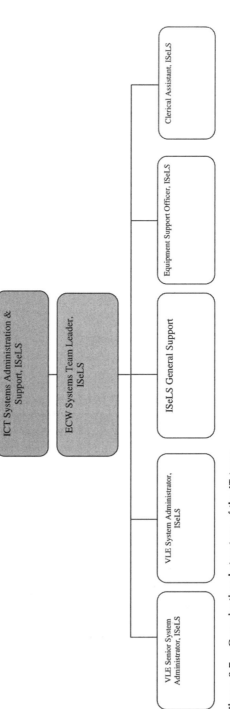

Figure 8.7. Organizational structure of the IT team.

Another priority was the continuous evaluation of the project. Again, this hadn't been done during Phase I, but with the second bid, Phase 2 created this opportunity. Another recognition was that the reasons behind the low retention rate on these courses needed to be analyzed and that students' use of the system needed to be monitored. So during the second phase of ECW, this team was set up (see figure 8.8). Their initial responsibilities were:

- to ensure students enjoy a quality learning experience from initial inquiry to application, graduation, and beyond;
- to highlight good practices and areas for improvement across all modules;
- to keep accurate details about the research activities of core and associate members of the e-College Research Unit; and
- to manage the administration for the e-moderator course

A major task performed by this team was to monitor students' overall use of the VLE and to pick up on students who were registering low or no activity either on the system or in the discussion forums. Then they liaised with the customer services team, who contacted those students and their e-moderator to see if there were solvable problems or a genuine withdrawal. The Evaluation Report had shown that 90% of staff felt that student non-participation in online discussion was a big issue in e-learning, so this new team helped to highlight this issue and began to tackle it in a very proactive manner.

The administration of ECW was a major task and was again being handled by already busy staff within the business school during ECW1. A newly formed dedicated team had a desire to consolidate and improve student recordkeeping and to have a good policy of knowledge management (see figure 8.9).

The Evaluation Report had highlighted several areas of improvement, which would mean that comprehensive information about staff and students and their nature of involvement with ECW would be readily available. This need for information to support the entire team became invaluable in all areas of student recordkeeping across the project. The sort of information initially requested from the Evaluation Report (p. 87)[22] was:

- Students' profiles by personal information
- Up-to-date information about who is delivering modules
- A module database that is fully accessible
- Monitoring student access
- Retention monitoring
- Staff skills database

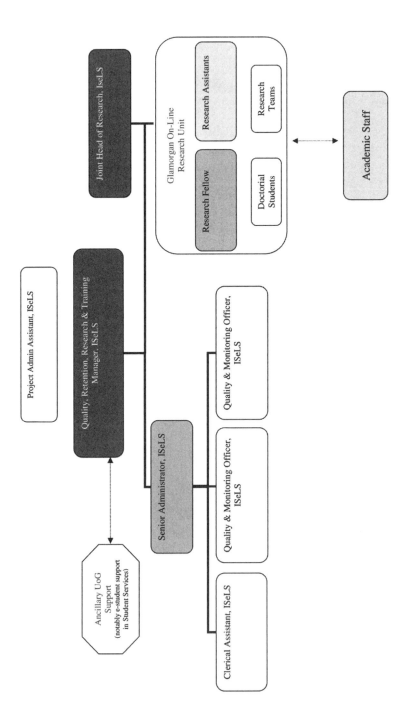

Figure 8.8. Organizational structure for quality and retention team.

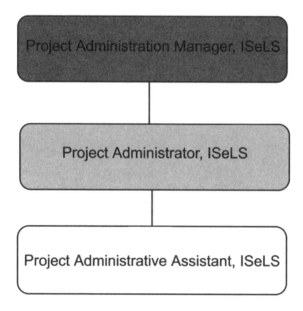

Figure 8.9.   Organizational structure for administration team.

The team was able to produce all this information in an accessible format for the life of the project, and it was to prove invaluable for moving into the next phase of blended learning at the university.

This team was initially kept within the Business School at the start of ECW2, but a communication gap with the Quality staff was soon recognized. This gap was having a negative impact on the project. Physical separation and this lack of shared information had led to duplicate record-keeping and overlapping databases. So the two teams were consolidated, improving the standard of administration by a recognizable degree.

LRC Improvements

The role of the Learning Resources Centre staff never altered in attitude, but the recruitment of a dedicated team for ECW meant that better systems and services were established to provide a higher quality of service to both staff and students. This new ECW2 structure (see figure 8.10) meant that a dedicated librarian role, in the learning resources delivery officer, would revise and maintain the ECW modules supported by an administrator whose main tasks were to obtain and deliver the physical and online resources.

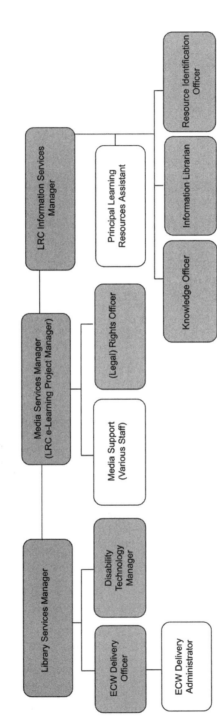

Figure 8.10. Organizational structure for the learning resources center (LRC) team.

Also, the area of support for the online resources and the people using them could be tackled. Previously students had used the normal helpdesk, where staff were untrained in the VLE and the concepts of online learning. Now the customer services team referred resource inquiries to staff who had an understanding of the difficulties of working online and were learning to communicate without face-to-face contact.

The evaluation of ECW1 has actually shown that students were happy with the online services, but on moving into ECW2, LRC staff suspected that students weren't really utilizing the full online resources available to them, but were using only what they were directed to through the module. This was confirmed during the first series of LRC inductions during ECW2, when third-year students indicated they were not aware of the LRC online resources that were available for their use.

Since one of the main goals of ECW was for students to gain information literacy skills, the librarians dedicated to ECW were poised to see this information gap with students and to address it directly. As with all other staff involved in the establishment of e-learning at the University of Glamorgan, the staff at the LRC were enthusiastic about the new methods of teaching and learning that promoted the established set of online resources. During ECW2 the resource section of the online modules was revised and simplified to draw attention to the wide variety of resources available to students working purely online.

Also recruited to the LRC team was a rights officer, whose time was meant to be in the majority dedicated to ECW, with a 20% slice dedicated to dealing with copyright issues across the rest of the university. LRC had recognized the importance of the copyright issue for online materials as far back as 1999. Subsequent visits to other institutions to investigate methods of clearing online material through such services as HERON[23] had meant the take-up of this service independently of this project. The clearance of digitized journal articles and book chapters was going to become essential in online delivery support.

It took a lot of effort to impart the importance of early LRC inclusion in the production process; this remains a challenge today, post-ECW. At least the role of the rights officer has been recognized over time, and prospective staff who wish to move into e-learning, or rather blended learning, are always alerted to the importance of working closely with the LRC.

Parallel to the support being given by the LRC staff, measures were put in place to create a knowledge base for students. A knowledge officer was appointed early on in ECW1 to develop a resource that would become an FAQ service and also a major component of capturing knowledge management issues related to e-learning. Initially, the officer's tasks were simply to record all student queries that went through the helpdesk. ECW2 saw the development of this service into a knowledge base with editing, recategorization, new search features, and promotion of the service. The officer was proactive rather than reactive.

This knowledge base of FAQs has now been integrated into the Blackboard VLE as a support for all users behind the help facility. It is being continually updated and looks at all aspects of student study.

The ECW project taught that the LRC team was integral to the e-learning production, delivery, and support system. It was proved that the LRC was one of the only sections involved in all aspects and stages of e- and blended learning, and this is a continuing truth.

COLLABORATION AS A PROJECT STANDARD

The teams or departments that were set up between the different phases of ECW produced a large volume of work and supported this group of students during their study. Perhaps the major challenge of the project was to create a blending of ideas and personalities into one e-learning team. For the most part, this seemed to have been achieved, and in the three major areas of design, delivery, and support it was possible at the end to identify with certainty several processes and instances that illustrate this merging and collaboration of individuals.

Design

During Phase 2 of ECW the design stage of an e-learning module became a process of revision rather than of creation. It was an evolution of material, with most of the modules delivered for the BA, MAPD, and Foundation courses being revised and improved before every recurring instance was launched.

Where any major changes were considered, there was a consultation process among the instructional designer, academic, librarian, and rights officer. At these meetings the implications of any changes were considered for the resources, copyright, and academic standards. Learning outcomes were considered and the amount of time available to obtain rights clearance or new online resources was reviewed. Through this consultation all the parties were aware of any consequences a change might bring. This created an awareness and also a record of the process of change, which gave an insight and point of reference to all the sections of the team.

The actual physical creation and revision of any e-learning module was undertaken using the content management system, or CMS. A comprehensive piece of software, which was designed and built within the ICT department of the e-learning team, it was extremely organic and grew with the project. All changes to the software were brought about through the advice of the teams who used the system, including the IDs, editors, and LRC staff. These revisions tackled some problems, but even at the time all personnel in the design process recognized that in the future a much more sophisticated system would be needed, especially one that could possibly link with our library management system and deal with copyright control.

The current reality is that beyond the project, the CMS is still being utilized and improved, as it has proved a very robust system. The LRC has taken the decision to use a new piece of software from our library management system that will allow the creation of live online reading lists that can be accessed at module level through the VLE. Thus, our access of the CMS is for review and consideration only, while our support resources are now accessed through the VLE at module level.

During ECW the CMS meant that all members of the team could access and alter the same information. Early guidelines prevented overwriting or deletion by mistake, so certain sections of staff could access only certain parts of a module. The library staff, for example, was the only section that could access the resources page and had complete control over its appearance and the information that was listed there. All this meant that modules could be revised simultaneously, which would save time and hopefully negate errors.

Delivery

The delivery of online modules to ECW students involved a wide range of administration processes that involved several sections across the e-learning team liaising to make the process as smooth as possible for both the potential and returning students. Initially, the administration and customer services team liaised with each other and the academics at all the partner institutions to arrange applications and interviews and to process records.

This process changed greatly from ECW1 to ECW2. Initially, it was all done by the administration team in the Business School, but the implementation of an independent ECW administration team made the needs of these students a priority. At all stages the process was supported by the customer services team, who kept in contact with students to make sure that they were kept up-to-date on their applications.

The student record system was shared by the administrators, quality and research teams, and the library team. The database began simply as one created in Microsoft Excel, but then, due to demands from all the users, it was rewritten as a more three-dimensional Microsoft Access database with reports attached to it. This move was to benefit all the different administrative needs of the team across both administration and library sectors.

Perhaps one of the most successful areas of collaboration at the delivery stage was in the induction process for both new and returning students to

ECW courses. This was the foundation of the course for students, and in e-learning it may be one of the few face-to-face experiences they will have. It gives them the tools they will need to start working, and it also is an important indication of what they can expect from the course. Initially, this process was not handled satisfactorily, and the one-day session was too intensive for students to absorb the necessary skills. For example, the library section provided too much information, and students often came away still unsure what resources were on offer to them. Another problem was that across different partner colleges there was a varied student experience, meaning that standards had not really been established; thus, the partnership was not working to its full potential.

It was decided that the induction must be lengthened for all the courses and standards created. An induction team was established with representatives from customer services, ICT, LRC, and the academic team. In each case a program was devised, and the administration team organized the practicalities of this. An ideal and regularized induction was offered across the new intake in all partner colleges as staff traveled to deliver their presentations as a team. For the LRC section, the decision was made to try and minimize the amount of information delivered and to concentrate on getting students to understand and learn to use resources available within the module and to offer an insight into the gateway (FINDit) that allowed them to reach further research and online resources. This meant that the e-learning team was presented as one service supporting students in their studies.

For the LRC, another excellent exercise in partnership was one with the partner college libraries. The distribution of books to the ECW students was necessary at the induction of every intake of students. Appropriate texts would be couriered out and distributed from the local library; the library staff on site would be involved in the process and would then be visible to the students studying at that college. This process worked well and the relationship meant a greater understanding on both sides of the nature of the institutions and the students who were affiliated to them.

Support

The customer services team led support in the project, and their public face was heavily promoted to students from first contact. However, support was actually distributed among several sections of the e-learning team, including ICT, LRC, and the academic staff.

All the teams received calls, but students were encouraged through the helpdesk to use the call management software that was established to record the nature and frequency of calls. The LRC and ICT staff, who have their own call references and lists, also contributed to this system. Thus, a particular call could be passed back and forth between teams to find the best person to answer a query and help the student.

The software, RMS, has become the premier call-logging software for all support teams across the university and is now being piloted among all blended learning staff, including academics, to try and capture all support calls and further build up the knowledge base.

Online support was expanded during the project through the work of all the teams. For example the knowledge officer's work, as previously mentioned, changed in nature through consultation with the customer services team and academic needs. It was also part of the new remit to monitor use of the service that was being encouraged for all support sections. The knowledge base covered a wide range of support needs, including technical, pastoral, and academic issues.

Coupled with this was a combined project by the LRC and the university's Centre for Lifelong Learning to create an online study skills module; in the new major intake at the start of the 2005 academic year, this was made available through every module being offered to ECW students as part of the resources section. This had sections on how to analyze information, how to write essays, exam preparation, information searching, managing your time, netiquette, plagiarism, referencing, and presenting your work. This module contributed greatly to the support of students, and all members of the support team used it to instruct students, so ultimately it became a team support mechanism.

These study skills modules were adapted during 2006 and rewritten into subject areas. They are now available to all schools as independent modules from the VLE and LRC websites. It is hoped that in the future they may become validated modules that can be taught and can yield students points toward their degrees.

THE CHALLENGES

The whole of ECW was a great challenge, firstly in creating an integrated team, and secondly in dealing with students whose learning needs are so different from the majority of what was then a traditional student population. It has to be noted now, however, that the definition of the traditional student is morphing and that soon the majority of the university population will no longer be the 18-year-old post-A-level undergraduate candidate.

For the ECW project two of the greatest challenges proved to be ICT and communication. Both of these were integral to the project, and both affected the staff and the students.

ICT

Perhaps one of the most difficult areas to deal with over the entire ECW project, both Phase 1 and 2, was the area of IT literacy. Much of the staff difficulty with the IT used for e-learning was due to a lack of training. The early days of e-learning saw many staff hired who didn't receive any kind of e-learning induction; instead, much training was "on the spot." There was some basic technical training, but this was purely operational. However, the need for a longer induction program was recognized, and a series of tutorials introducing staff to the history and place of e-learning showed them how to use the VLE, what a module consists of, how to use the resources, and what students face in their learning program. Staff who went through the induction program called their greater knowledge base invaluable.

It is now the case that the blended learning team offers a wide variety of staff training in using the VLE for teaching. This includes the LRC, which is trying to emphasize the benefits of online resources and how they can enhance the learning experience.

Perhaps the greater challenge was the ICT knowledge of the students. "In recent years, it has been commonly accepted that most students should possess basic Information Technology (IT) skills and the ability to use these skills competently within an educational setting. Arif (2001) however, warns that it should not be assumed that any given population is 'technology-conversant.' In fact, Arif (2001) maintains that many students entering University have had no exposure to the Internet and very little to IT generally. Participation in e-learning courses can therefore be seriously affected by the IT deficiencies of students and thus a significant contributor to withdrawal (Hara & Kling, 1999)."[24]

This assumption was not really recognized at the start of the project, but it soon became apparent that students were not always coping with the VLE and the ICT demands. In fact, an outcome of the evaluation was that, "more training in IT skills is needed at the start of the course" (Evaluation Report, p. 86).[25] This led to the new induction and training structure as indicated in the IT team section. Students needed the skills we had assumed they had, and such an inequality across a class will always prove difficult for online learning.

Once students had managed to get online, they began to encounter difficulties, as usability and reliability of the system was initially a major challenge. During ECW1 it proved to be one of the chief areas for complaint; however, evaluation showed that more recently there has been an encouraging trend toward improvement in all areas of ICT (Evaluation Report, p. 35).[26]

To tackle some of these issues, training in IT was changed. From being part of the three-day induction, it evolved into a set of tests at the interview stage that would lead to a period of training over four weeks if the students were not of adequate ability before they went into induction. "Reliable

Table 8.7. Reliability of ICT

Year of Enrollment	2001	2002	2003
Reliability of E-Learning Environment	D	C	A
Ease of use of E-Learning Environment	B	B	A
Ease of Use of Discussion Boards	B	B	A

technical support is crucial for both staff and students as they become familiar with e-learning, indeed students will readily give up if they are unable to get the technology to work and do not receive support (Alexander, 2001; McVay-Lynch, 2002)."[27] (See table 8.7.)

Communication

The other major challenge through both stages and affecting all members of the project, both staff and students, was communication. It has always been a major business problem for any institution to tackle, but during ECW it was wide-ranging, as we had so many partners and such a wide spread of students.

Many students had expressed their dissatisfaction during ECW1 with the way they were informed about potential problems and changes in the system, but the team made a positive impact on this communication breakdown by being very proactive in its approach. A whole new online module was created—Help and Support, which informed both students and staff about impending changes or difficulties in the system through an announcements feature. Students were frequently communicated with by phone or e-mail; even the setting up of a student newsletter to highlight useful features of the system and support services on offer was instrumental in making students more aware and hopefully increased the feeling of community. For students, who are communicating mainly through electronic means, these forms of contact proved popular, and so we had the opportunity to try some online support and to offer help using the virtual classroom on Blackboard, for example, which was an innovation for staff at the time. The virtual classroom offered real-time chat and demonstration and meant that students could receive direct and immediate responses, which they appreciated and utilized when it was available.

The customer services team, as previously mentioned, tackled communication about IT issues through announcements and proactive e-mailing. Because of this there developed a role for the ICT team within the induction process, as it was recognized that students needed to be aware that this team was there for them. So during induction a lot of information was passed about various aspects of ICT, including system requirements and care of one's PC (including virus and software needs); alongside this was a demonstration of the support services available and how they fit into the whole e-learning team.

For staff physically distributed, communication was mainly through e-mail and the phone, as face-to-face encounters were not always possible. However, there was a series of meetings of various groups to try and disseminate information and to discuss it. These were at various levels from department to project and proved invaluable means of communication.

The communication factor was always contentious, though. In ECW1, tight deadlines for preparing modules, which sometimes required 300 hours for certain staff members, created a great deal of tension. Many staff lacked an overall understanding of the hierarchy within ECW and experienced confusion and frustration regarding who ought to be contacted in order to complete certain tasks (Evaluation Report, p. 64). Staff relationships and communication in different areas were improved, though, with efforts to put structures in place and have everyone understand and appreciate the roles of their fellow team members.

A staff forum was set up on Blackboard, which centralized information for all staff participating in ECW, and this was used as a communication tool. Coupled with this was a move to use Microsoft Sharepoint, a piece of knowledge management software, to try and control the storage and sharing of information. Overall, the collaborative nature of the staff team was built through successful communication among the different sections and between the staff and students.

CONCLUSION

In this chapter, we discussed in depth the history of ECW during Phase I and II, how management structured different departments during both phases, and why that structure evolved. We have investigated issues such as collaboration as a project standard and challenges staff faced during ECW. Participation in ECW has required a major change in thinking about academic structure, services, and delivery by engendering a collaborative atmosphere, and many individuals involved in ECW experienced firsthand that their team efforts made work on this project more efficient for themselves and others.

Ultimately, the e-College Wales project was an experiment with a new educational paradigm and has taken an innovative approach in building a solid infrastructure for the Welsh economy based on providing free courses to those in greatest need of entrepreneurship training. It established the collaborative aspect of creating and delivering e-learning in an academic context.

The work of ECW is an environmental indicator reflecting the future direction of university courses. Not only will the blended learning approach be used for e-learning, it has become a standard at the University of Glamorgan. As time goes by, more aspects of technology will spread into traditional classroom teaching, and instructors will use e-mail, listservs, the VLE, podcasts, and new technology yet to come in order to communicate with their students. As technology overflow becomes more common, we predict students can benefit from partnerships between academics, librarians, and instructional designers, people who, rather than helping students individually, can provide feedback to one another in their respective areas of expertise and collaborate to better serve students. The success of the courses offered by ECW for many students is a statement about the enthusiasm of staff and the willingness to establish new working practices. Furthermore, it has been the base from which blended learning at the University of Glamorgan is moving forward.

NOTES

1. Structural Funds are the European Union's main instruments for supporting social and economic restructuring across the Union; http://www.dti.gov.uk/europe/structural.html.

2. Eligible areas are those that have less than 75% of EU average GDP. It is the highest level of regional funding available from the EU. It is aimed at promoting the development and structural adjustment of the EU regions most lagging behind in development; http://www.dti.gov.uk/europe/structural.html# objective_1.

3. Allan, B. (2002). *E-Learning and Teaching in Library and Information Services*. London, Facet Publishing.

4. Jones, P., Packham, G., & Miller, C. E-Learning for Enterprise Studies: The Case of Enterprise College Wales. *International Journal of Applied Entrepreneurship* 1(1). http://www.managementjournals.com/journals/entrepreneur/article3.htm (1 April 2008).

5. Objective One-Backed Enterprise Initiative: Digital Learning Project to Provide Education Online. *Western Mail*, 3 March 2001, Business section, p. 30.

6. Jones, D. (2004). Information Super-highwayman. *Red Pepper*. November, p. 31.

7. BBC History, http://www.bbc.co.uk/history/timelines/wales/decline.shtml.

8. Jones, Packham, & Miller.

9. Bachtler, J. "Objective 1: A Comparative Assessment." *Contemporary Wales*, vol. 15, no. 1, 2003.

10. Benfield, G. A Voluntary Sector Perspective on European Programs 2000–2006. *Contemporary Wales*, vol. 15, no. 1, 2002, p. 47.

11. Object One, Map of Wales, http://www.e-collegewales.co.uk/info/objective one.

12. *Further education* (FE) is the term used to describe education and training that takes place after the school-leaving age of sixteen. *Higher education* (HE) is the term used to describe the education and training that takes place at universities, colleges, and institutes offering studies at degree level and higher. See British Council: Education system, http://www.educationuk.org/.

13. Anna Chalkley, interview, 18 November 2004.

14. ECW1, Discussion Paper, p. 4.

15. ESF Bid Section 3.1.

16. ESF Section 4.4.

17. ESF Section 4.8.

18. E-College Wales Evaluation Report, 2003, Internal Document.

19. Jones, Norah. Evaluation of ECW One, a discussion paper, 6 June 2002.

20. European Social Fund Bid Section 4, 2000.

21. Bainton, Alan. *ECW Technical Issues*, PowerPoint Presentation, 2002.

22. Evaluation Report 2003.

23. See the website at http://www.heron.ingenta.com/.

24. Jones P., Packham G., Miller, C., et al. (2003). E-Retention: An Initial Evaluation of Student Withdrawals within a Virtual Learning Environment. Presentation at 2nd European Conference on E-Learning, Glasgow Caledonian University, Glasgow, Scotland. 6–7 November, 2003.

25. E-College Wales Evaluation Report, 2003.

26. Ibid.

27. Jones et al., *E-Retention.*

BIBLIOGRAPHY

Allen, B. *E-Learning and Teaching in Library and Information Services.* London: Facet Publishing, 2002.

Arif, A. "Learning from the Web: Are Students Ready or Not?" *Educational Technology & Society* 4, no. 4 (2001): pp. 32–38.

Bachtler, J. "Objective 1: A Comparative Assessment." *Contemporary Wales* 15, no. 1 (2003): pp. 30–40.

Benfield, G. "Voluntary Sector Perspective on European Programmes 2000–2006." *Contemporary Wales* 15, no. 1 (2003): pp. 45–50.

British Council Education system, http://www.educationuk.org/ (14 December 2005).

Davidson, J. "E-Learning Presentation for Am Minster for Education National Assembly for Wales." 2004.

DFEE. "European Social Fund 2000." 2000.

"Discussion Paper." University of Glamorgan, 2002. Internal Document.

(DTI), Department of Trade and Industry. The European Structural Funds. HMSO (Her Majesty's Stationery Office), 2002, http://www.dti.gov.uk/europe/structural .html (4 January 2006).

———. The European Structural Funds—Objective One. HMSO (Her Majesty's Stationery Office), 2002, http://www.dti.gov.uk/europe/structural.html#objective_1.

"European Social Fund Bid." University of Glamorgan, 2000. Internal document (application form).

"Evaluation Report." University of Glamorgan, 2003. Internal document.

"Forward Wales." *Western Mail*, 2000.

HERON, http://www.heron.ingenta.com (14 December 2005).

History, BBC. History of Wales. BBC History, 2004, http://www.bbc.co.uk/history/timelines/wales/decline.shtml (14 December 2005).

Hara, N., & Kling, R. "Students' Frustrations with a Web-Based Distance Education Course: A Taboo Topic in the Discourse." *CSI Working Paper* (WP 99-01-C1).

Jones, P., Packham, G., Miller, C., & Jones, A. (2004). An Initial Evaluation of Student Withdrawals within an e-Learning Environment: The Case of e-College Wales, Electronic Journal of E-learning, *2*(1): 113–120.

Jones, D. "Information Super-Highwayman." *Red Pepper*, November (2004): 31.

"Objective One-Backed Enterprise Initiative: Digital Learning Project to Provide Education Online." *Western Mail*, 3 March 2001, Business section, p. 30.

Outreach, University of Idaho Engineering. Guide 3: Instructional Development for Distance Education. Tania H. Gottschalk, 1995, http://www.uidaho.edu/eo/dist3.html.

Wales, e-College. E-College Wales Object One Area. 2004, http://www.e-collegewales.co.uk/info/objectiveone (14 December 2005).

9

A New Approach to E-Learning

The Learner-Centric E-Learning (LCeL) Group

Gregory Fleet, Daniel Downes, and Laura Johnson
University of New Brunswick, Saint John, Canada

INNOVATIA

The goal of any good design project is to create a system that provides the optimal balance of both human and system performance. This is as true in today's design projects as it was in the early days of human factors science at the start of the 18th century. Over the past 300 years, human factors science has continued to develop and spread its influence into a wide variety of areas (i.e., beyond the occupational issues to software, information design, and e-learning).

Today, many recognize, some pursue, but few understand how to apply the principles of human factors to design within their organizations. This problem lies at the feet of those who practice in the field. Specifically, how do we articulate this approach to design in a way that 1) can be understood and used by others and 2) can be applied in the strategic planning stages of a project?

There is a growing recognition that learning is a continuous, lifelong process. For example, Sanderson (2002) emphasizes the need for organizations to build a strategic foundation for e-learning by addressing the emerging approaches to e-learning in addition to synthesizing other learning efforts of the organization.[1] Learning organizations must concentrate on ingraining learning into the work culture. The key factors to balance, therefore, are the user (or learner) needs *and* the learner's learning environment. At the organizational level these same factors appear in the form of organizational needs or strategic goals, and the context within which new learning will be applied. It is not an overstatement to say that the creation of usable knowledge requires considerable coordination, investment, and planning.

However, it has been argued that there is a serious mismatch between the overabundance of features in technologically mediated learning systems and the lack or total absence of explanation on the pedagogy underlying the inclusion of these tools. Equally lacking are guidelines on how to design, develop, deliver, plan, and manage pedagogically sound e-learning materials. Finally, there are few processes or models by which to tie the need for learning with the goals of the corporation.[2]

This chapter describes how our Learner-Centric e-Learning (LCeL) project is planning to develop pedagogically sound *and* strategically significant e-learning tools. Our approach is to use user-centered design approaches to understand and develop best-in-class e-learning. In addition, we will use the *balanced scorecard* approach[3] to articulate the organizational needs (i.e., the processes whereby organizations identify their learning needs and expectations of e-learning tools). Therefore, this project is focused on the planning and creation of effective and performance-enhancing e-learning content that is beneficial to both the customer (or purchaser of content) and the learner (the person taking the course).

BACKGROUND

In 2002, Innovatia (a Canadian e-learning supplier) conducted research with one of its major customers. The findings revealed three key issues for the development of future e-learning offerings: the need to better understand the learner and organizational environment; when to use (and not use) collaboration tools; and the significant role simulations can play in e-learning. Later that year, Innovatia successfully applied for a federal grant with both government and university research partners (Canada's National Research Council and the University of New Brunswick), securing a four-year $3.4 million grant. The purpose of this research grant was to utilize a multidisciplinary research and design team to identify and apply the user-centric methods in the development of e-learning tools for training products in the telecommunications industry.

There are few references to *learner*-centered design approaches to distance education (e.g., describing the shift from educators disseminating knowledge in a classroom to the asynchronous self-directed character of online courses). In fact, there is little in the design literature that is concerned with the user-centered design of e-learning systems. Indeed, the learner-centric concept is yet to be coherently articulated.

What you find is that most approaches to adult learning are not learner-centered, knowledge-centered, assessment-centered, or community-centered. Yet organizations are increasingly concerned with the creation of "usable knowledge" among their employees in the pursuit of corporate strategies and goals. Usable knowledge is not just a list of disconnected facts; it is connected and organized around concepts to specify the context in which it is applicable.

Often the principles of user-centered design are sacrificed in favor of business needs, deadlines, and budgets. In our Learner-Centric e-Learning (LCeL) project, we are taking the time to validate the use of a thorough user-centered design approach. The goal of the LCeL project is to embed (learner-centric) design principles and practices throughout the planning, development, and delivery of online education by understanding the learners and their particular contexts when designing and delivering courses online.

Current user-centric models propose a three- or four-phase iterative research and design process.[4] In this chapter we describe the process we have adapted for use with our particular e-learning project. To this end, we have articulated a five-phase process:

1. Understand the organizational environment (strategies, goals, and needs)
2. Understand the learner environment (goals, needs, and motivations)
3. Design the total learning experience (using a holistic view of the learning process)
4. Evaluate and iterate (improve) the learning experience (with learners)
5. Measure the change in learners' readiness and in the business's return on investment (ROI) (against the organization's strategies, goals, and needs)

In this chapter we take a broad view of the user-centered design approach, with the goal of demonstrating the importance of understanding learners, their contexts, and the goals of the organizations within which they operate, in order to develop a practical e-learning strategy.

TRADITIONAL PRODUCT DESIGN AND DEVELOPMENT

One of the most widely adopted ideals in product design in recent years is the concept of mass customization. It has been applied in a wide range of industries, including e-learning.[5] The underlying concept of mass customization is that the product you design will eventually serve the particular needs of individual users. For many products, this traditional design approach is effective, and although products are mass-produced, they still meet individual needs. This process is well defined and concrete. The designated product team collects and analyzes user data and requirements from research efforts. They then use these data to eventually build their product.

While this approach is applicable and useful for many products, it is less applicable when creating and developing e-learning products. This assertion was founded on e-learning research conducted by the Canadian e-learning company Innovatia. Following the release of a library of new e-learning courses, the company conducted a series of informal customer interviews and visits to clients in an attempt to determine:

- end-user acceptance of the new courses
- an understanding of the broader context in which learners use the company's e-learning products

From the data collected throughout this research, the research team concluded that the following issues were roadblocks to creating a successful e-learning product and learner experience:

- the learner's familiarity with the technology (i.e., how familiar with and comfortable the learner is using the Internet and PC technology)
- the learner's familiarity with the content (i.e., the prior knowledge and experience with the e-learning content [or product])
- the learner's control of their learning environment (e.g., the time taking the course)

This e-learning research proved invaluable and resulted in the company implementing numerous process and product changes. However, more importantly, this research produced an unexpected yet welcome outcome: the recognition that we needed to better understand and focus on the actual learner.

THE CONCEPT OF LEARNER-CENTRICITY

Within the e-learning realm, the concept of learner-centricity can have various interpretations ranging from "the delivery of chunks of knowledge needed by each individual"[6] to individualized learning (the goal of the mass customization approach to product design). For the purposes of this chapter, learner-centricity is defined by the following: an awareness of different learning styles, application of adult learning principles, and the need to balance organizational goals and strategies with individual cognitive needs. The traditional human factors approach, when applied to e-learning, would move toward a more learner-centric model of education by using a variety of techniques throughout the design process, such as:

- the upfront data collection and analysis of the learner's requirements using human factors methodologies

- the development of e-learning prototypes using actual learners
- redesigning the prototypes based on ongoing testing with learners

FORMATION OF THE LEARNER-CENTRIC
E-LEARNING (LCeL) RESEARCH TEAM

In 2004, the Learner-Centric e-Learning (LCeL) Research Team was formed to determine how to incorporate human factors principles and product development strategies into e-learning courses and products. The funding of this project by the Atlantic Innovation Fund (http://www.acoa.ca/e/financial/aif/index.shtml) signals a recognition that e-learning requires unique research partnerships between the public and private sectors to bring together areas of expertise and different research strategies not found in traditional industrial research.

The expected outcome of this research is the development of an e-learning prototype that embodies the learner-centric approach to e-learning, as well as the creation of a content development model that articulates and defines this learner-centric approach.

The research team foresees the following learner (and organizational) benefits from this research:

- improved learner retention
- increased transfer of knowledge
- improved learner experience
- improved learner motivation
- transfer into performance enhancement

BACKGROUND TO OUR LCeL PROCESS

One of the difficulties in describing a learner-centric design process is that it behaves in two ways. On the one hand, it is a linear, sequential process, where a broad research phase is followed by a design phase, followed by the build phase. Yet throughout these phases, research and design can occur in parallel. In addition, design typically starts with simple sketches or ideas, and through a series of user testing, the design is refined into more detailed and complete ideas and prototypes. In fact, even during the build phase there can be ongoing research and design cycles, where the user input is used for the current build, or for future builds. Therefore, a learner-centric approach is defined as *both* a sequential and an iterative process model.

Given that this is an inherent aspect of user-centric approaches, there is the business question (and associated fears) of when to stop iterating the design and start building the product. These fears, as real as they are, are rarely warranted. Most projects are (severely) constrained by time in this fast-paced world of information technology, and this, combined with difficulties gaining access or finding appropriate users, often provides its own project management limits to the overall design-phase timeline.

Our own e-learning (LCeL) project has specific time and resource constraints, which has shaped the project plan and funding allocations. The remainder of this chapter will provide an inside look at our use of a learner-centric design approach within this four-year research grant timeline. We will return to our five-phase approach mentioned above. The first phase looks at the organizational *needs assessment*, by examining various aspects of the learner's environment.

LCeL Phase 1: Understand Business Environment

Corporate learning occurs in a business context with specific business goals, strategies, and plans. Therefore, the first two research phases are really two sides of the same (needs assessment) coin. On the one side, we must collect information to determine the broad business context and environment the learner works within (as described by our Phase 1). On the other side, we must collect information to understand and profile the types of learners and their specific learning needs for their work responsibilities (as we will address in our description of Phase 2 below).

In essence, this first phase studies the relationship between the specific business strategies needed to deliver the goals or mission of the organization, and the training needs of the employees required to meet those strategies. There are any number of ways one can assess (both qualitatively and quantitatively) a company's business strategies, yet given the popularity and level of acceptance within the information and communication technologies (ICT) sector (the main customer market for Innovatia), we will use Kaplan and Norton's[7] balanced scorecard framework to assist us with this assessment.

Developed in the early 1990s, the balanced scorecard (BSC) allows companies to measure (and therefore manage) their vision and strategy by balancing four perspectives of the organization:

- The customer perspective—how to present yourselves to customers in order to achieve your vision
- The internal business processes perspective—what specific business processes are required to meet customer (and shareholder) needs
- The learning and growth perspective—how to sustain a *learning organization* where employees and management can meet current needs and grow and learn to meet future needs

- The financial perspective—what measurements are required to accurately measure financial performance and communicate that assessment to shareholders

The BSC approach is a measurement-based process, so within each of these four perspectives, you articulate the objectives, measures, targets, and initiatives required to answer these questions.

We see two clear benefits of adopting this approach. First, as mentioned, it is a popular performance management tool used by many of the current and future clients of Innovatia. Second, it provides a common and accepted language to describe the specific details of the organization's business strategy (i.e., in relation to its employees' specific tasks and the learning needs to accomplish those tasks and meet the business strategy). Understanding this strategy is one of the main goals of this phase of our business needs assessment. Unfortunately, needs assessment in general, and user-centric design in particular, are processes that are easily misunderstood. There is also a fear that this multidisciplinary, at times qualitative approach to research lacks the credibility and rigor of a more quantitative approach. Therefore, BSC provides credibility to the learner-centric process (which is too often seen as fuzzy), and a shared language by which to communicate the organization's business strategies and needs, both within that business and between the business and the e-learning developer.

We will not provide a detailed description of how we will use the BSC approach in our research, though we will outline some of the key elements that further demonstrate the benefits of using this approach in an e-learning development process.

In order to perform the business needs assessment (and using the language of the BSC), we see three broad tasks:

1. Identify the business processes that create value for the organization (i.e., the value associated through meeting the customer's needs and/or satisfying the business goals and vision).
2. Identify and develop detailed competency profiles of the (various) strategic jobs associated with Task 1.
3. Determine what specific training is needed to support learners (so they can meet the business's specific and defined strategic needs, as well as provide them a context for a positive learning and growth experience).

Ultimately, the first phase of the LCeL design approach identifies the key learner groups and their role to meet the company's strategy and vision, and then measures their current readiness to perform that role. In other words, we perform a human capital (skills, training, and knowledge), information capital (systems, databases, networks), and organizational capital (leadership, culture, teamwork) audit to identify both organizational readiness and to provide a baseline for our post-e-learning readiness in Phase 5. The development and nurturing of human capital is, indeed, the most important reason for an organization's investment in e-learning. We will return to this point at the end of the chapter.

LCeL Phase 2: Understand the Learner's Environment

Phase 1 looked at the business from the four perspectives of customer needs, internal organizational needs, learning needs, and financial requirements, goals, and expected results. Phase 2 revisits the learning and growth perspective, seeking to understand (measure and describe) in detail all the important dimensions that affect the learner. While Phase 1 looked broadly at performing a *business* needs assessment, Phase 2 focuses specifically on the *learner* needs assessment (both individually and collectively).

E-learning programs aimed at organizations are concerned with a particular kind of learner—adults. Understanding adult learners is crucial in the development of effective e-learning tools, content, and environments. What are the unique characteristics of adult learning?

1. Adult learners are capable of self-directed learning (understood as the ways in which learners set goals, look for appropriate resources, decide on learning styles, and evaluate their own progress).
2. Meta-cognition plays an important role in adult learning. *Meta-cognition* simply means thinking about thinking, or understanding "how learning will be conducted, what learning will occur, and why learning is important."[8] Adult learners are more capable and more engaged when they learn how to learn.[9] Brookfield[10] argues that being skilled at learning will promote lifelong learning. In this way, a meta-cognitive approach also supports self-directed learning.
3. Adult learners show a preference for problem solving as an educational strategy, specifically involving knowledge that is presented in a real-life context.[11] Again, such an approach to learning makes sense when we recognize that adult learners are motivated to seek new knowledge for the practical purpose of solving problems in their professional or personal lives.[12]
4. Adult learners come to the classroom with background knowledge and experience that reinforces their self-identity.[13] Prior experience of the learner impacts learning in creating individual differences, providing rich resources, creating biases, and providing adult self-identity.[14] Prior subject knowledge improves the learner's ability to ask the right questions and to evaluate the results of his or her inquiry.[15] Pre-

existing knowledge affects the learner's ability to remember, reason, problem-solve, and acquire new knowledge.[16]

Learning style can be thought of as the combination of the learner's motivation, task engagement, and information-processing habits. Cognitive controls take place only after the learner becomes engaged in the task.[17]

Learning styles are varied. Gardner (1983) proposed that humans are born with at least seven intelligences, which allows extraordinary flexibility in developing the competency necessary to meet the intellectual demands of their cultures.[18] These intelligences are *verbal/linguistic, musical/rhythmic, logical/mathematical, visual/spatial, bodily-kinesthetic, interpersonal,* and *intrapersonal.* According to Gardner's multiple intelligences theory, these intelligences evolved for the purpose of solving problems and fashioning products necessary for human survival.[19] By participating in an environment that is nourishing for all the intelligences, adults can experience a richness and enjoyment in learning they thought they had outgrown or, in many cases, had never experienced.[20]

Other research suggests that problem-based learning may be particularly suited for adult learners because adults have a fully developed working memory, they are interested in contextual issues (current events, social conditions, etc.), and they can distinguish reality from fantasy (in most situations). Adults have a context for meaning because they have had adult experiences of anger, guilt, and other emotions, and have experienced social relationships. Finally, adult learners come to education having already learned to recognize and solve many problems.[21]

Huang (2002) identifies a number of issues that are particularly important for developing online education:

1. Learner isolation; individual learning at a distance is a basic design for online learning. Often this is assumed to be a strength of e-learning, because the "user" is in control of the flow of learning. However, as we have seen, learning is a social activity, and the e-learning environment must compensate in some way for the learner's isolation.
2. Learners are unable to determine the quality and authenticity of their learning. This criticism can be addressed using the pedagogical insights of constructivism and cognitive apprenticeship.
3. Instructors must notice the reality of physical distance between learners and themselves and must be prepared to change their role from consultant, guide, resource provider, etc., as the situation dictates. Learner support becomes a crucial component in effective e-learning.[22]

Huang's major criticism of current practice is that educators and course creators *predetermine* authentic learning in their instruction. Information is not provided by the real world but comes from instructors' and developers' ideas. Simulations and collaborative settings may be effective tools for dealing with this criticism.

Learning style is one of the most common measurements in developing customized learning materials. Unfortunately, there is no standard assessment approach or tool that is widely accepted by scholars or practitioners.[23] In general, the questionnaires measure either the preferred mode of learning (perceptual channels such as auditory learner, visual learner, kinesthetic learner, etc.) or the preferred cognitive mode of learning (e.g., theorist, pragmatist, reflecter, etc.). The LCeL research team is currently comparing these various methods and developing a measurement tool that will meet our particular needs.

The balanced scorecard also provides a method for detailing the learner needs. Kaplan and Norton[24] use the language of measuring learner (and collectively, business) readiness to perform specific jobs or activities by defining only three competency measurement areas: learner knowledge, learner skills, and job value. The uniqueness they add to our process is the quantification of how many employees perform that (strategic) job, and a single score (out of 100) summarizing the baseline readiness for all employees in that job category.

Drawing together these insights about learning as they apply to adults, in the LCeL approach, we will profile the learner(s) by measuring their:

Learning style: How they *prefer* to learn

Learning skills: Their *ability* to learn

Learning motivation: Their *desire* to learn

Immediate learning environment: Opportunities, peers, support systems

Broader management environment: Cultural support, role models

Included in these specific assessments will be an understanding of past learning experience(s), including e-learning experiences, in order to assess their level of interest (or disinterest) in using online and/or blending learning approaches.

An effective e-learning system supports the learner in her or his development of competence in a particular area of inquiry. To develop competence, students must: (a) achieve a solid foundation of factual knowledge; (b) understand facts and ideas in the context of a conceptual framework; and (c) organize knowledge in ways that facilitate retrieval and application.[25]

Having completed the needs assessment (of the business and the learners) and calculated a baseline readiness, our LCeL process moves on to the initial design phase. There are two possibilities at this point. On the one hand, there may already be developed learning content, and the task is to understand how to tweak or customize that content to the specific business and learner needs. On the other hand, new e-learning content might need to be developed to meet the new or particular need of the business. We will discuss our Phase 3 with this latter scenario in mind.

LCeL Phase 3: Design the Total Learner Experience

There are numerous aspects to this phase, which work together to design a learning solution that delivers a rich, easy-to-use, holistic, and integrated learning experience.

From a design standpoint, this phase means bringing all the research and analysis together and exploring ways they can be combined to maximize learning. Clearly, there is no one solution that can be arrived at during this phase, but rather multiple solutions, each a unique balance of strengths and weaknesses, benefits and limitations. Time and resources, as well as creativity, will limit how many learning solutions can be imagined, but the design team should explore as many solutions as possible. The team should also identify and articulate the specific trade-offs that individual solutions require, for the benefit of future design iterations.

There is no easy way to prescribe the design process itself, since it is a highly creative venture, though the standard user-centric design approach does provide some useful recommendations. A multidisciplinary design team is essential to represent the various perspectives and disciplines required in building the learning experience.[26] Currently, there is no one discipline or background that can represent the technical, psychological and social, business and marketing, and design and usability expertise required at the design stage. Therefore, it is common to see user-centric design teams representing a variety of backgrounds. The literature also recommends an iterative approach, where early ideas are compared, contrasted, and then combined to create newer ideas. Again, time and budget constraints will play a significant role in limiting the number of iterations.

Now let us return to some specifics about the LCeL design approach. Given the goal of designing a rich e-learning experience through a multidisciplinary, iterative design process, what raw materials (data and perspectives) are used by this team?

First, of course, we bring together the needs assessment research gathered during Phases 1 and 2, detailing all the individual and contextual background.

Second, not only do we need a learner- and business-centric focus, but we need to explore design solutions that are knowledge-centered (i.e., how is knowledge represented and what is the context for the knowledge), as well as assessment-centered (i.e., how to measure progress and provide appropriate feedback to the learner). Particular learning circumstances may also benefit from a community-centered approach (i.e., communities of practice or other social interactions that could enrich the individual learning). Finally, multimedia simulations that allow the learner to experience and practice within a realistic yet non-mission-critical environment can provide clear learning benefits.

A third aspect to designing a total learner experience is to understand that the learning is truly a part of a larger holistic, integrated way of life. According to IBM's User-Centered Design team, "everything a [learner] sees, hears, and touches [must be] designed together."[27] Yet this goes beyond the exploration of how the various human senses play a role in learning, to also seeing the specific learning tasks in the context of an ongoing learning life cycle, whether that life cycle is specific to an individual or to the organization.

It is, perhaps, unreasonable to assume that e-learning systems can support all intelligences and all styles of learning. Indeed, by its very design, an Internet environment requires students to utilize reflective observation (learning by watching and listening) and abstract conceptualization (learning by thinking).[28] Nevertheless, a study by Aragon, Johnson, and Shaik[29] found that online learning can be as effective as face-to-face learning in many respects, even though students have different learning-style preferences.

Structure of Cognition

Knowledge comes coded and connected to the activity and environment in which it is developed. Knowledge is situated, being in part a product of the activity, context, and culture in which it is developed and used. Classroom tasks, therefore, can completely fail to provide the contextual features that allow *authentic activity* (the application of knowledge in a real-world context). At the same time, students may come to rely on features of the classroom context, in which the task is now embedded, that are wholly absent from and alien to authentic activity.[30]

Cognitive apprenticeship supports learning in a particular domain by enabling students to acquire, develop, and use cognitive tools in authentic domain activity. Through this process, apprentices learn the culture of practice. Social interaction is a critical component of this type of situated learning. As the novice is socialized into the community of practice, she or he becomes more active and engaged within the culture and gradually assumes the role of expert.[31] Salmon (2002) explored reflective practice in which individuals interpret events and then frame their interpretations into suitable actions. This process enables practitioners to be prepared for professional situations.[32]

Of particular interest to developers of e-learning tools is the use of real-world simulations as a form of authentic assessment in cognitive apprenticeship. Simulations can determine the degree of transfer of classroom knowledge to typical real-life situations.[33]

Social presence has been defined as the degree of awareness of another person in an interaction and the consequent appreciation of an interpersonal relationship.[34] Three dimensions of social presence—social context, online communication, and interactivity—have been identified as important elements in establishing a sense of community among online learners.[35]

1. For an individual, social connectedness has been shown to be an important determinant of economic success and of physical and psychological well-being.[36] In order to form a community, "virtual" or "real," participants need a common purpose: it is in this connection that the use of the Internet for online education may be especially relevant.[37]

2. Interaction tools such as chat rooms support adult learners, stressing the importance of high information-carrying capacity in media for collaborative tasks, the need for high salience of others' presence in tasks that are highly interpersonally involving, and building shared mental models through dynamic, patterned discourse with others.[38]

3. Simulations help people "learn while doing" by providing information coordinated with or embedded in people's activities, information in the "language" of tasks and activities. Companies are increasingly using simulations to replicate processes that otherwise need to be witnessed on expensive hardware. Simulations provide a realistic context for exploration and experimentation. Such processes allow the learner to construct his or her own mental model of the environment. The interactive quality of microworlds allows learners to experience immediate results as they create models or try out new theories.[39]

The goal of this phase is to explore and finally produce some e-learning design ideas that can be tested with learners. If we see this design process as a linear progression, then the Phase 3 ideas are learner-tested in Phase 4 before moving the design specifications to full development and production. But a user-centric design approach in general (and our LCeL process in particular) is also iterative. Therefore, the design team starts with a larger number of low-fidelity ideas (e.g., pencil drawings) and through learner feedback and reaction refines and consolidates these ideas into fewer, more detailed ideas: Phase 4.

LCeL Phase 4: Evaluate and Iterate the Learner Experience

The earliest testing and evaluation with learners may not, in fact, examine specific design ideas at all. They may seek to confirm specific scenarios and tasks that are important to the learner and his or her environment. In the user-centered design literature, this exploration is called task analysis and use case research. That this form of evaluation comes at the beginning of

Phase 4 underlines the nonlinear aspects to our LCeL approach. Our own plan is to introduce conceptual designs at the same time as confirming specific task and use case data.

This phase of testing and evaluation therefore includes redesign and refinement of the learning experience. This process involves moving from what are called low-fidelity prototypes (pencil sketches, flowchart logic, simple animations) to higher-fidelity and more detailed design prototypes, while narrowing the number of design ideas to the specific needs of the learners and by the technical and organizational limitations of the business environment.

Finally, the design team will have a rich enough learning solution that can be tested in more realistic scenarios using usability tests and beta trials.

In our LCeL research project, our plan deliberately stops short of describing the development and production phase. At the end of Phase 4, and throughout Phase 5, a separate team at Innovatia will begin to build our learner-tested learning solution based on the design specifications discovered and articulated throughout Phases 3 and 4.

LCeL Phase 5: Measure Change in Learner Readiness and Business ROI

During our fifth and final research and design phase, we return to the baseline measurements we gathered during Phase 1. Our goal now is to show how our LCeL learning solution has improved the readiness of the organization, and therefore the return on investment of the employee training.

The balanced scorecard approach again shows its usefulness, with its focus on performance outcomes as well as its ability to measure the readiness of employees to meet the organization's strategic goals. In addition, the BSC allows for the comparison of pre- and post-training measures in a return-on-investment framework.

Benefits and Risks of E-Learning

The benefits of e-learning are numerous. It provides consistent content, can be updated easily and quickly, can lead to an increased retention and a stronger grasp of the subject, and can be easily managed for large groups of students.[40]

At the pedagogical level, online courses can provide a risk-free simulation environment—a forum where learners can make mistakes without directly exposing themselves, eventually receiving feedback on the consequences of their actions. This characteristic is particularly valuable when trying to learn soft skills, such as leadership and decision-making.[41]

The risks of e-learning must also be recognized. It may cost more to develop, may require new skills in content producers, and has yet to clearly demonstrate a return on investment.[42] The real value of e-learning lies not in its ability to train just anyone, anytime, or anywhere, but in the ability to train the right people to gain the right skills or knowledge at the right time. Only then can e-learning yield a justifiable return on investment, considering the costs incurred in implementing it.[43]

What Do We Expect to Find?

The LCeL project is just wrapping up the first year of its four-year research program. This places us in the second phase of our LCeL approach (see above). Interestingly, we are also involved in a smaller design project, where we will pilot all five phases with a smaller number of learners and with a smaller learning solution design project. Our plan has us moving into Phase 3 of the research plan by the end of 2005, as well as having validated our complete LCeL approach with a small project.

Even at this early stage in the research, there are several sets of expectations that can be identified. At the concrete or practical level, we anticipate that our process of gathering data about adult learners and about the organizations they operate in will greatly improve the benefits of e-learning for participants in our courseware. Our intention is to change the way we think about developing e-learning materials by actively incorporating a planning component in the design process itself. For people engaged in e-learning (and for organizations choosing e-learning strategies), such an approach would fit the learner's experience with the specific strategies and goals of their organizations.

At a broader level, the LCeL approach offers one way to achieve the oft-quoted goal of a "learning culture" by recognizing that organizations must create a climate of support for their members engaged in e-learning. At this point, we suggest that through e-learning an organization build on its human capital—the primary resource of the knowledge society.

Lifelong learning is an asset to enterprises in a knowledge economy. This is indeed one of the primary reasons to invest in e-learning (as discussed in Phase 1 of the LCeL process above). The promotion of a learning culture within an organization is intended to increase that organization's intellectual or human capital. This concept is derived from the broader notion of social capital.

Standard definitions describe human capital as the "ability, skill and knowledge of individuals which is used to produce goods and services." Attributes include emotional and mental health of individuals.[44] The term *social capital* is used to describe the resources that are made available to individuals or groups by virtue of networks and their associated norms and trust. It has also been used to describe the networks themselves.[45] Nahapiet and Ghoshal (1998) define social capital as "the sum of the actual and potential resources embedded within, available through, and derived from the network of relationships possessed by an individual or social unit."[46] The *structural dimension* of social capital refers to the "impersonal linkages between people or units." The *relational dimension* identifies the features of personal relationships, including trust, trustworthiness, norms and sanctions, obligations and expectations, identity and identification. The *cognitive dimension* refers to shared language, codes, and shared narratives within the organization.[47]

Learning occurs when social capital is built, that is, when the set of interactions calls upon existing knowledge and identity resources and adds to them.[48] The development of social capital involves three components: the interaction between participants, the resources potentially available to that interaction, and the desired outcomes of the interaction.[49] Balatti and Falk found that most, if not all, outcomes required participants to engage in interactions that developed stores of knowledge and identity resources available to them in ways that permitted them to act differently from their norm.[50]

Content required for organizational development and knowledge transfer is unlikely to be found in the catalogues of a third-party vendor. Such content must be developed to cater to the specific requirements of an organization (e.g., language and cultural requirements).[51] Granular information is essential to the delivery of the right information, to the right person, in the right amount. It is thus important for organizations embarking on an e-learning development project to develop a strategy and a systems framework prior to any specific technology acquisition.[52]

Thus, to create and maintain a learning culture, we need to encourage individuals to develop lifelong learning attitudes and to see their needs as part of the organizational goals. Further, organizations must look to e-learning solutions that help them develop support structures and a supportive culture for lifelong learning.

SUMMARY

What is new about the LCeL approach to e-learning design? We have taken a broad view of the typical user-centric design process in an attempt to define and apply this to e-learning. Our approach is three-pronged: we address the learner context, learner styles, and organizational validity. At the level of context, e-learning must be mindful of the needs of learners within an organizational context. Further, we must balance client needs (organizational) with the learner's needs for education without sacrificing one to the other. It has been suggested that tools like the balanced scorecard are useful in assessing organizational needs. At the level of learner styles, we have applied some general adult learning principles with an awareness of different cognitive styles to incorporate technologies, techniques, and methods to provide scaffolding for adult learners. Finally, the LCeL Group has the particular task of proving its results in a business context—that the process described above can be operationalized and incorporated into the business practices of our industrial partner. At a broad level, this involves demonstrating that the investment in such a learner-centric approach can have effects on employee performance, ones measurable using tools such as the balanced scorecard.

NOTES

1. P. E. Sanderson, "E-Learning: Strategies for delivering knowledge in the digital age," *Internet and Higher Education* 5, no. 2 (2002): 18.

2. T. Govindasamy, "Successful implementation of e-learning: Pedagogical considerations," *Internet and Higher Education* 4, no. 3–4 (2001): 288.

3. R. Kaplan and D. Norton, *The Balanced Scorecard: Translating Strategy into Action* (Boston: Harvard Business School Press, 1996).

4. See, for example, P. Morville and L. Rosenfeld, *Information Architecture for the World Wide Web: Designing Large-Scale Web Sites* (New York: O'Reilly, 2002); J. Nielsen, *Usability Engineering* (San Francisco: Morgan Kaufmann, 1994); Jeffrey Rubin, *Handbook of Usability Testing* (New York: John Wiley & Sons, 1994); S. Isensee, C. Righi, and K. Vredenbrug, *User-Centered Design: An Integrated Approach* (New York: Prentice Hall PTR, 2002).

5. S. Teeravarunyou and K. Sato, "User Process Based Product Architecture," proceedings of the World Congress on Mass Customization and Personalization, Hong Kong, October 1–2, 2001.

6. E. Berglund, "The learner-centric approach to enterprise education," *Chief Learning Officer Magazine* (April 2004). Accessed from http://www.clomedia.com (20 January 2005).

7. Kaplan and Norton, *The Balanced Scorecard*.

8. M. S. Knowles, E. F. Holton, and R. A. Swanson, *The Adult Learner: The Definitive Classic in Adult Education and Human Resource Development* (Houston: Gulf Publishing Company, 1998); D. L. Conrad, "Engagement, excitement, anxiety, and fear: Learners' experiences of starting an online course," *American Journal of Distance Education* 16, no. 4 (2002), 205–226.

9. J. D. Bransford, A. L. Brown, and R. Cocking, *How People Learn: Brain, Mind, Experience and School* (Washington, DC: National Academy Press, 2003).

10. S. B. Brookfield, *Becoming a Critically Reflective Teacher* (San Francisco: Jossey-Bass, 1995).

11. Knowles et al., *The Adult Learner*.

12. H. S. Huang, "Toward constructivism for adult learners in online learning environments," *British Journal of Educational Technology* 33, no. 1 (2002): 27–37; see also Knowles et al., *The Adult Learner*.

13. J. Cromley, *Learning to Think, Learning to Learn: What the Science of Thinking and Learning Has to Offer Adult Education* (National Institute for Literacy, 2000).

14. Knowles et al., *The Adult Learner.*

15. J. McDonald, N. Heap, and R. Mason, "Have I learnt it?: Evaluating skills for resource-based study using electronic resources," *British Journal of Educational Technology* 32, no. 4 (2001): 419–433.

16. See, for example, Cromley, *Learning to Think, Learning to Learn;* Bransford et al., *How People Learn;* and B. Dalgarno, "Interpretations of constructivism and consequences for computer assisted learning," *British Journal of Educational Technology* 32, no. 2 (2001): 183–194.

17. S. Aragon, D. Johnson, and N. Shaik, "The influence of learning style preferences on student success in online versus face-to-face environments," *American Journal of Distance Education* 16, no. 4 (2002): 229–230.

18. H. Gardner, *Frames of Mind: The Theory of Multiple Intelligences* (New York: Basic Books, 1983).

19. J. Brougher, "Creating a nourishing learning environment for adults using multiple intelligence theory," *Adult Learning* 8, no. 4 (1997): 28.

20. Ibid., 29.

21. Cromley, *Learning to Think, Learning to Learn.*

22. Huang, "Toward constructivism for adult learners," 27–37.

23. B. A. Soloman and R. M. Felder, "Index of Learning Styles Questionnaire," *NC State University,* http://www.engr.ncsu.edu/learningstyles/ilsweb.html (15 November 2004); see also "VARK: A Guide to Learning Styles," 2001, http://www.vark-learn .com/english/page.sp?p=questionnaire (15 November 2004); and Peter Honey, "Learner Needs Analysis Questionnaire," http://www.peterhoney.com/learning (10 October 2004).

24. Kaplan and Norton, *Balanced Scorecard.*

25. Bransford et al., *How People Learn.*

26. Isensee et al., *User-Centered Design.*

27. Ibid.

28. Aragon et al., "The influence of learning style preferences," 242.

29. Ibid., 244.

30. Bransford et al., *How People Learn.*

31. R. Corbett and J. Kearns, "Implementing Activity-Based Learning" (paper presented at the TCC 2003: Eighth Annual Teaching in the Community Colleges Online Conference, April 2003).

32. G. Salmon, "Mirror, mirror, on my screen . . . exploring online reflections," *British Journal of Educational Technology* 33, no. 4, 380.

33. Corbett and Kearns, "Implementing Activity-Based Learning," 7.

34. C. H. Tu and M. S. McIsaac, "The relationship of social presence and interaction in online classes," *American Journal of Distance Education* 16, no. 3 (2002): 134.

35. Ibid., 131.

36. D. Timms, S. Ferlander, and L. Timms, "Building Communities: Online Education and Social Capital" (paper presented at the EDEN 10th Anniversary Conference, Stockholm, Sweden, June 2001), 1.

37. Ibid., 3.

38. G. DeSanctis, A.-L. Fayard, M. Roach, and L. Jiang, "Learning in online forums," *European Management Journal* 21, no. 5 (October 2003): 566.

39. Dalgarno, "Interpretations of constructivism and consequences," 193–194; C. McLoughlin and J. Luca, "A learner-centered approach to developing team skills

through web-based learning and assessment," *British Journal of Educational Technology* 33, no. 5 (2002): 571–582.

40. V. Cantoni, M. Cellario, and M. Porta, "Perspectives and challenges in e-learning: Towards natural interaction paradigms," *Journal of Visual Languages & Computing* 15 (2004).

41. Ibid., 4.

42. Ibid., 4.

43. Govindasamy, "Successful implementation of e-learning," 288.

44. Jo Balatti and Ian Falk, "Socioeconomic Contribution of Adult Learning to Community: A Social Capital Perspective" (paper presented at the Wider Benefits of Learning: Understanding and monitoring the consequences of adult learning, Lisbon, Portugal, September 2001), 2.

45. Ibid.

46. J. Nahapiet and S. Ghoshal, "Social capital, intellectual capital, and the organizational advantage," *Academy of Management Review* 23, no. 2 (1998): 243.

47. Balatti and Falk, "Socioeconomic Contribution of Adult Learning to Community," 3–4.

48. Ibid., 4.

49. Ibid., 4–5.

50. Ibid., 15.

51. Johan Ismail, "The design of an e-learning system: Beyond the hype," *The Internet and Higher Education* 4, no. 3–4 (2001): 332.

52. Ismail, "The design of an e-learning system," 335.

10

Maintaining Quality Education while Reducing Costs

Jeffrey Trzeciak, Wayne State University, Michigan

Recent economic downturns, rising health care costs, and inflation rates have formed "the perfect storm" for educational institutions, resulting in the worst fiscal news for higher education in years. It is estimated that over the last four years alone, states have experienced shortfalls totaling nearly $235 billion. In response to this economic crisis, state legislatures have cut state appropriations to higher education, resulting in stagnant or even dramatically reduced operating budgets.[1]

Responses from the higher-education community to these budget pressures generally vary. Some have chosen to make up for shortfalls by raising tuition and imposing new fees. Others are reducing or eliminating opportunities for student financial aid. Frustrated with skyrocketing costs and unconvinced that state colleges are spending wisely, many state legislators have moved to cap tuition under pressure from constituents concerned about affordability.[2] In addition, there is some fear that the cost of college may be outstripping students' ability to pay, may be affecting their college choice, may influence their decision to attend full-time, and may impact their time to graduation. For some low- and middle-income families, the barriers are just too hard to overcome, causing them to postpone or even eliminate tertiary education as an option, which then causes a decline in actual enrollment and results in a further budget deficit.

Some institutions have turned to enrollment increases as one possible solution and are actively recruiting students, thus expanding capacity. Ohio University president Roderick McDavis has stated, "We must now look at ways to raise revenue, and increased enrollment is an option to consider."[3] Yet these enrollment increases, primarily at the freshmen level, are creating a demand for which universities do not have resources (added instructors and facilities). As a result of these increases, institutions have typically asked instructors to teach more classes, add more sections, and increase class sizes. In effect, work harder, not smarter.

In addition, tuition increases do not make up for the loss of state support, which generally subsidizes the cost of education on a per-student basis. Adding students can actually result in a decrease in revenue due to an increased demand for services, resources, and facilities. So, what can an institution do?

In order to accommodate growth and contain costs through use of existing human, financial, and institutional resources, universities must reexamine traditional approaches. Conventional wisdom must be challenged. How do institutions increase capacity while containing costs and continuing to provide quality education? Some are turning to online education and technology-infused courses. Institutions that have invested heavily in improving administrative systems (registration, financial aid, etc.) are now hoping that technology will facilitate some of the same improvements on the academic side of the house as well.

Yet critics and proponents alike share a common concern about the quality of technology-enhanced education. After all, this is not the first time that technology has been hailed as a magic bullet for effective teaching and learning at an affordable rate. At various times in the 20th century, television, radio, 16-mm film, and other technologies were heralded as the saviors of modern education. Throughout this period institutions have invested heavily in the various technologies as they have become available in the hopes of reducing costs and improving student performance. But for most, technology simply became another expense associated with "facilities." In his landmark 1999 comparison of online versus traditional face-to-face instruction, Thomas L. Russell coined the phrase "no significant difference phenomenon"[4] to articulate what he found in his studies; that technology does not necessarily improve student performance. In most cases, technology was an add-on that resulted in little change.

There is some evidence to suggest that improved performance and cost reduction, while at first glance at odds with each other, can be achieved through careful and deliberate planning. Institutions must be ready and wiling to make changes in how they approach instruction. While change is occurring on multiple fronts and at an ever-increasing pace, many institutions have not yet made fundamental shifts in the classroom. Now more than ever, it is important for institutions to assess, plan, and reflect.

Is there a formula that institutions follow that will assure success? There is one model that is proving to be successful for many: the Roadmap to Redesign (R2R) from the Center for Academic Transformation.

What makes this model successful? The model has elements of the traditional instructional design model (ADDIE) but has been modified to meet the needs of institutions to reduce costs while improving quality. For example:

- It analyzes institutional readiness and conducts activity-based costing.
- It designs a curriculum that is learner-based, not instructor-based.
- It develops resources at a reduced cost through integration of technology-assisted activities based on institutional circumstances.
- It implements redesigned courses based on past successes, partnering new institutions with those that are experienced with the redesign process.
- It evaluates its success by comparing costs and outcomes in its course planning and course structure forms.

No one methodology is a panacea, and there is no guarantee of success. However, the Roadmap to Redesign is a proven method that can be implemented by different institutions with differing needs to address the complex issues that face them. Drawing on experiences at Wayne State University, this paper focuses on how institutions can use Roadmap to Redesign principles and ADDIE, an instructional design model, to improve outcomes and reduce costs.

ABOUT THE CENTER FOR ACADEMIC TRANSFORMATION

The Center for Academic Transformation at Rensselaer Polytechnic Institute is one example of a program of system redesign that can result in institutional cost savings while maintaining and even improving student performance.

The mission of the center is to provide expertise and support for academic institutions interested in "the capabilities of information technology to transform their academic institutions"[5] through innovative and cost-effective applications of technology. A primary objective is to improve quality while reducing costs, particularly in large introductory classes. The R2R program is based on five essential principles: whole course redesign, active learning, individualized assistance, time on task, and prompt feedback. It accomplishes its mission by partnering newer redesign programs with institutions experienced at course redesign using proven methods to enhance teaching with technology.

To what do participants in this program attribute their success? The emphasis for redesign is focused on learning outcomes, not on new technologies. Carol Twigg, in "New Models for Online Learning," focuses on the impact of projects on learning outcomes as well as increased course-completion rates, improved retention, student attitudes, and satisfaction as measures of success.[6]

ABOUT WAYNE STATE UNIVERSITY

WSU is a large, urban, research university in Detroit, Michigan, with a strong teaching and service mission. Located in the heart of the Detroit Cultural Center, the main campus encompasses more than 203 acres, with more than 100 residential, research, and education buildings. While the main campus is located in the heart of the city, five extension centers offer educational opportunities to students throughout the metropolitan region.

The university's roots date back to 1868, with the founding of the Detroit College of Medicine. Since then, the university has long been a vehicle for the region's cultural, social, economic, and educational transformation. The university is the tenth-largest employer in Detroit, with more than 7,700 regular staff and more than 2,100 student employees. In particular, the university is committed to the revitalization of southeastern Michigan through innovative teaching and research programs enhanced with technology and developed in support of the citizens who will live and work in the region. For example, a new 75-acre "Tech Town," adjacent to the main campus, is expected to attract 60 new businesses and generate more than 2,000 new jobs.

WSU is recognized as a doctoral extensive institution according to the Carnegie Classification of Institutions of Higher Education. As such, it offers a wide range of baccalaureate programs and is committed to graduate education through the doctorate. The university offers courses in more than 600 disciplines that lead to degrees in more than 350 programs from 12 different schools and colleges. The neighboring College of Medicine is the largest single-campus medical school in the country, annually enrolling more than 1,000 students.

Student enrollment is growing and the student body is Michigan's most diverse. Currently more than 33,000 students are taught by more than 2,600 faculty members. More than 20,000 of these students are undergraduates, while approximately 13,000 are graduate students. These students come to WSU with a wide and varied background. While many of them come from southeastern Michigan, WSU also serves a large student population from areas throughout Michigan, across the United States, and from abroad. The WSU student body includes those of traditional college age as well as many older students. Many students are of the first generation in their family or neighborhood to attend a university.

With the opening of the first undergraduate residence halls in over 30 years, WSU has recently started to see steady increases in the freshmen class. At the same time, WSU, like other U.S. universities, faces decreased funding from the state, leaving it to serve more students with fewer resources.

As a nationally ranked university with a teaching and service mission, WSU recognizes the importance of providing opportunities for students from disadvantaged educational backgrounds while continuing to maintain high expectations for educational achievement. It seeks to employ new techniques and innovative technologies that promote effective teaching and learning, in particular for its nontraditional student body.

STEP ONE IN THE ADDIE PROCESS: ANALYSIS

In spring 2004, the WSU Mathematics Department and the University Library System applied for and were accepted to participate in the R2R. As a large urban institution with a diverse student population, WSU was an ideal candidate, for three reasons identified in its mission statement: "first, it uses its metropolitan locale as a setting for basic and applied research and fosters the development of new knowledge of urban physical and social environments; second, it employs its locale as a teaching laboratory and incorporates metropolitan area materials into its curriculum; and third, it brings knowledge to bear to assist and strengthen the metropolitan area."[7]

WSU is also ideal for the R2R program due to its growing student body. President Irvin Reid has indicated that further growth in the student body will be expected in fall 2005, with a future student body reaching 40,000, an increase of nearly 8,000. Moving to a model whereby the computer lab will accommodate all students enrolled in the course has eliminated the need to locate classrooms and faculty for additional sections of this very important course.

R2R recognizes the importance of analysis before beginning the redesign process. Prospective applicants must go through a rigorous application process that requires them to analyze their "readiness" before being accepted into the program. Readiness criteria include an analysis of the impact on learning outcomes, potential cost savings, faculty experience with innovative approaches, and broad institutional support. Throughout this application process the center provides advice and assistance to the prospective applicants.

The center's program relies on a systematic approach to course redesign that allows the program participants to share experiences and resources. In addition to a focus on large, introductory courses, the participants have other attributes in common as well. These include a commitment to whole course redesign; active learner-focused instruction; use of instructional hardware and software; mastery of specific learning objectives; on-demand individualized assistance; and alternate staffing models that incorporate peer mentors and course assistants as well as instructors.

Despite some common elements, the participants have taken different approaches to implementing whole course redesign. These "models" can be broken down into the following: the "supplemental model," which supplements traditional lectures with computer-based resources; the "replacement model," which replaces some lectures with computer-mediated instruction; the "emporium model," which replaces traditional lectures with a computer-lab-based model; the "fully online model," which places all instruction in a Web-based environment; and the "buffet model," which gives the learner the option of choosing from any of the above, based on his or her individual learning style.

Each institution is expected to redesign its courses using materials that have been developed by the center, evaluating and revising them as necessary to meet local needs. The institutions are also encouraged to form teams of instructors, IT staff, assessment experts, and administrators. The institutions are also encouraged to work collaboratively amongst themselves, sharing resources and experiences.

Wayne State University has a collaborative environment that encourages and supports faculty members' support of integration of technology into courses. First, the Office for Teaching and Learning provides workshops on the pedagogy and design associated with technology integration in courses. These workshops include such topics as designing for online communication and collaboration; multimedia for your course; creating and preparing digital images; designing inclusive college teaching; and creating an online presence, among others. In addition to workshops, the Office for Teaching and Learning provides a drop-in multimedia computer lab for faculty in which they can develop the technology enhancements for their courses with assistance from an on-site instructional designer.

Second, the University Libraries provides staff for additional workshops through the Office for Teaching and Learning, including Electronic Reserves and Improving Student research skills; it also provides assistance to faculty as they use electronic media in the classrooms. The Library Computing and Media Services Unit provides one-on-one instruction to faculty using electronic technology in large lecture classes, and manages the streaming of over 100 audio lectures per week. Library Computing and Media Services also provides support for more than 700 computers available in labs and open public spaces in the libraries. The unit has a history of working together with faculty and students to provide computing environments that are conducive to teaching and learning.

Third, the university's Computing and Information Technology division provides infrastructure support for the campus installation of Blackboard in addition to providing a helpdesk that assists faculty with using Blackboard for their courses.

In 2003, the university made major investments in large lecture classrooms. Twenty-seven large lecture halls were completely retrofitted to allow faculty to teach using the newest equipment available. Computing and Information Technologies allocated over $275,000 from technology fee money to the project, which was managed by Library Computing and Media Services. The provost has recently allocated more than $260,000 in additional funding for upgrading technology equipment in another large classroom building.

In summer 2002, the University Libraries, the Office for Teaching and Learning, and Computing and Information Technology collaborated to develop and provide a weeklong intensive institute for faculty who wished to develop their skills in using technology to enhance instruction. The provost sponsored the institute and provided a laptop to each faculty member who participated. Twenty faculty members were chosen from an applicant pool of over 40. Faculty came expecting to leave with a product that could be used in class, and they did. Although not offered in summer 2003, the program was replaced by Innovation grants for 20 faculty per semester. These grants provide funding ($5,000) for faculty who want to enhance classes with technology. This year the grants focused on lower-level, large lecture classes. Award winners are able to take advantage of workshops and personal assistance offered by the Office for Teaching and Learning as well as library staff and Computing and Information Technology (Blackboard) staff.

The university has had a Teaching and Learning Roundtable group for many years. Membership in the group comes from many departments on campus, in addition to the Libraries, the Office for Teaching and Learning, and Computing and Information Technology. Each year the TLTR convenes a conference centered on the theme of enhancing teaching through technology.

In fall 2003 the provost (who joined WSU in June 2003) convened a broad-based committee to determine how to create an even better technology resource center for the campus. This committee will recommend a centralized location for some activities and some staff from the Office for Teaching and Learning, the University Libraries, and the Computing and Information Technologies Unit, with the possibility of others as well. Co-chaired by the dean of the University Libraries and the executive director of Computing and Information Technologies, this committee will complete its work this spring.

The provost, the University Libraries, Computing and Information Technologies, and the Office for Teaching and Learning are all committed to providing support for the Redesign project because it will have a long-term positive effect on the instruction for our students.

At Wayne State University, the Mathematics Department has a long tradition of dealing with curricular issues in a collegial setting. Departmental by-laws specify that an undergraduate committee "shall determine suitable lower and upper division courses (the latter in conjunction with the departmental graduate committee) and develop suitable syllabi for undergraduate courses." The curriculum is highly standardized at the lowest levels and progressively less so as one passes through the curriculum. There is committee oversight of even the most advanced courses, though only at a general level.

Prior to the redesign, only one full-time faculty member was assigned to teaching Mathematics 0993. All other instructors were adjunct faculty. Regular full-time faculty members readily accept this curricular change, because the need for standardization at this level is well understood.

MAT 0993 has been improved and supervised in recent years by one of the Mathematics faculty in consultation with the associate chair of the department and in response to the Undergraduate Committee's review. This same faculty member has recently investigated the delivery of courses such as this at other universities, with special emphasis on computer-based instruction. The chair and associate chair of the department are involved in developing the revision of this course, and other faculty input will be given as needed.

STEP TWO IN THE ADDIE PROCESS: DESIGN

In the fall 2003 semester, 812 students took Mathematics 0993. Of that total, 39% received a satisfactory grade, 40% received an unsatisfactory grade, and 21% withdrew (table 10.1). Of the 812 students registered, 5% received As, 18% received Bs, and 16% received Cs (table 10.2).

As part of the university's general education requirements, students are expected to achieve an advanced placement score of "2" or higher on the mathematics placement exam or to complete Mathematics 0993, the core

Table 10.1.   Math 0993 Lecture/Lab Enrollment, Fall 2003

Withdrawn	21%
Satisfactory	39%
Unsatisfactory	40%
Total	100%

Table 10.2.   Math 0993 Lecture/Lab Grades, Fall 2003

A	5%
B	18%
C	16%
W	21%
U	40%
Total	100%

competency course for mathematics at WSU. This requisite applies to all students, including transfers and guests.

The courses offered by the Department of Mathematics serve multiple purposes. They supply the mathematical preparation necessary for students specializing in the physical, life, and social sciences, in business administration, in engineering, and in education. All students entering WSU who intend to take mathematics classes at the 0995 level or above must achieve a satisfactory score on the Mathematics Placement Exam. However, many students who enter Wayne State are not prepared for college-level mathematics. For those students, MAT 0993 is offered as a remedial course that allows them to satisfy the university's mathematics competency requirement. It is an introductory, high-enrollment course.

MAT 0993 identifies explicit learning outcomes. They are: understanding real number systems, including integers, fractions, decimals, percentages, irrational numbers, and ratios; understanding basic algebra, including operations on real numbers, order of operations, factoring, algebraic fractions, solving equations and inequalities, word problems, graphing lines and slope, exponents, polynomials, and scientific notation; and understanding basic geometry.

While Mathematics 0993 carries no degree credit, students who plan to take Mathematics 0995 or higher must pass the course to advance. Approximately 1,600 students take it each year. Prior to fall 2004, courses were divided into sections of approximately 30 students, each taught by a combination of graduate teaching assistants (GTAs) and adjunct faculty (AF). The traditional class met four hours per week, during which time students were expected to meet with their instructor for two hours to receive instruction and then to meet with a student tutor for the remaining two hours, to work on problems in small groups. Course topics included real numbers, integers, fractions, decimals, percentages, solving equations, word problems, and basic geometry. Students were expected to complete three hourly exams and complete some quizzes and/or graded homework. Students were also expected to complete a comprehensive group final exam.

Students enter MAT 0993 with a wide variety of skills and experiences. WSU was seeking to redesign the course to include the ability to provide individualized instruction, geared toward different learning styles, while at the same time standardizing learning outcomes. Computer-based instruction was identified as one potential solution. In fall 2004, a redesigned course was taught, using a computer-mediated, individually paced approach based on the Roadmap to Redesign, a three-year FIPSE-funded program.

Some estimates place the annual costs of pre-algebra mathematics at $50 billion annually, most going to instructors' salaries.[8] These courses are well suited to the type of redesign facilitated by the R2R program. They are often required courses, are taught by adjunct faculty in multiple sections, have standard curricula, and enroll large numbers of students.

The "emporium model" of R2R allowed us to completely redesign the course; allowing for reduced costs and increased performance while also accommodating a growing enrollment. It provides for standardization through the use of a proven software program that can be installed in an open access computer lab, and at the same time, it is an individualized, self-directed approach that accommodates a variety of learning styles while encouraging active learning. All sections are now computer-based, using online materials. Instead of offering multiple sections of no more than 30 students each, one large 100-seat computer lab was established in the Science and Engineering Library. The new facility was built at a cost of more than $500,000 in construction and equipment. The lab is staffed by a math lab coordinator (with a mathematics background) and graduate teaching assistants, as well as undergraduate assistants (UAs). In addition, students can access the software from their home computers and from additional workstations located in any of the five campus libraries.

The redesign of the MAT 0993 course created significant savings in personnel and classroom utilization. Adjunct faculty members are no longer needed for the numerous sections of the course, and graduate teaching assistant numbers have been reduced as well. The resulting savings is the equivalent of approximately $79 per student. Additional savings have also resulted from the use of fewer classroom facilities. Because these classrooms can now be scheduled for other courses, the university has seen increased availability of scarce classroom space during the busiest times of the days.

STEP THREE IN THE ADDIE PROCESS: DEVELOPMENT

In order to minimize unnecessary institutional expenses associated with course redesign, MyMathLab from Pearson Education, Inc. was selected as the instructional software. MyMathLab is delivered in the CourseCompass system, which allows for easy implementation of administrative functions. The software also makes it easy to do minor customizations that have already been done for the pilot sections. Sections not being used have been deleted, homework assignments have been chosen, and tests and quizzes have been selected from the large test-bank. Customizations will be revisited each term. Students pay a $35 lab fee, which covers the entire cost.

The MyMathLab software is also learner-centered, providing individualized and automatic feedback. Exercises are immediately marked as wrong or right. If the answer is incorrect the student has the option of "walking through" the problem with computer assistance. A new similar problem is then provided to give the student another chance at mastery of the concept. The student is encouraged to delay submission of the assignment until 100% mastery has been achieved. Although this allows the students to be self-directed, we also require attendance and assignment due dates to provide some structure for the students in this new course. In order to assure sufficient time on task, students are required to spend 5 hours per week in the lab.

Students take a quiz after every two sections of the text. Four exams and one comprehensive final are also required. The students must complete all quizzes and tests within the lab. All quizzes and tests are graded as soon as they are submitted. Quizzes can be immediately reviewed by the student and continue to remain available for review throughout the semester. Tests may be reviewed, but not until after everyone in the course has completed the test. The testing takes place over a 3-day period.

Students are allowed to work ahead and complete the course faster than the regular semester schedule, but they cannot take longer than the term to complete the course. Students are able to view their progress through a summary, which indicates exactly where the student stands at all points during the term.

STEP FOUR IN THE ADDIE PROCESS: IMPLEMENTATION

Despite being computer-based, students are required to register for an individual section of the class, which is then assigned to an adjunct faculty or graduate teaching assistant whose responsibilities include:

- Being available in the computer lab for five hours each week at assigned times.
- Monitoring student progress.
- Sending e-mail to students regularly, discussing progress, and arranging meetings as necessary.
- Submitting early academic assessment warnings and final grades.

At least one undergraduate assistant is hired to cover each of the 65 hours that the lab is open during the term. In addition, at least one instructor and one student assistant are also available at all times that the lab is open to provide individual assistance to the 100 students (maximum) as needed.

Students are required to spend a minimum of five hours per week in the computer lab. Each hour of attendance contributes 1 point toward the 980 out of 1,400 points required to pass the class. Additional attendance points can be earned for additional hours of attendance, up to a maximum of 10 points per week (70 additional points in total).

All graded homework, quizzes, and tests have deadlines for submission, after which the grade becomes a zero. These deadlines keep students proceeding at a pace sufficient to complete the course on schedule. The deadlines are not extended for any reason, but students are allowed to drop several homework scores and quiz scores to allow for illness and other unexpected difficulties. If a test is missed, the final exam score can be used to replace the missing grade. These strict rules help to keep students from procrastinating and also keep the instructor's workload to a minimum.

Each student is assigned to an adjunct faculty member or graduate teaching assistant whose responsibilities include being available in the lab, monitoring student progress, communicating with students regularly, discussing progress and arranging meetings as necessary, giving early academic assessment warnings, and assigning final grades. The self-directed course provides for individualized assessment and immediate feedback. Students can immediately know about deficiencies and take measures to correct them. Individual exercises are immediately checked for accuracy, and students have the option of "walking through" the problem with computer assistance. A new, similar problem is then provided to give the student another chance at mastery of the concept. The student is encouraged to delay submitting the assignment until 100% mastery is attained.

All quizzes and tests are automatically graded as soon as they are submitted. Students can immediately review quizzes, which remain available for review throughout the semester. Tests may be reviewed, but not until after everyone in the course has completed the test. The testing takes place over a 3-day period.

STEP FIVE IN THE ADDIE PROCESS: EVALUATION

This new design has allowed us to increase the number of students enrolled in the course while actually reducing the instructional cost per student. Our calculations indicate that the cost per student has dropped by almost $80 for the redesigned course. In addition to this savings, we have benefited from needing fewer classrooms. Some classrooms have been redeployed to other courses and departments to accommodate future growth in enrollment.

Some of the savings also resulted from changing the mix of personnel teaching the class. Because of using the computer lab model, fewer adjunct faculty and graduate teaching assistants were required. The savings of approximately $137,700 from the adjunct salaries have been returned to the central pool for part-time faculty in other departments that must increase sections to accommodate increased enrollments.

For the purpose of comparing costs, the following traditional face-to-face courses were analyzed.

Winter 2003 (W03)	309 students
Spring/Summer 2003 (SS03)	188 students
Fall 2003 (F03)	812 students
Fall 2004 (F04)	910 students

In total, 1,309 students were enrolled in 46 sections during the 2003 academic year. Higher enrollments are expected in the future as general enrollment increases.

In fall 2004, 910 students were enrolled. By comparing fall 2003 with fall 2004, the redesign reduced the cost per student from approximately $185 to $106. This comparison is outlined in detail below.

COST COMPARISON

The traditional face-to-face course is taught by a variety of individuals. Graduate teaching assistants are paid a stipend for each semester they provide services to the department. The estimate for the amount of time this requires varies by job; therefore, the hourly rate for GTAs varies by job performed. The same is true for adjunct faculty. They are paid a set amount for each credit hour. But when the job responsibilities differ, so does the hourly rate.

1. Faculty course coordinator for the traditional course. The faculty lab manager will assume this responsibility in the redesign course.
2. Graduate Teaching Assistant/Adjunct Faculty Supervision Committee, comprised of six members. This committee supervises all traditional teaching done by GTAs and AF. The faculty lab manager will take over this responsibility in the redesign.
3. Faculty lab manager for the redesign course. This is a new position that incorporates coordinating the course and supervising GTAs and AF as well as teaching 11 sections per year.
4. Adjunct faculty teaching one traditional section (paid for two credit hours).
5. Adjunct Faculty teaching two traditional sections (paid for four credit hours). Times are adjusted to account for overlap of office hours, lesson plan preparation, and test writing.
6. Adjunct Faculty teaching one traditional section at an extension site (paid for four credit hours). They do both the lecture and the lab parts of the class.

7. Adjunct Faculty teaching one redesigned section at an extension site (paid for three credit hours). GTA teaching two traditional sections.
8. New GTAs assigned as assistants in a traditional section. They do the same job as the UA, plus some practice teaching and test writing and grading. This is not a full assignment. Additional duties are assigned.
9. GTAs with a Winter/Spring–Summer contract assisting in a Spring/ Summer traditional section. Since they missed the fall training, they cannot be assigned as primary instructors. This is a very light load but is considered a full assignment.
10. GTAs teaching two redesigned sections. The hourly rate is a little higher than (8), since the new course requires slightly less work for each GTA, an added bonus of the redesign.
11. Undergraduate assistants working with students in both the traditional and redesign sections. Office support staff for the traditional course not needed for the redesign.
12. The Math Resource Center for the traditional course provides tutoring by UAs. It is assumed that few students will use this facility in the redesigned model, since they have access to one-on-one tutoring in the new computer lab.

For the purpose of this study, the Center for Academic Transformation breaks down the costs into two categories: course preparation and course delivery. At Wayne State University, our traditional course was taught to 1,337 students at a cost of $185 per student, for a total of $247,493.

The redesigned course is offered in our new 100-computer lab and also at an extension-site lab with 24 computers. Course content is the same for both, but there is no flexibility in when students may attend at the extension site. In the main lab, students may attend anytime during the 65 hours that the lab is open, with a minimum of five hours per week required. At the extension site, students will attend twice each week, at set times, for two and a half hours each time. Adjunct instructors will staff the extension site. Students select a section number based on the orientation time, which takes place the first two days of the semester. An instructor is assigned to each 50-student section. The instructor is responsible for monitoring student progress and attendance (all recorded on the computer), communicating with students via e-mail, arranging meetings as necessary, and submitting early academic assessment and final grades.

Through this redesign process, Wayne State University was able to reduce the per-student costs for the class from $185 to $106, a savings of $79 per student.

INDICATIONS OF SUCCESS

To date, all indications are that the program has been successful. In fall 2004, 910 students registered for the course, for an increase in total students of 98. By the end of the first term, approximately 80 students were able to finish the class early, 1 as early as the third week. It appears that for some of our students this new course allows them to move more quickly through the materials, completing the course at their own pace.

Of those registered, 53% successfully completed the course, 20% were unsuccessful and 27% withdrew. In other words, more students were registered and of those who were registered, a greater percentage completed the course successfully in 2004 than those who were successful in 2003 (table 10.3).

In addition, in 2004 a larger percentage of students received a grade of A, B, or C than in 2003 (table 10.4). While the median for the final exam remained the same, the mean for the final exam and both the median and mean for the course all increased from 2003 to 2004 (figure 10.1).

In addition, students also appear to be more engaged with the material. Instructors reported fewer disruptions caused by disengaged students. As a result, the lab manager and assistants were able to focus more on providing instruction and support to the students.

REMAINING CHALLENGES

We associate many of the remaining challenges with the facility and with issues of the "start-up," and we expect that with time many of these problems

Table 10.3.   Computer Lab Enrollment, Fall 2004

Withdrawn	27%
Satisfactory	53%
Unsatisfactory	20%
Total	100%

Table 10.4.   Computer Lab Grades, Fall 2004

A	8%
B	19%
C	26%
W	27%
U	20%
Total	100%

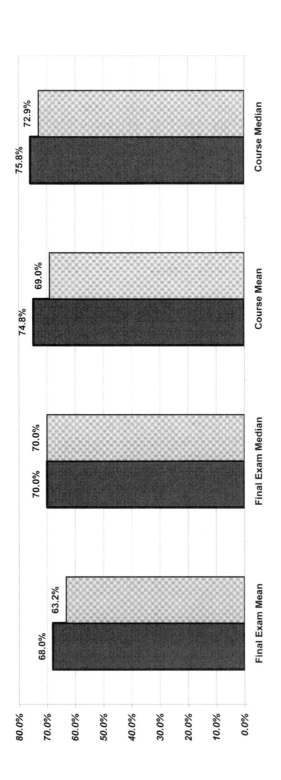

Figure 10.1. Math 0993 Computer Lab in fall 2004 vs. Lecture/Lab in fall 2003

will be resolved. Other problems can be grouped into categories such as "Student Preparation" and "Technical Issues."

Student Preparation

As with any traditional course, students often do not plan well for assignments and tests. However, the result in the "math emporium" is that we sometimes have long lines. We are currently considering "time management" training opportunities for the students. In the meantime, students also have access to other computers throughout the university. For those who choose to or need to wait, we have provided seating. Next semester we plan on staggering due dates more, so that there are due dates every day of the week.

We provided a two-hour orientation that was lecture-based, which some students did not follow or ignored. For the next orientation, the students will review the syllabus themselves by answering 20 questions for a 20-point quiz. They will receive an additional five points for answering questions about navigating through CourseCompass. And finally, they receive five points for emailing their instructor, assuring us that they have activated their WSU email and know how to use it.

Start-Up Issues

We believe these issues can be easily and permanently resolved with some coordination. Hopefully, knowledge of these problems will help others avoid them.

We must further coordinate with the registrar to avoid confusion at the beginning of the term. The location of the lab and required attendance for an orientation session were unclear on the students' class schedule.

The *Student Evaluation of Teaching*, previously available only in print, had to be revised to reflect the difference in delivery from the traditional model, and had to be made available online.

We hired 24 instructors and student assistants to work in the lab with our 1,000 students. Only two of them were familiar with the setup from the pilot. We ran a two-hour training that everyone attended, but it was still chaotic until everyone learned the system. In future semesters we will try to keep about half of the trained people. More training is necessary, especially with people who do not have strong computer skills.

Technical Issues

These are problems primarily related to the technology. However, some of them can be attributed to student time management issues and our own procedural issues. These technical issues are resolvable as well and, once addressed, should not affect future terms. It is important for those still in the developmental stage to anticipate technology problems and have a plan in place to cover them.

We selected MyMathLab, which occasionally marks correct answers wrong because they are not in the form that the computer accepts. We are investigating alternatives for fall 2005.

We experienced some unplanned downtime during the term. The downtime affected the students who procrastinated. We added a note to our syllabus that deadlines would not be extended unless CourseCompass was down for 30 minutes or more. We are also considering adding time management training opportunities for students. Sometimes the downtime occurs in the middle of testing. We now have paper-and-pencil tests available as a backup.

We count attendance as 5 percent of the grade, requiring accurate records. Our computer program to track attendance has some bugs that need to be resolved.

We require students to register for tests but have not yet implemented an online test registration site. Currently, registration is handled manually. We are exploring options through campus systems such as a training database offered through our implementation of Pipeline. As you can see, many of these issues are relatively simple to overcome. While they created some problems for us, we are not surprised, since this is a new model for us. We hope to have them all resolved by fall 2005 and have even begun discussing a redesign for an additional course, Math 0995, Intermediate Algebra, for a total of 1,200 students.

Universities today are struggling with competing demands associated with increased costs, increased enrollments, and reduced budgets. As a result, many have turned to technology in the hope of reducing costs of instruction while also improving student learning outcomes and increasing retention. A variety of approaches have been taken, ranging from "technology-enhanced" instruction to fully online instruction. Successful implementation will depend on careful planning using instructional design models that place the emphasis on improved student outcomes. Following models such as those developed and promoted by the Center for Academic Transformation can provide the necessary framework for institutions to move forward with reasonable assurance of success.

NOTES

1. "A Brighter Financial Picture for Colleges," *Chronicle of Higher Education* 51, no. 1 (2004), 3. http://chronicle.com/free/almanac/2004/nation/nation.htm.

2. A. Klein, "States Move to Limit Increases in Tuition," *Chronicle of Higher Education* 50, no. 26 (March 5, 2004), A1.

3. J. Jeffrey, "Ohio University considers increasing enrollment to maintain availability of quality education," Ohio University Outlook. http://www.ohio.edu/outlook/04-05/257n-045.cfm.

4. T. Russell, *No Significant Difference Phenomenon* (Raleigh: North Carolina State University, 1999).

5. C. Twigg, "Mission Statement," National Center for Academic Transformation. http://www.center.rpi.edu/.

6. C. Twigg, "Improving Learning and Reducing Costs: New Models for Online Learning," *EDUCAUSE Review* 38, no. 5 (2003), 28–38. http://www.educause.edu/ir/library/pdf/erm0352.pdf (April 26, 2005).

7. "Mission Statement," Wayne State University. http://www.wayne.edu/MissionStatement.htm (March 20, 2005).

8. J. Evelyn, "Wider Adoption of Instructional Software Is Inevitable, College Official Says," *Chronicle of Higher Education* 51, no. 28 (March 18, 2005).

Index

Note: Italic page numbers refer to illustrations.

About the Editors and Contributors

Sue Abbott is the learning support librarian at the University of Glamorgan, working in the area of blended learning. She was previously the learning resources delivery officer for the E-College Wales Project, library systems manager at Glamorgan, and librarian at the School for Lifelong Learning at the University of Birmingham. Her professional interests include user support and international and children's librarianship.

Stephanie Sterling Brasley is manager of Information Literacy Initiatives at the California State University, Los Angeles Office of the Chancellor. In this position she develops initiatives that forward information literacy and information and communication technology (ICT) literacy goals of the twenty-three campuses. Her primary research interests lie in applying e-learning to improve student engagement and learning and assessing student learning. She has been heavily involved in the development of the ETS iSkills (formerly ICT literacy) assessment tool to evaluate students' abilities to solve information problems in a digital environment. Ms. Brasley is currently leading a system-wide effort to create a repository of digital learning objects for information/ICT literacy to promote information competence amongst CSU students.

Daniel M. Downes is a fellow of the Royal Society of Arts. He is associate professor of information and communication studies at the University of New Brunswick at Saint John. His research explores issues pertaining to cultural diversity, communication technologies, and the regulation of the new media economy. He has published articles on intellectual property and copyright, new media regulation, and the changing nature of the audience. Dr. Downes is the author of *Interactive Realism: The Poetics of Cyberspace* (2005).

Gregory J. Fleet, Ph.D., is associate professor in the faculty of business at the University of New Brunswick, Saint John. Dr. Fleet's current research explores a variety of aspects of how the Internet continues to challenge businesses and institutions, communities, and individuals. His work explores the use of new Web 2.0 tools both in the classroom and in business; the transformational impacts of high-speed Internet in rural New Brunswick; the death of the traditional Web browser; and user-centered design, cognitive apprenticeship, and social bookmarking in e-learning. He teaches MMCC 6610 (technology, communication, and cooperation) in the MMCCU program.

Christina Goff held the position of research instruction librarian at Golden Gate University in San Francisco from 2001 to 2007. She is currently working at Los Medanos College in Pittsburg, California, as instruction librarian and is now teaching a for-credit, online research and information literacy skills course. Her professional interests include information literacy, instructional design, and helping make the academic library more approachable for students.

Laura Johnson works as a senior product manager for TELUS in Calgary, Canada. Her current focus is on the design and development of integrated solutions aimed at small to medium business markets.

Stella Lee has worked in the field of e-learning, blended learning development, training, project management, and educational technology implementation in Europe, Asia, and North America for more than ten years. She is a regular speaker at international conferences and has presented in the United States, Canada, England, Germany, Brazil, China, India, Malaysia, and Singapore. Her areas of expertise include mobile learning, instructional design, adaptable learning objects, user-centered design, information architecture, and e-learning project planning and management.

Roderick MacLeod, MA, DipLib, MCILIP, is senior subject librarian at Heriot-Watt University. He edits the Internet resources newsletter, manages the TechXtra service (a free service for technology information), and is a past manager of the Pilot Engineering Repository (PerX) project and EEVL, the Internet Guide for Engineering, Mathematics, and Computing. He currently provides management support for the JISC-funded ticTOCs project and subject advice for the Gold Dust project. He was the Information World Review Information Professional of the Year in 2000 and has led initiatives that have won three marketing and publicity awards. He coedited the 4th edition of *Information sources in engineering*, published by KG Saur, which was chosen by the Engineering Libraries Division of the ASEE as 2006 Best Reference Work. He has written and presented on topics such as engineering information resources, RSS, and branding, and his home page is http://www.hw.ac.uk/libwww/libram/roddy.html.

Rosemary McGill was a reference and instruction librarian at California State University, Fullerton, since 1999. Prior to joining CSUF, Ms. McGill was a reference librarian at several community colleges in California, including Chaffey, Barstow, Victor Valley, Riverside, and the University of California Riverside. Ms. McGill was a member of the CARL and CARL/ABLE academic business librarian's exchange and was awarded an MLS degree from San Jose State University, Fullerton Program. Rosemary McGill recently passed away after an extended battle with cancer. As the book editors, and on behalf of the rest of the contributors, we would like to express our sincere condolences and warm wishes to all her friends and family, who will truly miss her presence.

Elaina Norlin currently works at OCLC as the manager for new initiatives and outreach. She is responsible for developing new programs in the areas of digital and preservation services, managing our member outreach activities through new partnerships and professional collaborations, and implementing new services to better meet the day-to-day needs of OCLC Eastern member libraries. Elaina comes to OCLC from the Institute of Museum and Library Services (IMLS), where she served as a senior program officer from 2003 to 2006. From 1997 to 2003, she was on the faculty at the University of Arizona Library, Tucson, as associate librarian. Elaina has authored several books, including *Usability Testing for Library Web Sites: A Hands-On Guide* (2001, ALA Editions). Elaina frequently consults with libraries on a variety of topics, including Web design and usability, and grants development. Elaina obtained her M.S. in library and information science, as well as her B.S. in advertising, from the University of Illinois at Urbana-Champaign.

Rose Roberto served as e-learning resources librarian at the University of Glamorgan from 2004 to 2005. She currently works at the University of Oxford in the Bodleian Library and has worked professionally in other research institutions, such as the NASA/Jet Propulsion Laboratory in California and the Natural History Museum in London. She is a native Californian who moved to the UK in 2003. Her research interests include special libraries, information architecture, and digitization of cultural material for greater access.

Tiffini Travis is associate librarian at California State University, Long Beach. She received her MLS from the University of California at Los Angeles in 1998. As a librarian at CSULB, she has been involved in online as well as traditional bibliographic instruction. Ms. Travis attended ACRL's Immersion Program at Kent State University, where she learned about implementing information literacy courses. She has been an instructor at the General Education Institute at CSULB. Her research interests include information literacy, student use of the Internet for research, and website usability. She has published an article in *College & Research Libraries* entitled "Testing the Competition: Usability of Commercial Information Sites Compared to Academic Library Web Sites." She has presented on all topics at various local, national, and international conferences.

Jeffrey Trzeciak is the university librarian at McMaster University in Hamilton, Ontario, Canada. As such he is responsible for the management of the Thode Science and Engineering Library, Innis Business Library, and Mills Library for the Social Sciences and Humanities. As one of the top research libraries in North America, the McMaster University Library is a member of the Association of Research Libraries and the Canadian Association of Research Libraries.